ACROSS SOUTH AMERICA

LECTOR HOUSE PUBLIC DOMAIN WORKS

ACROSS SOUTH AMERICA

HIRAM BINGHAM

ISBN: 978-93-5342-116-8

First Published: 1911

LECTOR HOUSE LLP
E-MAIL: lectorpublishing@gmail.com

RIO FROM THE CORCOVADO

ACROSS SOUTH AMERICA

AN ACCOUNT OF A JOURNEY FROM BUENOS
AIRES TO LIMA BY WAY OF POTOSÍ

WITH NOTES ON BRAZIL, ARGENTINA,
BOLIVIA, CHILE, AND PERU

BY

HIRAM BINGHAM

YALE UNIVERSITY

WITH EIGHTY ILLUSTRATIONS
AND MAPS

1911

Published April 1911

THIS VOLUME IS
AFFECTIONATELY DEDICATED

TO
THE MOTHER OF
SIX LITTLE BOYS

PREFACE

IN September, 1908, I left New York as a delegate of the United States Government and of Yale University to the First Pan-American Scientific Congress, held at Santiago, Chile, in December and January, 1908-09. Before attending the Congress I touched at Rio de Janeiro and the principal coast cities of Brazil, crossed the Argentine Republic from Buenos Aires to the Bolivian frontier, rode on mule-back through southern Bolivia, visiting both Potosí and Sucre, went by rail from Oruro to Antofagasta, and thence by steamer to Valparaiso. After the Congress I retraced my steps into Bolivia by way of the west coast, Arequipa, and Lake Titicaca. Picking up the overland trail again at Oruro, I continued my journey across Bolivia and Peru, via La Paz, Tiahuanaco, and Cuzco, thence by mules over the old Inca road as far as Huancayo, the present terminus of the Oroya-Lima Railroad. At Abancay I turned aside to explore Choqquequirau, the ruins of an Inca fortress in the valley of the Apurimac; an excursion that could not have been undertaken at all had it not been for the very generous assistance of Hon. J. J. Nuñez, the Prefect of Apurimac, and his zealous aide, Lieutenant Caceres of the Peruvian army. I reached Lima in March, 1909.

The chief interest of the trip lay in its being an exploration of the most historic highway in South America, the old trade route between Lima, Potosí, and Buenos Aires. The more difficult parts of this road were used by the Incas and their conqueror Pizarro; by Spanish viceroys, mine owners, and merchants; by the liberating armies of Argentina; and finally by Bolivar and Sucre, who marched and countermarched over it in the last campaigns of the Wars of Independence.

Realizing from previous experience in Venezuela and Colombia that the privilege of travelling in a semi-official capacity would enable me to enjoy unusual opportunities for observation, I made it the chief object of my journey to collect and verify information regarding the South American people, their history, politics, economics, and physical environment. The present volume, however, makes no pretence at containing all I collected or verified. Such a work would be largely a compilation of statistics. The ordinary facts are readily accessible in the current publications of the ably organized Pan-American Bureau in Washington. Nevertheless, I have included some data that seemed likely to prove serviceable to intending travellers.

Grateful acknowledgment for kind assistance freely rendered in many different ways is due to President Villazon of Bolivia, the late President Montt of Chile, and President Leguia of Peru; to Secretary, now Senator, Root and the officials of the Diplomatic and Consular Service; to Professor Rowe and my fellow delegates to the Pan-American Scientific Congress; and particularly to J. Luis Schaefer, Esq., W. S. Eyre, Esq., and their courteous associates of the house of W. R. Grace & Co. Although business houses rarely take the trouble to make the path of the scientist or investigator more comfortable, it would be no easy task to enumerate all the favors that were shown, not only to me, but also to the other members of the American delegation, by Messrs. Grace & Co. and the managers and clerks of their many branches.

Acknowledgments are likewise due to the officials of the Buenos Aires and Rosario Railroad, the Peruvian Corporation, and the Bolivia Railway; and to Colonel A. de Pederneiras, Sr. Amaral Franco, Don Santiago Hutcheon, Sr. C. A. Novoa, Sr. Arturo Pino Toranzo, Dr. Alejandro Ayalá, Captain Louis Merino of the Chilean army, Don Moises Vargas, Sr. Lopez Chavez, and Messrs. Charles L. Wilson, A. G. Snyder, U. S. Grant Smith, J. B. Beazley, D. S. Iglehart, John Pierce Hope, Rankin Johnson, Rea Hanna, and a host of others who helped to make my journey easier and more profitable.

I desire also to express my gratitude, for unnumbered kindnesses, both to Huntington Smith, who accompanied me during the first part of my journey, and to Clarence Hay, who was my faithful companion on the latter part.

Some parts of the story have already been told in the "American Anthropologist," the "American Political Science Review," the "Popular Science Monthly," the "Bulletin of the American Geographical Society," the "Records of the Past," and the "Yale Courant," to whose editors acknowledgment is due for permission to use the material in its present form.

HIRAM BINGHAM.

YALE UNIVERSITY, NEW HAVEN, CONN.
20 November, 1910.

CONTENTS

LIST OF ILLUSTRATIONS

MAPS

THE AUTHOR'S ROUTE ACROSS SOUTH AMERICA

ACROSS SOUTH AMERICA

CHAPTER I

PERNAMBUCO AND BAHIA

There are two ways of going to the east coast of South America. The traveller can sail from New York in the monthly boats of the direct line or, if he misses
that boat, as I did, and is pressed for time, he can go to Southampton or Cherbourg
and be sure of an excellent steamer every week. The old story that one was obliged
to go by way of Europe to get to Brazil is no longer true, although this pleasing
fiction is still maintained by a few officials when they are ordered to go from Lima
on the Pacific to the Peruvian port of Iquitos on the Amazon. If they succeed in
avoiding the very unpleasant overland journey via Cerro de Pasco, they are apt
to find that the "only feasible" alternative route is by way of Panama, New York,
and Paris!

Personally I was glad of the excuse to go the longer way, for I knew that the
exceedingly comfortable new steamers of the Royal Mail Line were likely to carry
many Brazilians and Argentinos, from whom I could learn much that I wanted to
know. They proved to be most kind and communicative, and gave me an excellent
introduction to the point of view of the modern denizen of the east coast whose
lands have received the "golden touch" that comes from foreign capital, healthy
immigration, and rapidly expanding railway systems. I was also fortunate in finding on board the Aragon a large number of those energetic English, Scots, and
French, whose well-directed efforts have built up the industries of their adopted
homes, until the Spanish-Americans can hardly recognize the land of their birth,
and the average North American, who visits the east coast for the first time, rubs
his eyes in despair and wonders where he has been while all this railroad building
and bank merging has been going on. If there were few Germans and Italians on
board, it was not because they were not crossing the ocean at the same time, but
because they preferred the new steamers of their own lines. I could have travelled
a little faster by sailing under the German or the Italian flag, but in that case I
should not have seen Pernambuco and Bahia, which the more speedy steamers
now omit from their itinerary.

The Brazilians call the easternmost port of South America, Recife, "The Reef,"
but to the average person it will always be known as Pernambuco. Most travellers

who touch here on their way from Europe to Buenos Aires, prefer to see what they can of this quaint old city from the deck of the steamer, anchored a mile out in the open roadstead. The great ocean swell, rolling in from the eastward, makes the tight little surf boats bob up and down in a dangerous fashion. It seems hardly worth while to venture down the slippery gangway and take one's chances at leaping into the strong arms of swarthy boatmen, whom the waves bring upward toward you with startling suddenness, and who fall away again so exasperatingly just as you have made up your mind to jump.

Out of three hundred first-cabin passengers on the Aragon, there were only five of us who ventured ashore, — three Americans, a Frenchman, and a Scotchman. The other passengers, including several representatives of the English army — but I will say no more, for they afterwards wrote me that, on their return journey to England, the charms of Pernambuco overcame their fear of the "white horses of the sea," and they felt well repaid.

Pernambuco is unquestionably one of the most interesting places on the East Coast. From the steamer one can see little more than a long low line of coast, dotted here and there with white buildings and a lighthouse or two. To the north several miles away, on a little rise of ground, is the ancient town of Olinda, founded by the Portuguese in the sixteenth century, a hundred years before Henry Hudson stepped ashore on Manhattan Island. By the time that our ancestors were beginning to consider establishing a colony in Massachusetts, the Portuguese had already built dozens of sugar factories in this vicinity. Then the Dutch came and conquered, built Pernambuco and, during their twenty-five years on this coast, made it the administrative centre for their colony in northeast Brazil. Their capital, four miles north of the present commercial centre, is now a village of ruined palaces and ancient convents. The Dutch had large interests on the Brazilian seaboard and carried away quantities of sugar and other precious commodities, as is set forth in many of their quaint old books. The drawings which old Nieuhof put in his sumptuous folio two centuries ago are still vivid and lifelike, even if they serve only to emphasize the great change that has come over this part of the world in that time.

Now, three trans-Atlantic cables touch here, and it is a port of call for half a dozen lines of steamers. The old Dutch caravels used to find excellent shelter behind the great natural breakwater, the reef that made the port of Recife possible. No part of the east coast of Brazil possesses more strategical importance, and modern improvements have deepened the entrance so that vessels drawing less than fifteen feet may enter and lie in quiet water, although the great ocean liners are obliged to ride at anchor outside. Tugs bring out lighters for the cargo, but the passengers have to trust to the mercy of the surf boats.

It took six dusky oarsmen to pull us through the surf and around the lighthouse that marks the northern extremity of the reef, into the calm waters of the harbor. On the black reef a few rods south of the lighthouse stands an antiquated castle, which modern guns would make short work of, but which served its purpose admirably by defending the port against the sea rovers of the seventeenth century. Opposite this breakwater, on two or three "sea islands" whose tidal rivers cut them off from the mainland, the older part of Pernambuco is built.

It was with a feeling of having miraculously escaped from the dangers of a very stormy voyage, that we clambered up the slippery stone stairs of the landing stage and entered the little two-storied octagonal structure which serves the custom house as a place in which to examine incoming passengers. This took but a moment, and then we went out into the glaring white sunlight of this ancient tropical city and began our tour of inspection.

Immediately in front of us was a line of warehouses three or four stories high and attractively built of stone. They give the water-front an air of permanency and good breeding. Between them and the sea-wall there was a tree-planted, stone-paved area, the Rialto of Recife, where all classes, from talkative half-tipsy pieces of foreign driftwood to well-dressed local merchants, clad in immaculate white suits, congregate and gossip. Beyond the sea-wall a dozen small ocean steamers lay inside the harbor, moored to the breakwater; while numbers of smaller vessels, sloops, schooners, and brigantines were anchored near the custom house docks or in the sluggish Rio Beberibe, which separates Recife from the mainland.

As we wandered through the streets past the Stock Exchange, the naval station, and the principal business houses, we saw various sights: a poorly dressed Brazilian, of mixed African and Portuguese descent, carrying a small coffin on his head; barefooted children standing in pools of water left in the paved sidewalks by the showers of the morning; bareheaded women, with gayly colored shawls over their shoulders; neat German clerks dressed in glistening white duck suits; lounging boatmen in nonde script apparel; and everywhere long, low drays loaded with bags of sugar, each vehicle drawn by a single patient ox whose horns are lashed to a cross-piece that connects the front end of the thills. Those who moved at all moved as if there were abundant time in which to do everything, and as though the hustle and bustle of lower New York never existed at all. The scene was distinctively Latin-American. One must be careful not to say "Spanish-American" here, for if there is one thing more than another that the Brazilian is proud of, it is that he is not a Spaniard and does not speak Spanish. However, the difference between the two languages is not so great and the local pride not so strong but that the obliging natives will understand you, even if you have the bad taste to address them in Spanish. They will reply, however, in Portuguese, and then it is your turn to be obliging and understand them, if you can.

West of Recife, on another island and on the mainland, are the other public buildings, parks, and the finest residences. A primitive tram-car, pulled by mules, crosses the bridge and jangles along toward the suburbs, which are quite pretty, although some of the houses strive after bizarre color-effects which would not be appropriate in the Temperate Zone. There are fairly good hotels here, and there is quite a little English colony. But it is not a place where the white man thrives. The daily range of temperature is very small, and it is claimed that the average difference between the wet and dry season is only three degrees.

From Pernambuco there radiate three or four railways, north, west, and south. None of them are more than two hundred miles long, but all serve to gather up the rich crops of sugar and cotton for which the surrounding region is noted, and bring them to the cargo steamers that offer in exchange the manufactured products of Europe and America. If one may judge from the size of the custom house and the busy scene there, where half a dozen steam cranes were actively engaged in unloading goods destined to pay the annoyingly complex Brazilian tariff, the business of the port is very considerable. It seemed quite strange to see such mechanical activity and such a modern customs warehouse so closely associated with the narrow, foul-smelling streets of the old town. But it gives promise of a larger and more important city in the years to come, when the new docks shall have been built and still more modern methods introduced.

Yet even now there are over one hundred and fifty thousand people in the city, and the mercantile houses do a good business. The clerks move slowly, and there is little appearance of enterprise; but one must always remember, when inclined to criticise the business methods of the tropics, that this is not a climate where one can safely hurry. Things must be done slowly if the doer is to last any length of time. The commercial traveller who comes here full of brusque and zealous activity, will soon chafe himself into a fever if he is not careful. These are easy-going folk, and political and commercial changes do not affect them seriously. They are willing to stand governmental conditions that would be almost in tolerable to us, and their haphazard methods of business are well suited to their environment. The European, although proverbially less adaptable than the American, is forced by keener competition at home to adjust himself as best he may to the local conditions here and elsewhere in South America. His American colleague, on the other hand, has as yet not felt the necessity of learning to meet what seems to him ridiculous prejudice.

Emblematic of this Brazilian trade are the primitive little catamarans in which the fishermen of Recife venture far out into the great ocean. The frail little craft are only moderately safe, and at best can bring back but a small quantity of fish. They are most uncomfortable, and their occupants are kept wet most of the time by the waves that dash over them. Furthermore, a glimpse of them is as much of Pernambuco as most steamship passengers get. It is only by venturing and taking the trouble to go ashore that one can see the modern custom house dock on the other side of Recife, and learn the lesson of the possibilities of commerce here.

We left Pernambuco in the afternoon and reached the green hills of the coast near Bahia the next morning. The steamers pass near enough to the shore to enable one to make out, with the glasses, watering-places and pretty little villas that have been built on the ocean side of the peninsula by the wealthier citizens of Bahia. At the end of the promontory, just above the rocks and the breakers, is the picturesque white tower of a lighthouse. Unfortunately, it did not avail to save a fine German steamer that was lying wrecked on the dangerous shoals near the entrance to the harbor when we passed in.

As we steamed slowly around the southern end of the low promontory, the city of Bahia gradually came into view, its large stone warehouses lining the water-front, its lower town separated by a steep hill, covered with gardens and graceful palms, from the upper city, conspicuous with the towers and cupolas of numerous churches and public buildings.

On the left, as one enters the harbor, rises the interesting island of Itaparica, which England once offered to take in payment of a debt due her by Portugal. It bears a resemblance to Gibraltar in more ways than one, but it was not destined to become a British stronghold. A favorite resort of the citizens of Bahia, it is called "the Europe of the poor," because it has a genial climate and is frequented by those who cannot afford to cross the Atlantic.

As we leave it on our left, in front of us, and to the north, lies the magnificent bay that has given the city its name. It lacks the romantic mountains that make Rio so famous, yet its beautiful blue waters are most alluring, dotted as they are here and there with the white sails of fishing-boats and catamarans.

We have to anchor a mile from the shore, and a steam launch carrying the port officials soon comes alongside. The local boatmen, whose little craft, suited only to the quiet waters of the bay, bear no resemblance to the seaworthy surf boats of Pernambuco, line up at a distance of half a mile, awaiting the signal which permits them to hoist sail and race for the steamer. It is a pretty sight, enlivened by the shouts of the boat crews. Some boats are loaded with delicious tropical fruits that are eagerly bargained for by our steerage passengers, most of whom are Spanish peasants on their way to harvest the crops of Argentina. Others are anxious to take us ashore. And after the usual delay, we make a deal with a boatman, a lazy fellow who wastes a lot of time trying to sail in against the wind while his more energetic competitors are rowing. On the way we pass half a dozen steamers and a few sailing vessels, and steer carefully between scores of huge lighters and dozens of smaller craft. In place of the steel steam cranes which we saw at Pernambuco, on the wharves are numerous wooden cranes worked by hand.

We land on slippery wooden stairs, and hurry across the blistering hot pavements of the street to rest for a few moments in the shade of the large warehouses and wholesale shops that crowd the lower town. Some of the signs are decidedly bizarre and scream as loudly for patronage as the limits of modern Frenchified Portuguese art will permit. There is none of the picturesqueness of Pernambuco, and we soon betake ourselves to one of the cog railways where, for a few cents, we are allowed to scramble into a bare little wooden passenger coach and be yanked up the steep incline by a cable that looks none too strong for its purpose. Once in the upper city, the narrow streets of commerce seem to be left behind, and we are in broader thoroughfares, with here and there a green park full of palms and other tropical plants. There are churches on every side,

LOOKING DOWN INTO THE LOWER CITY, BAHIA

some of them wonderfully decorated and most attractive. Bahia is not quite so old as Pernambuco, its foundation dating only from the middle of the sixteenth century; but it early became the religious and intellectual centre of Portuguese-America, and it is still noted for its literature and culture, although long ago passed in the race by Rio.

The glaring white sunlight throws everything into bold relief and makes the shadows seem unusually dark and cool. On the corners of the streets are little folding stands bearing a heavy load of toothsome confectionery. Their barefooted coal-black owners, clad generally in white, lean against the iron posts of the American Trolley Car System and watch patiently for the trade that seems sure to come to him who waits. On every side one sees black faces.

In fact, Bahia is sometimes popularly spoken of as the "Old Mulattress," in affectionate reference to the fact that more than ninety per cent of its two hundred thousand people are of African descent. For over two centuries Bahia monopolized the slave trade of Brazil. Her traders continued to be the chief importers of negroes down to the middle of the nineteenth century. It is said that as many as sixty thousand slaves were brought in within a single year.

We took one of the American-made trolleys and soon went whizzing along through well-paved streets and out into the suburbs. Here villas, fearfully and wonderfully made, like the baker's best wedding cake in his shop window, attest to the local fondness for rococo extravagance. In general, however, the principal buildings appear to be well built, and are frequently four or five stories in height.

The architecture of Bahia is decidedly Portuguese, much more so than that of Pernambuco, which still bears traces of its Dutch origin and even reminds one of Curaçao. Some of the villas in Bahia are strikingly like those in Lisbon. And there are other likenesses between the Portuguese capital and this ecclesiastical metropolis of Brazil. Both are situated on magnificent estuaries, and present a fine spectacle to the traveller coming by sea. Both have upper and lower towns, with hills so steep as to require the services of elevators and cog or cable railways to connect them. The upper town of each commands an extensive view of the shipping, the roadstead, and the surrounding country. But here the similarity ends; for Lisbon is built on several hills, while Bahia occupies but a single headland, the verdure-clad promontory which shelters the magnificent bay.

Bahia is the centre for a considerable commerce in sugar and cotton, cocoa and tobacco. These are brought to the port by land and water, but chiefly by the railroads that go north to the great river San Francisco and west into the heart of the state. There are many evidences of wealth in the city, and there is certainly an excellent opportunity for developing foreign trade. One looks in vain, however, for great American commercial houses like those which mark the presence of English, French, and German enterprise. Nevertheless the electric car line, with its American equipment, gives a promise of things hoped for. And there is a decided air of friendliness toward Americans on the part of the Brazilians whom one meets on the streets and in the shops. There is none of that "chip on the shoulder" attitude which the Argentino likes to exhibit toward the citizens of the "United States of North America." The Brazilian appears to realize that Americans are his best customers, and he is desirous of maintaining the most friendly relations with us.

CHAPTER II
RIO, SANTOS, AND BRAZILIAN TRADE

Two days' sail from Bahia brought us within sight of the wonderful mountains that mark the entrance to the Bay of Rio de Janeiro. As one approaches land, the first thing that catches the eye is the far-famed Sugar Loaf Mountain which seems to guard the southern side of the entrance. Back of it is a region even more romantic, a cluster of higher mountains, green to their tops, yet with sides so precipitous and pinnacles so sharp one wonders how anything can grow on them. The region presents, in fact, such a prodigious variety of crags and precipices, peaks and summits, that the separate forms are lost in a chaos of beautiful hills.

The great granite rocks that guard the entrance to the harbor leave a passage scarcely a mile in width. At the base of the Sugar Loaf we saw a fairy white city romantically nestling in the shadow of the gigantic crag. It is the new National Exposition of Brazil.

Once safely inside the granite barriers, the bay opens out and becomes an inland sea, dotted with hundreds of islands, a landlocked basin with fifty square miles of deep water.

On the northern shores of the bay lies the town of Nictheroy, the capital of the state. Its name per petuates the old Indian title of the bay, "hidden water." The name of the capital of the Republic, on the south side of the bay, carries with it a remembrance of the fact that when first discovered, the bay was mistaken for the mouth of a great river, the River of January.

Since the early years of the sixteenth century, Rio has been conspicuous in the annals of discovery and conquest. Magellan touched here on his famous voyage round the world. The spot where he landed is now the site of a large hospital and medical school. French Huguenots attempted to find here a refuge in the time of the great Admiral Coligny. As one steams slowly into the harbor, one passes close to the historic island of Villegagnon, whose romantic story has been so graphically told by Parkman.

Hither came the King of Portugal, flying from the wrath of Napoleon. Here lived the good Emperor Don Pedro II, one of the most beneficent monarchs the world has ever seen. And into these waters are soon to come Brazil's new Dreadnoughts, about which all the world has been speculating, and which have made Argentina almost forget the necessities of economic development in her anxiety to keep up with Brazil in the way of armament.

An elaborate system of new docks, that has been in the course of construction for a long time, has not been completed yet; so we anchor a mile or more from the shore, not far from a score of ocean steamers and half a hundred sailing vessels. Before the anchor falls we are surrounded by a noisy fleet of steam launches, whose whistles keep up a most in fernal tooting. A score of these insistent screamers attempt to get alongside of our companion-way at the same time. In addition, half a hundred row-boats attack the ladder where some of the steerage passengers are trying to disembark.

We had heard, before entering the port, that there were several hundred cases of smallpox here, besides other infectious diseases. Yet this did not prevent everybody that wanted to, and could afford the slight cost of transportation, from coming out from the shore and boarding our vessel. Such a chattering, such a rustling of silk skirts and a fluttering of feathers on enormous hats, such ecstatic greetings given to returning citizens! Such ultra-Parisian fashions!

On shore we found the marks of modern Rio—electric cars, fashionable automobiles, well-paved streets, electric lights, and comfortable hotels—very much in evidence. Were it not for the blinding sunlight that fairly puts one's eyes out in the middle of the day, one could readily forget one's whereabouts. To be sure, if you go to look for it, there is the older part of the city which still needs cleaning up according to modern ideas of sanitation. But if you are content to spend your time in the fashionable end of the town or speeding along the fine new thoroughfares in a fast motor car, it is easy to think no more of Rio's bad record as an unhealthy port.

The city of Rio is spread over a large peninsula that juts out from the south into the waters of the great bay. Across the peninsula, through the centre of the busiest part of the city, the Brazilians have recently opened a broad boulevard, the Avenida Central. Fine modern business blocks have sprung up as if by magic, and the effect is most resplendent. The spacious avenue is in marked contrast with the very narrow little streets that cross it. One of them, the Rua Ouvidor, the meeting-place of the wits of Rio, is in many ways the most interesting street in Brazil. Here one may see everybody that is anybody in Rio.

At one end of the Avenida Central is Monroe Palace, which once did duty at an International Exposition, and more recently was the meeting-place of the third Pan-American Conference, made notable by the presence of Secretary Root. Beyond the showy palace to the east there are a number of little bays, semi-circular indentations in the shore, which have recently been lined with splendid broad driveways, where one may enjoy the sea breeze and a marvellous view over the inland sea to the mountains beyond.

At the far end of the new parkway rises the ever-present Sugar Loaf, at whose feet are the buildings of the National Exposition. They are wonderfully well situated, lying as they do on a little isthmus wedged in between two gigantic rocks, with the ocean on one side and the beautiful bay on the other. The buildings themselves are not particularly remarkable, being decorated in the gorgeous style of elaborate whiteness that one is accustomed to associate with expositions.

The crowds I saw there were composed exclusively of Brazilians, most of whom had apparently visited the grounds many times and accepted them as the fashionable evening rendezvous. Each of the states of Brazil had a building of its own in which to exhibit its products, and there was a theatre, a "Fine Arts" building, a Hall of Manufactures, and a sad attempt at a Midway. An entire building was devoted to the manufactures and exports of Portugal. All other buildings were devoted to the states or industries of Brazil, making the prejudice in favor of the mother country all the more noticeable.

A change is coming over the foreign commerce of Rio. Twenty years ago, the largest importing firms were French and English. Many of these have practically disappeared, having been driven out by Portuguese, Italian, and German houses. The marked leaning toward goods of Portuguese origin is very striking and naturally difficult to combat.

Brazil has recently established in Paris an office for promoting the country and aiding its economic expansion. This office is publishing a considerable literature, mostly in French, and will undoubtedly be able to bring about an increase of European commerce and that immigration which Brazil so much needs. The completion of the new docks will greatly help matters.

But besides new docks Rio needs a reformed customs service. Every one is agreed that the most vexatious thing in Rio is the attitude of the custom house officials. Either because they are poorly paid or else simply because they have fallen into extremely bad habits, they are allowed to receive tips and gratuities openly. The result may easily be imagined.

THE CORCOVADO FROM RIO

A few days after my arrival, an American naturalist, thoroughly honest but of a rather short temper, was treated with outrageous discourtesy, and his personal effects strewn unceremoniously over the dirty floor of the warehouse by angry inspectors, simply because he was unwilling to bribe them. There was no question as to his having any dutiable goods.

The population of Rio is variously estimated at between seven and eight hundred thousand, but her enthusiastic citizens frequently exaggerate this and speak in an offhand way of her having a million people. They are naturally reluctant to admit that Rio has any fewer than Buenos Aires.

The suburbs of Rio are remarkably attractive. On the great bay, dotted with its beautiful islands, are various resorts that take advantage of the natural beauties of the place, and cater to the pleasure-loving Brazilians. From various ports on the bay, railroads radiate in all possible directions, going north into the heart of the mining region and west through the coffee country to Saõ Paulo. The terminus of a little scenic railway is the top of one of the highest and most remarkable of the near-by peaks, the Corcovado. The view from the summit can scarcely be surpassed in the whole world. The intensely blue waters of the bay, the bright white sunlight reflected from the fleecy cumulous clouds so typical of the tropics, the verdure-clad hills, and the white city spread out like a map on the edge of the bay, combine to make a marvellous picture.

No account of Rio, however brief, would be com plete without some reference to the "Jornal do Comercio," the leading newspaper of Brazil, whose owner and editor, Dr. J. C. Rodriguez, is one of the most influential men in the country. In addition to guiding public opinion through his powerful and ably edited newspaper, he has had the time to attend to numerous charities and to the collection of a most remarkable library of books relating to Brazil. He has recently taken high rank as a bibliographer by publishing a much sought after volume on early Braziliana, basing his information largely on his own matchless collection.

Another well-edited paper is "O Paiz," which like the "Jornal do Comercio" has its own handsome edifice on the new Avenida Central. A subscription to it for one year costs "thirty thousand reis" —a trifle over nine dollars! As in the case of other South American newspapers, its offices are far more luxurious and elaborate than those of their contemporaries in North America. These southern dailies give considerable space to foreign cablegrams, so much more, in fact, than do our own papers, that it almost persuades one that we are more provincial than our neighbors.

Santos, the greatest coffee port in the world and the only city in Brazil having adequate docking facilities, is a day's sail from Rio. It is separated from the ocean by winding sea-rivers or canals. The marshes and flats that surround it, and the bleaching skeletons of sailing vessels that one sees here, are sufficient reminders of the terrible epidemics that have been the scourge of Santos in the past. Stories are told of ships that came here for coffee, whose entire crews perished of yellow fever before the cargo could be taken aboard, leaving the vessel to rot at her moorings. All of this is changed now, and the port is as healthy as could be expected.

Yet the town is not attractive. It lacks the picturesque ox-drays of Pernambuco and the charming surroundings of Rio. The streets are badly paved and muddy; the clattering mule-teams that bring the bags of coffee from the great warehouses to the docks are just like thousands of others in our own western cities. The old-fashioned tram-cars, running on the same tracks that the ramshackle suburban trains use, are dirty but not interesting. Prices in the shops are enormously high. In fact, on all sides there is too much evidence of the upsetting influence of a great modern commerce.

A long line of steamers lying at the docks taking on coffee is the characteristic feature of the place, and a booklet that has recently been issued to advertise the resources of Brazil bears on its cover a branch of the coffee tree, loaded with red berries, behind which is the photograph of a great ocean liner, into whose steel sides marches an unending procession of stevedores carrying on their backs sacks of coffee. It not only emphasizes Brazil's greatest industry, but it is also thoroughly typical of Santos.

Most of the coffee is grown in the mountains to the north, and comes to Santos from Saõ Paulo on a splendidly equipped British-built railway. The line is one of the finest in South America. It rises rapidly through a beautiful tropical valley by a gradient so steep as to necessitate the use of a cable and cogs for a large part of the distance. The powerhouses scattered at intervals along the line are models of cleanliness and mechanical perfection.

Notwithstanding the fact that America is by far the greatest consumer of Santos coffee, the greater part of the local enterprises are in British hands. The investment of British capital in Brazil is enormous. It has been computed that it amounts to over six hundred million dollars. Americans do not seem yet to have waked up to the possibilities of Brazilian commerce, or to the fact that the question of American trade with Brazil is an extremely important one.

It is only necessary to realize that the territory of Brazil is larger than that of the United States, that the population of Brazil is greater than all the rest of South America put together, and that Brazil's exports exceed her imports by one hundred million dollars annually, to understand the opportunity for developing our foreign trade.

Brazil produces considerably more than half of the world's supply of coffee, besides enormous quantities of rubber. The possibilities for increased production of raw material are almost incalculable. It is just the sort of market for us. Here we can dispose of our manufactured products and purchase what will not grow at home.

We have made some attempts to develop the field, even though our knowledge is too often limited to that of the delightful person who knew Brazil was "the place where the nuts come from!" We have

THE HARBOR OF SANTOS

little conception of the great distances that separate the important cities of Brazil and of the difficulties of transportation.

A story is told in Rio of an attempt to go from Rio to Saõ Paulo by motor, over the cart-road that connects the two largest cities in the Republic. The trip by railway takes about twelve hours. The automobile excursion took three weeks of most fearful drudgery. Needless to say, the cars did not come back by their own power.

It is more difficult for a merchant in one of the great coast cities of Central Brazil to keep in touch with the Amazon, than it is for a Chicago merchant to keep in touch with Australia.

Furthermore, to one who tries to master the situation, the coinage and the monetary system seem at first sight to present an insuperable obstacle. To have a bill for dinner rendered in thousands of reis is rather confusing, until one comes to regard the thousand rei piece as equivalent to about thirty cents.

Another and much more serious difficulty is the poor mail service to and from New York. To the traveller in South America, unquestionably the most exasperating annoyance everywhere is the insecurity and irregularity of the mails. The Latin-American mind seems to be more differently constituted from ours in that particular than in any other. He knows that the service is bad, slow, and unreliable. But it seems to make little difference to him, and the only effort he makes to overcome the frightfully unsatisfactory conditions is by resorting to the registered mail, to which he intrusts everything that is of importance. Add to this fact the infrequency of direct mail steamers from the United States to the East Coast, and it may readily be seen where lies one of the most serious obstacles in the way of extending our commerce with Brazil.

A marked peculiarity of the Brazilian market is its extreme conservatism. Brazilians who have become accustomed to buying French, English, and German products are loath to change. American products are unfashionable. The Brazilian who can afford it travels on the luxuriously appointed steamers of the Royal Mail, and he and his friends regard articles of English make as much more fashionable and luxurious than those from the United States.

This is largely due to the lack of commercial prestige which we enjoy in the coast cities of Brazil. The Brazilians cannot understand why they see no American banks and no American steamship lines. Our flag never appears in their ports except as it is carried by a man-of-war or an antiquated wooden sailing vessel. To their minds this is proof conclusive that the American, who claims that his country is one of the most important commercial nations in the world, is merely bluffing.

Such prejudices can only be overcome by strict attention to business, and this attention our exporters have in large measure not yet thought it worth while to give. The agents that they send to Brazil rarely speak Portuguese, and are unable to compete with the expert linguists who come out from Europe. Frequently they even lack that technical training in the manufacture of the goods which they are trying to sell, which gives their German competitors so great an advantage.

Still more important than commercial travellers in a country like Brazil, is the establishment of agencies where goods may be attractively displayed. An active importer told me that, in his opinion, the most essential thing for Americans to do was to maintain permanent depots or expositions where their goods could be seen and handled. Relatively little good seems to result from the use of catalogues, even when printed in the language of the country, owing to the insecurity of the mails and the absence of American banks or express companies which would insure the delivery of goods ordered.

Finally, it is disgraceful to be obliged to repeat the old story of American methods of packing goods for shipment to South America. This fact has been so often alluded to in many different publications that it might seem as though further criticism were unnecessary. Unfortunately, however, in spite of repeated protests, American shippers, forgetful of the almost entire absence of docks and docking facilities here, continue to pack their goods as if they were destined for Europe.

At most of the ports, lighters have to be used. These resemble small coal barges, into which the goods are lowered over the side of the vessel. Often more or less of a sea is running, and notwithstanding all the care that may be used the durability of the packing-cases is tested to the utmost. I saw a box containing a typewriter dumped on top of a pile of miscellaneous merchandise, from which it rolled down, bumping and thumping into the farther corner of the barge. Fortunately, this particular typewriter belonged to a make of American machines whose manufacturers have learned to pack their goods in such form as to stand just that kind of treatment. The result is that one sees that brand of machine all over South America.

The American consul in Rio, Mr. Anderson, has been doing a notable service in recent years by sending north full and accurate reports of business conditions in Brazil, and our special agent, Mr. Lincoln Hutchinson, has written excellent reports on trade conditions in South America. To the labors of both these gentlemen I am greatly indebted for information on this subject.

CHAPTER III
BUENOS AIRES

WE left Santos late on a Tuesday afternoon, and after two pleasant days at sea entered the harbor of Montevideo on Friday morning. It was crowded with ships of all nations, and we were particularly delighted to see the American flag flying from three small steamers. Could it be possible that the flag which had been so conspicuous for its absence from South American waters, was regaining in the twentieth century the preëminence it had in the early years of the nineteenth? Alas, no; the boats were only government vessels in the lighthouse service, towing lightships from the Atlantic to the Pacific coast. They had stopped here to coal, for Montevideo is a favorite port of call for steamers bound through the Straits of Magellan. Ever since the days when it was the home of active smugglers, who were engaged in defying Spain's restrictive colonial policy, Montevideo has been a prosperous trading centre. To-day, clean streets, new buildings, electric cars, fine shops, elaborate window displays, well-dressed people, and excellent hotels mark it as modern and comfortable.

It is difficult to realize that this is the capital of Uruguay, "one of the most tumultuous of the smaller revolutionary states of South America." The Amer ican is chagrined to find that the Uruguayan gold or paper dollar is worth two cents more than our own. And the Englishman is most annoyed to find the "sovereign" at a discount. But chagrin gives way to frank amazement at the high prices which the Montevidean is willing to pay for his imported luxuries.

The republic is small but there is no waste land, and the railroads bring in quantities of wool and food-stuffs destined for the European market. More than three thousand steamers enter the port annually. Most of them belong to the eighteen British lines that touch here. No wonder the city is wealthy and has attractive shops and boulevards. To be sure, the harbor improvements, not completed yet, have been greatly retarded by the most flagrant kind of political graft. But what American city, from New York to San Francisco, has a clean record in this particular?

Splendidly equipped steamers, resembling our Fall River boats, ply nightly between Montevideo and Buenos Aires, in order to accommodate the increasing numbers who wish to do business in both cities.

A generation ago the traveller to Buenos Aires was obliged to disembark in the stream seven or eight miles from the city, proceed in small boats over the shallow waters, and then clamber into huge ox-carts and enjoy the last mile or two of his journey as best he could. Since then, extraordinary harbor improvements, costing millions of dollars, have been completed, and ocean steamers are now able

THE DOCKS OF BUENOS AIRES

to approach the city through dredged channels. Yet such has been the phenomenal growth of the port that the magnificent modern docks are already overcrowded and the handling of cargo goes on very slowly, retarded by many exasperating delays. The regular passenger and mail steamers are given prompt attention, however, and the customs house examination is both speedy and courteous, in marked contrast to that at Rio. In years to come, the two other important ports of Argentina—Rosario, higher up the Rio de la Plata, and Bahia Blanca, farther down the Atlantic coast—are destined to grow at a rapid rate because of the better docking facilities they will be able to afford.

Bahia Blanca in particular is destined to have a great future, as it is the natural outlet for the rapidly developing agricultural and pastoral region of southern Argentina.

Buenos Aires, however, will always maintain her political and commercial supremacy. She is not only the capital of Argentina, but out of every five Argentinos, she claims at least one as a denizen of her narrow streets. Already ranking as the second Latin city in the world, her population equals that of Madrid and Barcelona combined.

Hardly has one left the docks on the way to the hotel before one is impressed with the commercial power of this great city. Your taxicab passes slowly through crowded streets where the heavy traffic retards your progress and gives you a chance to marvel at the great number of foreign banks, English, German, French, and Italian, that have taken pos session of this quarter of the city. With their fine substantial buildings and their general appearance of solidity, they have a firm grip on the situation. One looks in vain for an American bank or agency of any well-known Wall Street house. American financial institutions are like the American merchant steamers, conspicuous by their absence. The Anglo-Saxons that you see briskly walking along the sidewalks are not Americans, but clean-shaven, red-cheeked, vigorous Britishers.

In England they talk familiarly of "B.A." and the "River Plate"; disdaining to use the Spanish words Argentina, Uruguay, Paraguay, and Buenos Aires. To hear them you might suppose they were speaking of something they owned, and you would not be so very far from the truth. What Mexico owes to American capital and enterprise, the countries and cities of the Rio de la Plata owe to Great Britain. British capitalists have not been slow to realize the possibilities of this great agricultural region. They know its potentiality as a food-producer, and they have covered it with a network of railways much as we have covered the prairies of Illinois and the plains of Kansas. Of the billion and a quarter dollars of British capital invested in Argentina, over seven hundred millions are in railways. Thousands of active, energetic young Englishmen, backed by this enormous British capital, have aided in the extraordinary progress which Argentina has made during the past generation.

In some ways this is an English colony. The majority of the people do not speak English, except in the commercial district, and the Englishman is here on sufferance. But it is his railroads that tie this country together. It is his enterprises that have opened thousands of its square miles, and although the folly of his ancestors a century ago caused him to lose the political control of this "purple land," the energy of his more recent forebears has given him a splendid heritage. Not only has he been able to pay large dividends to the British stockholders who had such great faith in the future of Argentina, he has made many native Argentinos wealthy beyond the dreams of avarice.

Land-owners, whose parents had not a single change of clothes, are themselves considering how many motor cars to order. Their patronage sustains the finely appointed shops which make such a brave display on Florida and Cangallo Streets. These streets may be so narrow that vehicles are only allowed to pass in one direction, but the shops are first class in every particular and include the greatest variety of goods, from the latest creations of Parisian millinery to the most modern scientific instruments. Fine book shops, large department stores, gorgeous restaurants, expensive to the last degree, emphasize the wealth and extravagance of the upper classes.

On the streets one may hear all of the European languages. In the business district it is quite as likely to be English as Spanish, and in the poorer quarters Italian is growing more common every day. The speech of the common people is nominally Spanish, very bad Spanish. In reality it is a hybrid into which Portuguese, Italian, and Indian words and accents have entered to disfigure the beautiful Castilian.

When Rio cut her Avenida Central through the middle of her business district, she had in mind the Avenida 25 de Mayo of Buenos Aires, a typical imitation Parisian Boulevard that was opened not many years ago to facilitate traffic and beautify the city. On the Avenida, as in Rio, the leading newspaper has its luxurious home.

All the world has heard of "La Prensa" and its marvellously well-appointed building where distinguished foreigners are entertained, lectures are given, and all sorts of advertising dodges are featured. It was "La Prensa" that had the news of President Taft's election two minutes after it was known in New York. Many Porteños, as the people of Buenos Aires are called, think the columns of "La Prensa" are too yellow and that its business methods are almost too modern. They prefer the more dignified pages of the "Nacion."

The hotels on the Avenida are not up to the standard of three of those on the narrower thoroughfares. In fact, it would be hard to find more comfortable hostelries than the Grand or the Palace. The new Phœnix Hotel, one of the first skyscrapers to be erected here, promises even greater comforts and is to be the rendezvous of the British colony.

There are many theatres and they have a brilliant season, which begins in June. The pleasure-loving Porteños are willing to pay very high prices for the best seats, and managers can offer good

AVENIDA DE MAYO, BUENOS AIRES

salaries to tempt the best performers to leave Europe. Variety shows are popular and carried to an extreme with which we are not familiar in the United States.

Some of them are poor copies of questionable Parisian enterprises. But even these are not as bad as the moving picture shows that have captured Buenos Aires. Public opinion is astonishingly lax in the southern capital. Exhibitions of shocking indecency are countenanced, that would no longer be tolerated in Europe or North America. In this matter Buenos Aires also offers a marked contrast to Santiago de Chile where morals are on a much higher plane, thanks to the Catholic Church, which unfortunately seems to have lost its grip here.

The Porteño has not only forgotten his religion, he seems also to have lost the pleasing manners of his Castilian ancestors. I have been in eight South American capitals and in none have I seen such bad manners as in Buenos Aires. Nowhere else in South America is one jostled so rudely. Nowhere else does one see such insolent behavior and such bad taste. Santiago, Lima, Bogotá, and Caracas seem to belong to a different civilization. To be sure, none of them are as rich and prosperous. But in all of them good society is a much more ancient concern than in this overgrown young metropolis.

Here the newly rich are in full sway and their ideas and instincts seem to predominate. On Sunday afternoon, all the world dashes madly out to the race course, where it exercises its passion for gambling to the fullest capacity. In the Jockey Club inclosure are gathered the youth and beauty, the wealth and fashion of the city. And yet the ladies carry the artificial tricks of feminine adornment to such an amazing extent that it is almost impossible to realize that they belong to the fashionable world and not to the demi-monde. The races that I attended drew an audience of thirty thousand. One race had a first prize amounting to fifteen thousand dollars. The horses seemed to be of a rather heavier build than ours but they did not interest the spectators. Facilities for betting were provided on an elaborate scale. There were no bookmakers, and the odds depended entirely on the popular choice, as is commonly done in Europe. The gate receipts and the proceeds of the "percentage" are enormous and have enabled the Jockey Club to build one of the most luxurious and extravagant club houses in the world.

After the races, hundreds of motor cars and carriages promenade slowly up and down that part of the parkway which society has decreed shall be her rendezvous. Here one sees an astonishing display of paint and powder illuminating the faces of the devotees of a fashion which decrees that all ladies must have brilliant complexions. The effect is very unpleasant. I suppose it is simply another evidence of the newness of modern Buenos Aires. Very few wealthy families have a long-established social position. Culture and refinement are at a discount. Otherwise it is difficult to imagine how any society can tolerate such artificiality. This garish Sunday parade is quite a swing of the pendulum from the old days when Creole ladies, mod estly attired in lovely black lace mantillas, walked quietly to church and home again, as they still do in most South American cities.

It is hardly necessary to speak of the more usual evidences of great wealth, palatial residences that would attract attention even in Paris and New York, charming parks beautifully laid out on the shores of the great Rio de la Plata, and a thousand luxurious automobiles of the latest pattern carrying all they can hold of Parisian millinery.

One does not need to be told that this is a city of electric cars, telephones, and taxis. These we take for granted. But there is a characteristic feature of the city that is unexpected and striking: the central depots for imported thoroughbreds. Only a few doors from the great banks and railway offices are huge stables where magnificent blooded horses and cattle, sheep and pigs, which have brought records of distinguished ancestry across the Atlantic, are offered for sale and command high prices.

These permanent cattle-shows are the natural rendezvous of the wealthy ranchmen and breeders who are sure to be found here during a part of each day while they are in town. So are foreigners desirous of purchasing ranches and reporters getting news from the interior. The cattle-fairs offer ocular evidence of the wealth of the modern Argentino and the importance of the pastoral industry. There are over a hundred million sheep on the Pampas. Cattle and horses also are counted by the millions.

The problems of Argentine agriculture and animal industries are being continually studied by the great land-owners, who have already done much to improve the quality of their products.

During my stay in Buenos Aires, it was my privilege to visit an agricultural school in one of the neighboring towns. The occasion was the celebration of its twenty-fifth anniversary. The festivities were typically Spanish-American. An avenue of trees was christened with appropriate ceremonies, being given the name of the anniversary date. To each tree a bunch of fire-crackers had been tied. At the beginning and end of the avenue a new sign-post bearing its name had been put up and veiled with a piece of cheese cloth. A procession consisting of the officials of the school and of the National University of La Plata, with which the school is affiliated, alumni and visitors, formed at the school-buildings after the reading of an appropriate address, and marched down the new avenue following the band. As we progressed, the signs were unveiled and the bunches of fire-crackers touched off. At the far end, in a grove of eucalyptus trees, a collation was served, and we were entertained by having the fine horses and cattle belonging to the school paraded up and down. The school has an extensive property, is doing good work, and shows a practical grasp of the needs of the country.

Argentina has worked hard to develop those industries that are dependent upon stock-raising. The results have amply justified her. The exportation of frozen meat from Argentina amounts to nearly twenty million dollars annually. Only re cently one of the best known packing-houses of Chicago opened a large plant here and is paying tribute to the excellence of the native stock. Every year Argentina sends to Europe the carcasses of millions of sheep and cattle as well as millions of bushels of wheat and corn, more in fact than we do. Of all the South American republics, she is our greatest natural competitor, and she knows it. Nevertheless, she lacks adequate resources of iron, coal, lumber, and water power, and notwithstanding a high protective tariff, can never hope to become a competitor in manufactured products. Argentina exports more than three times as much per capita as we do, and must do so in order to pay for the necessary importation of manufactured goods. It also means that she will always find it to her advantage to buy her goods from England, France, and Germany, where she sells her food-stuffs. Brazil can send us unlimited amounts of raw materials that we cannot raise at home, while at present Argentina has little to offer us. Yet we are already buying her wool and hides, and before long will undoubtedly be eating her beef and mutton, as England has been doing for years.

The banks of Buenos Aires have learned to be extremely conservative. For a long time this city was a favorite resort of absconding bank cashiers from the United States, and stories are told of many well-dressed Americans who have come here from time to time without letters of introduction but with plenty of money to spend, who have been kindly received by the inhabitants, only to prove to be undesirable acquaintances. What we consider "old-fashioned and antiquated" English bank methods are the rule, and it frequently takes a couple of hours to draw money on a letter of credit even when one has taken the pains to notify one's bankers beforehand that the letter was to be used in South America. Personally, I have found American Express checks extremely useful in all parts of South America and have had no difficulty in getting them accepted in Buenos Aires. In the interior it is more difficult unless one comes well introduced. But the necessity for letters of introduction is quite generally recognized all over the continent. Strangers who have "neglected to supply themselves with credentials," frequently turn out to be fugitives from justice.

Another local peculiarity noticeable also in Chile, is that many of the citizens bitterly begrudge us our attempted monopoly of the title of "Americans." They catalogue us at all possible times under "N" instead of "A." They also speak of us as North Americans or as "Yankis," and they call our Minister the "North American Minister," quite ignoring the existence of Mexico and Canada.

Certain Americans who are desirous of securing an increase of our trade with South America and of placating in every possible manner the South Americans, overlooking the practical side of the question, have acquiesced in the local prejudice and speak of themselves as North Americans, even though they do not address their letters to the "United States of North America."

The fact that the South American refuses to grant us our title of "Americans" is really an indirect compliment. It is chiefly owing to the industry and intelligence of the citizens of the United States, that the word "American" has come to have a complimentary meaning, —far more complimentary in fact than it had fifty years ago when distinguished foreigners were wont to use that adjective as a peculiarly opprobrious epithet. With this change in the significance of the term has come a natural desire on the part of the South Americans to apply it to themselves. They reason that they have as good a right, geographically, to the term as we have, and they wilfully forget that each of their republics has in its legal title a word which conveniently and euphoniously characterizes its citizens. The people of the United States of Brazil are called Brazilians, and those of the United States of Mexico are Mexicans by the same right that those of the United States of America are Americans. To be sure, the world generally thinks of our country as the United States, quite forgetful that there are several other republics of the same name. It is a pity that a euphonious appellation cannot be manufactured from one or both of those two words. We cannot distinguish ourselves by the title "North American," as that ignores the rightful claim to that title which the denizens of the larger part of this continent, the Mexicans and Canadians, have in common with us. It is difficult to see how we are to avoid calling ourselves Americans even if it gives offence to our neighbors. It is not a point of great importance and it seems to me that in time, with the natural growth of Chile and the Argentine Republic, their citizens will be so proud of being called Chilenos or Argentinos that they will not begrudge us our only convenient and proper title.

There is another point, however, in their criticism of us which is more reasonable and on which they might be accorded more satisfaction. I refer to that part of our foreign policy known as the Monroe Doctrine. Many a Chileno and Argentino resents the idea of our Monroe Doctrine applying in any sense to his country and declares that we had better keep it at home. He regards it as only another sign of our overweening national conceit. And on mature consideration, it does seem as though the justification for the Monroe Doctrine, both in its original and its present form, had passed. Europe is no longer ruled by despots who desire to crush the liberties of their subjects. As is frequently remarked, England has a more democratic government than the United States. In all the leading countries of Europe, the people have practically as much to say about the government as they have in America. There is not the slightest danger that any European tyrant will attempt to enslave the weak republics of this hemisphere. Furthermore, such republics as Mexico, Argentina, Brazil, Chile, and Peru no more need our Monroe Doctrine to keep them from being robbed of their territory by European nations than does Italy or Spain. If it be true that some of the others, like the notoriously lawless group in Central America, need to be looked after by their neighbors, let us amend our outgrown Monroe Doctrine, as has already been suggested by one of our writers on international law, so as to include in the police force of the Western Hemisphere, those who have shown themselves able to practice self-control. With our lynchings, strikes, and riots, we shall have to be very careful, however, not to make the conditions too severe or we shall ourselves fail to qualify.

The number of "North Americans" in Buenos Aires is very small. While we have been slowly waking up to the fact that South America is something more than "a land of revolutions and fevers," our German cousins have entered the field on all sides.

The Germans in southern Brazil are a negligible factor in international affairs. But the well-educated young German who is being sent out to capture South America commercially, is a power to be reckoned with. He is going to damage England more truly than Dreadnoughts or gigantic airships. He is worth our study as well as England's.

Willing to acquaint himself with and adapt himself to local prejudices, he has already made great strides in securing South American commerce for his Fatherland. He has become a more useful member of the community than the Englishman. He has taken pains to learn the language thoroughly, and speak it not only grammatically but idiomatically as well; something which the Anglo-Saxon almost never does. He has entered into the social life of the country with a much more gracious spirit than his competitors and rarely segregates himself from the community in pursuing his pleasures as the English do. His natural prejudices against the Spanish way of doing things are not so strong.

His steamers are just as luxurious and comfortable as the new English boats. It is said that even if the element of danger that always exists at sea is less on the British lines, the German boats treat their passengers with more consideration, giving them better food and better service. No wonder the Spanish-American likes the German better than he does the English or American. Already the English residents in Buenos Aires, who have regarded the River Plate as their peculiar province for many years, are galled beyond measure to see what strides the Germans have made in capturing the market for their manufactured products and in threatening their commercial supremacy. And neither English nor Germans are going to hold out a helping hand or welcome an American commercial invasion.

Meanwhile the Argentinos realize that their country cannot get along without foreign capital, much as they hate to see the foreigner made rich from the products of their rolling prairies.

Politically, Buenos Aires and Argentina are in the control of the native born. They have a natural aptitude for playing politics, and they much prefer it to the more serious world of business. This they are quite willing to leave to the foreigner.

They realize also that they greatly need more immigrants. The population is barely five per square mile, and as a matter of fact, is practically much less than that for so large a part of the entire population is crowded into the city and province of Buenos Aires. Consequently they are doing all they can to encourage able-bodied immigrants to come from Italy and Spain.

And the immigrants are coming. My ship brought a thousand. Other ships brought more than three hundred thousand in 1908. Argentina is not standing still. Nor is she waiting for "American enterprise." During 1908 considerably more than two thousands vessels entered the ports of the republic. Four flew the American flag.

CHAPTER IV

ARGENTINE INDEPENDENCE AND SPAN-
ISH-AMERICAN SOLIDARITY

O_N the 25th of May, 1910, the Argentine nation in general, and Buenos Aires in particular, observed with appropriate ceremonies the one hundredth anniversary of their independence. Great preparations were made to insure a celebration that should suitably represent the importance of the event.

In 1810 Buenos Aires had been a Spanish colony for two hundred and fifty years following her foundation in the sixteenth century. But the Spanish crown had never valued highly the great rolling prairies drained by the Rio de la Plata. There were no mines of gold or silver here, and Spain did not send her colonists into far-away America to raise corn and wine that should compete with Spanish farmers at home. Buenos Aires was regarded as the end of the world. All persons and all legitimate commerce bound thither from Spain were obliged to go by way of Panama and Peru, over the Andes, across the South American continent, before they could legally enter the port of Buenos Aires. The natural result of this was the building up of a prosperous colony of Portuguese smugglers in southern Brazil. Another result was that no Spaniards cared to live so far away from home if they could possibly help it, and society in Buenos Aires was not nearly so brilliant as in the fashionable Spanish-American capitals of Lima, Santiago, or Bogotá.

During the closing years of the eighteenth century the Spaniards became convinced of their short-sighted policy and made Buenos Aires an open port. The English were not slow to realize that this was one of the best commercial situations in South America, and that far from being the end of the world, as the Spaniards thought, it was a natural centre through which the wealth of a large part of South America was bound to pass. The great Mr. Pitt, who was most interested in developing British commerce with South America, felt that it would probably be necessary to introduce British manufactures in the wake of a military expedition, and decided to seize Buenos Aires, which was so poorly defended that it could easily be captured by a small resolute force.

Accordingly in June, 1806, an attack was made. The Viceroy, notwithstanding repeated warnings, had made no preparations to defend the city, and it was captured without difficulty. There was great rejoicing in London at the report of the victory, but it was soon turned to dismay by the news of a disgraceful and unconditional surrender. The sudden overthrow of the English was due largely to the ability of a local hero named Liniers who played successfully on the wounded pride of the Porteños.

The significance of the episode is that it gave to the Porteños the idea that the power of Spain could be easily overthrown, and that they actually had the courage and strength to win and hold their own independence.

Hardly had the city recovered from the effects of its bombardment by the English before events, destined to produce a profound change throughout South America, commenced to attract attention in Spain. Napoleon inaugurated his peninsula campaigns, and the world beheld the spectacle of a Spanish king become the puppet of a French emperor. In July, 1809, a new Viceroy, appointed by the Spanish cortes then engaged in fighting against Napoleon, took possession of the reins of government in Buenos Aires. In the early months of 1810, Napoleon's armies were so successful throughout the Spanish peninsula that it seemed as if the complete subjection of Spain was about to be accomplished.

On May 18, the unhappy Viceroy allowed this news from Spain to become known in the city. At once a furor of popular discussion arose. Led by Belgrano and other liberal young Creoles, the people decided to defy Napoleon and his puppet king of Spain as they had defied the soldiers of England. On the 25th of May, the Viceroy, frightened out of his wits, surrendered his authority, and a great popular assembly that crowded the plaza to its utmost capacity appointed a committee to rule in his stead. So the 25th of May, 1810, became the actual birthday of Argentina's independence, although the acts of the popular government were for six years done in the name of Ferdinand, the deposed king of Spain, and the Act of Independence was not passed by the Argentine Congress until 1816.

No sooner had Buenos Aires thrown off the yoke of Spain than she began an active armed propaganda much as the first French republic did before her. Other cities of Argentina were forcibly convinced of the advantages of independence, and the armies of Buenos Aires pressed northward into what is now southern Bolivia. It was their intention to drive the Spanish armies entirely out of the continent, and what seemed more natural than that they should follow the old trade route which they had used for centuries, and go from Buenos Aires to Lima by way of the highlands of Bolivia and Peru. But they reckoned without counting the cost. In the first place the Indians of those lofty arid regions do not take great interest in politics. It matters little to them who their masters are. Furthermore, their country is not one that is suited to military campaigns. Hundreds of square miles of arid desert plateaux ten or twelve thousand feet above the sea, a region suited only to support a small population and that by dint of a most careful system of irrigation, separated by frightful mountain trails from any adequate basis of supplies, were obstacles that proved too great for them to overcome. Their little armies were easily driven back. On the other hand, when the royalist armies attempted to descend from the plateaux and attack the patriots, they were equally unsuccessful. The truth is that southern Bolivia and northern Argentina are regions where it is far easier to stay at home and defend one's self than to make successful attacks on one's neighbors. An army cannot live off the country as it goes along, and the difficulties of supplying it with provisions and supplies are almost insurmountable. The first man to appreciate this was José San Martin.

It is not too much to say that San Martin is the greatest name that South America has produced. Bolivar is better known among us, and he is sometimes spoken of as the "Washington of South America." But his character does not stand investigation; and no one can claim that his motives were as unselfish or his aims as lofty as those of the great general to whose integrity and ability the foremost republics of Spanish South America, Argentina, Chile, and Peru, owe their independence.

San Martin was born of Spanish parents not far from the present boundary between Argentina and Paraguay. His father was a trusted Spanish official. His mother was a woman of remarkable courage and foresight. His parents sent him to Spain at an early age to be educated. Military instincts soon drew him into the army and he served in various capacities, both in Africa and later against the French in the peninsula. He was able to learn thoroughly the lessons of war and the value of well-trained soldiers. He received the news of the popular uprising in Argentina while still in Spain, and soon became interested in the struggles of his fellow-countrymen to establish their independence. In 1812 he returned to Buenos Aires where his unselfish zeal and intelligence promptly marked him out as an unusual leader. The troops under him

THE USPALLATA PASS

became the best-drilled body of patriots in South America.

After witnessing the futile attempts of the patriots to drive the Spanish armies out of the mountains of Peru by way of the highlands of Bolivia, he conceived the brilliant idea of cutting off their communication with Spain by commanding the sea power of the West Coast. He established his headquarters at Mendoza in western Argentina, a point from which it would be easy to strike at Chile through various passes across the Andes. Here he stayed for two years governing the province admirably, building up an efficient army, organizing the refugees that fled from Chile to Mendoza, making friends with the Indians, and keeping out of the factional quarrels that threatened to destroy all proper government in Buenos Aires. In January, 1817, his army was ready. He led the Spaniards to think that he might cross the Andes almost anywhere, and succeeded in scattering their forces so as to enable him to bring the main body of his army over the most practical route, the Uspallata Pass.

The expedition was successful, and in 1818 San Martin had the satisfaction of administering such a decisive defeat to the Spaniards at Maipo as to insure Chilean independence. With the aid of a remarkable soldier of fortune, Thomas Cochran, Earl of Dundonald, and an interesting group of Anglo-Saxon seamen, San Martin drove the Spaniards from the West Coast and captured the city of Lima. The aid which was given him by Buenos Aires and Chile was not sufficient to enable him to penetrate the great Andes of the interior and totally destroy the last Spanish army. He sought Bolivar's aid, but that proud Liberator would only come as Commander-in-chief. So, rather than sacrifice the cause of independence, San Martin, with unexampled self-effacement, gave up his well-trained veterans to Bolivar and Sucre and quietly withdrew to his modest home in Argentina. His unwillingness to enter into political squabbles, his large-minded statesmanship, and his dignified bearing did not endear him to his fellow countrymen, and he was forced to pass the declining years of his life in Europe, an exile from his native land.

The history of the period is full of petty personal rivalries and absurd political squabbles. Against these as a background the magnificent figure of San Martin, efficient soldier, wise statesman, and unselfish patriot, stands out plainly distinct. His achievements are worthy to be remembered with those of the greatest heroes of history. His character, the finest that South America has ever produced, has few equals in the annals of any country.

For many years he was disliked by his fellow patriots because he openly expressed the belief that they were not fit for pure democratic government. Since his day many South Americans agree with him.

The most serious criticism, however, which we can lay at the door of the South American is his lack of political cohesion. The border provinces are everlastingly rebelling against the decrees of the central government. Furthermore, when the Spanish colonies secured their independence, they either did not combine or else combining soon fell apart. The reason for this lack of solidarity may be found in the history of the Hispanic race and in the geographical conditions that exist in the southern continent.

In criticising South American habits of mind and political tendencies, one must remember that the moral and intellectual characteristics that form the soul of a people have been developed by its entire past and represent the inheritance of its ancestors. For the motives of its conduct, one must look to its history.

Historically, the Hispanic race was led to develop individualistic rather than coöperative action. The forces at work in the peninsula were centrifugal rather than centripetal. A small handful of brave mountaineers were almost the only inhabitants of the peninsula that were able to defy the Moorish conquerors. The process of the Christian re-conquest of Spain was so slow that it took nearly eight centuries for her to grow from the lonely, rocky fastness of Covadonga to the group of Christian kingdoms that embraced the entire peninsula. During these eight hundred years, preceding the Conquest of America, the Spaniards fought almost continuously against an ever-present enemy. This developed a strong municipal spirit, for the towns on the frontier were in constant danger of attacks from the Moors, and it was necessary to grant them very considerable powers. As the boundaries of Christian Spain extended southward, new cities came to be frontier posts, but the old ones retained the powers and the semi-independence they had previously gained.

The result was a race of men devoted primarily to their cities; only secondarily to the province or kingdom to which their city belonged, and quite incidentally to Spain as a geographical and linguistic unit. Such a racial tendency could not help developing that disregard of large national interests in preference to petty local concerns which has been a most unfortunate trait in the history of the South American republics. For while it may be true that the conception of the city as the soul of the native country has always been effective from the point of view of the development of civilization, it has been disastrous in its effect on national progress. It was just that loyalty to the municipality that prevented the growth of the Greek Empire.

Another result of the eight hundred years of Christian warfare against the infidel Moor, was the development of moral and physical qualities that made possible the marvellously rapid conquest of America by small companies of conquistadores. Brave, bigoted, courageous, accustomed to continuous hostilities, ardently devoted to a cause for which they were willing to lay down their lives, fighting to the last ditch, it is not surprising that the ancestors of the South Americans were able to achieve such wonderful results in the early sixteenth century.

Only a vigorous and rising nation could have accomplished the great work of exploring, conquering, and colonizing America which was done at that time.

As a matter of fact, a wonderful transformation was then taking place in Spain. The marriage of Ferdinand and Isabella had united by personal bonds what had formerly been a handful of detached kingdoms. These countries each had their own laws, their own peculiar customs and separate administrative systems. Some of the provinces were inhabited by people of different stock. The process of unification was almost contemporaneous with the conquest and colonization of America.

For a career destined to be as great as that of any of the larger empires of history, Spain had at the beginning of the colonizing period an inadequate political organization. Spanish racial unity and religious uniformity were of recent growth. The European progenitors of the conquerors did not fight for Spain as a whole, but rather as citizens of a municipality or as vassals of a petty king. The spirit of a centralized, unified government whose citizens are willing to sacrifice everything for the sake of their nation, did not run in their blood. They belonged to a fragmentary and embryonic group of nations. Spain did not adopt a policy of centralization long enough before the acquisition of her American colonies to allow the results of such a change in methods of government to affect popular habits of thought. In the meantime, South America was being colonized by men who had no sense of racial unity and few tendencies towards concerted political action.

Hence it is not at all surprising that their descendants, the heroes of the Wars of Emancipation, did not find it easy or natural to unite under one government. It was in accordance with the history of their race that they should form separate political establishments. It was also in accordance with that Spanish colonial policy which forbade communication between the different colonies and in no way encouraged a community of interests.

Historically then, there was little to cause the South American colonies on achieving their independence, to unite, even had they not been separated by tremendous natural obstacles.

Although the basins of the Amazon, the La Plata, and the Orinoco offered many thousands of miles of navigable highways, the masses of water were too copious and too irregular to be controlled until the era of steam navigation. In the great valleys east of the Andes, the excessive fertility of the soil has produced an enormous area of continuous woodlands, a mass of vegetation that has defied the efforts of centuries to effect clearings and roads. This densely timbered and sparsely inhabited region keeps Venezuela from having any dealings with Bolivia more effectually than if an absolute desert lay between them.

There is nothing that separates one of the United States from another that is at all comparable to the lofty chain of the Andes and the impenetrable jungle that lies for hundreds of miles on the eastern slope of the Cordillera. The more one considers the matter, the more it seems as though nature could not have placed more impassable obstacles in the way of intercommunication if she had set out with that definite purpose in view. In comparison with the difficulties of travelling from Lima, the centre of the old Spanish domain, to Buenos Aires, a journey from New York to Charleston in the days of the Ameri can revolution was a mere pleasure jaunt, and yet it seemed difficult enough at that time! Nowhere in the English colonies existed such impediments to communication as the deserts of northern Chile and southern Peru, the swamps of eastern Colombia and western Venezuela, the forests of Ecuador, Peru, and Bolivia, or the gigantic chain of the Andes whose lowest point for thousands of miles is ten thousand feet above the sea.

The founders of the original thirteen English colonies not only inherited racial unity but providentially built their homes on a short strip of coast and occupied a homogeneous country, no larger than a single Spanish colony. Their union followed as a matter of course.

It was quite otherwise in South America. For, as though it were not enough that the tendency of the race was towards building up individual communities rather than federations, as though the laws forbidding the colonists from trading with one another and from travelling from one colony to another were not a sufficient preventive of union, all the forces of nature, mountains, rivers, deserts, swamps, and even winds, combined to promote the isolation of the new republics. The top of the highest mountain in the thirteen English colonies was not half as high as the lowest point in the ranges of lofty mountains that separated the Spanish colonies; nor one third as high as the Uspallata Pass by which Chile is connected with Argentina.

It is not for us to criticise the South Americans for having failed to unite and form a great nation. Our ancestors were favored by nature with a region that is comparatively accessible in all parts. It is not any more creditable to the English colonists that they united than it is discreditable to the Latin-Americans that they did not. In both cases, racial characteristics, aided by diverse policies of colonial administration made a foundation for growth which by an extraordinary coincidence, was in every possible way favored by local geographical conditions.

The English colonists, on securing their independence, had been acquainted with one another for generations; had fought side by side in the French and Indian wars; had intermarried, built up social and business friendships; united in sending agents to the mother country and in sending representatives to Congresses where the leading men of each colony came to know one another's desires and aspirations. Placed by fate on a narrow strip of coast less in length than the seaboard of Chile alone, enabled by nature to communicate both by sea and land, separated from one another by neither deserts nor lofty mountains, what more likely than that they should have followed their natural traditions and formed a single nation? The difficulties in the way of the South American colonists following such an example were stupendous. Scattered over an enormous area, separated by the greatest natural boundaries that nature has produced, it was scarcely to be expected that they too should not follow the traditions of their race and build up local governments instead of forming a federation.

The historical and geographical reasons that pre vented the formation of confederations have also mitigated against the building up of strong national governments. The citizen is still inclined to favor the affairs of his city rather than the good of his country. He finds it easier to be loyal to the local chieftain than to the central government. The cure for this, however, is already in sight. The energy and enterprise of English, French, and German capitalists are overcoming the obstacles that nature has placed in the way of intercommunication.

In time, aided by steam and electric systems of transportation, some of the Southern Republics may even unite with others. But before this comes about it may confidently be expected in the near future that the development of new transportation facilities will make possible the growth of strong national feeling and will prevent the states from falling apart. It will certainly make revolutions less frequent and bring a condition of stability that will even attract American capital and greatly augment European immigration.

CHAPTER V
THE TUCUMAN EXPRESS

For nearly three centuries the most important trade-route in South America was the overland trail from Buenos Aires to Lima by way of the silver mines of Potosí. The system of travel for both passengers and freight was well established. In 1773 there was published a little book called "El Lazarillo," "The Blind Man's Guide," which contains full information for travellers going from Buenos Aires to Lima with exact itineraries and "with some useful notes for those new business men who traffic by means of mules." The road with its post-houses, its relays of mules, and its provisions for the comfort of man and beast is well described. Buenos Aires is credited with having twenty-two thousand souls, of whom "ninety-nine are orphans and sixty-eight are in jail!"

I should have liked nothing better than to have been able to follow "The Blind Man's Guide" from post-house to post-house along the entire distance. But alas, since the days of railways, many of the road-houses that formerly offered "good accommodations to travellers," have disappeared, and it is necessary to go as the world goes and take the train—when there is one.

On November 13, 1908, accompanied by Mr. Huntington Smith, Jr., I left Buenos Aires for Bolivia. The first stage of the journey, seven hundred and twenty miles, was by train to Tucuman, over the tracks of the Buenos Aires and Rosario R. R., one of the oldest and richest railways in Argentina. Our train was made up entirely of vestibuled sleeping and dining cars.

Among the first-class passengers was a newly arrived Spanish mercantile clerk and a French commercial traveller. I noticed more French in Argentina and Brazil than on the West Coast or in the northern countries. Especially in the large cities, they, with the Germans and English, have been very active in promoting local enterprises.

In the first fifteen miles out from Buenos Aires we saw numbers of villas shaded by groves of eucalyptus trees standing in the midst of the owner's broad acres. There is considerable evidence of market gardening and general agriculture. So far as we could see from the train, the roads are very bad and have not improved since the days of the woe-begotten travellers who had to cross these plains in ox-carts.

When Edmund Temple, the breezy secretary of the Potosí, La Paz & Peruvian Mining Association, crossed Argentina on his way to Bolivia in 1825, he was struck with the immense number of "hoppers" that they passed on the Pampas. He says the locusts covered the road and adjacent parts for miles. In those days, pasturage was plenty, and cultivated fields were scarce, so nobody cared very much. It is only with the increasing importance of crops that the Argentinos have come to regard the swarms of locusts as a great pest, and have spent many thousands of dollars fighting them. They are now planning to build a fence of sheet zinc, costing several million dollars, to keep back the "hoppers." Some modern travellers have had their trains delayed by locust swarms on the tracks, but we saw comparatively few.

Our first stops were at suburban towns, which are more attractive than one would suppose in a country that is so flat. At one of them, on the River Tigre, the English colony has made boating fashionable, with festivals like those at Henley. We had showers in the course of the morning, but the country over which we passed looked rather dry.

A characteristic feature of the Pampas are the modern windmills with their steel frames. Most of them are of American make, for despite our backwardness in some lines, we have been peculiarly successful in supplying Argentina with windmills. In fact, we have almost monopolized that particular business. Fortunately, our manufacturers seem also to excel in the production of small and inexpensive motors, such as are particularly desired on farms and ranches where, owing to the extreme difficulty of getting workmen, there is an excellent market for labor-saving machinery. Notwithstanding this encouraging feature, for every million dollars' worth of goods which Argentina imports from the United States, she imports six millions from Europe.

Many of the interior towns have their own electric lighting plants. The agents of German manu facturers have been far-sighted in following up new concessions and in getting large contracts for the installation of German machinery. It takes a good many windmills to equal one electric lighting plant.

Our train made a short stop at Rosario, the second largest city in Argentina. Owing to its advantageous situation at the bend of the Paraná River, it has become a most important port.

Accessible throughout the year to vessels drawing sixteen feet, it is the terminus of many trans-Atlantic lines which bring European manufactured goods here in exchange for wheat and cattle. Some ore from Bolivia is also shipped from here. On our mule trip in Southern Bolivia we saw hundreds of animals laden with huge packing-cases from Europe marked "via Rosario."

The other important new port in Argentina is Bahia Blanca, which is situated several hundred miles south of Buenos Aires and is connected by railways with the newly opened regions in northern Patagonia. There is no scarcity of good agricultural land as yet undeveloped. Were the government of Argentina as well managed for the interests of the individual farmer as the governments of our western states, there is no question that Argentina would secure a much higher grade of immigrant. The opportunities are truly magnificent, but I was repeatedly told by foreign residents who are engaged in farming, that there are many unpleasant features. The truth of the matter is that the Argentino is too fond of keeping political power in his own hands. He does not understand all that is meant by a constitu tional democratic form of government. It is not his fault, for his race history, as we have seen, has given him other inheritances and prejudices. Nevertheless he is learning.

Leaving Rosario we plunged into the heart of a great agricultural and pastoral region. The heat and dust were rather trying. The humidity was considerable, being about eighty per cent in our car. In truth, we experienced all the various annoyances to which one is subject when crossing our western plains, in a moderately slow train. We had been told that this Tucuman express was "the finest train in America." Some of the young Englishmen on our steamer were extremely enthusiastic over it and assured us that we could have nothing so fine in the United States. Consequently we were somewhat disappointed to find the standard of comfort not any greater than it was on our western trains fifteen years ago.

There is one thing, however, in which the "B. A. and R." is ahead of most American railroads. At each station are one or two very large sign-boards conveniently placed so that the stranger has no difficulty in ascertaining whether he has reached his destination or not. And there are other little things along the line that make one feel the presence of railway officials carefully trained in English railway methods. It goes without saying that the road is largely owned in England and has Anglo-Saxons for its principal officers.

Argentina has about thirteen thousand miles of railway operated under some twenty companies. One thousand seven hundred miles are owned by the government, but by far the larger part of the railway system is controlled by British capitalists. A little more than half of the mileage consists of the very broad five and a half foot gauge. The remainder is one metre or less. The three gauges necessitate considerable transferring of freight and passengers.

To one who is accustomed to thinking of Argentina as a rich but undeveloped region, it seems incredible that she should have fifty thousand freight-cars and two thousand passenger-coaches. It is still more astonishing to learn that every year her railways carry thirty million passengers, and thirty million tons of freight, of which about one third are cereals. During the year 1906, the receipts from the passenger traffic amounted to more than $18,000,000, and from freight traffic to something over $55,000,000. Statistics are dry and uninteresting except as they open our eyes to conditions of which we have formed but a small conception. The extremely rapid growth of the Argentine railways is shown by the fact that while in 1884 the capital invested did not amount to $100,000,000, it now amounts to over $700,000,000.

So far as killing people is concerned, the Argentine railways do not come up to our record, although they do fairly well. In 1905 they killed, all told, two hundred and eighteen persons, and in 1906, two hundred and fifty. This is a heavier percentage per passenger carried than in the United States.

Towards evening we left the farming country and entered a barren region where great stretches of perfectly flat land seemed to promise splendid results if it could be irrigated.

The dust increased, and we were glad enough to be hauled over these dry pampas of Santa Fé and Santiago del Estero in a night, instead of being obliged to spend a fortnight on them following a slow-moving Spanish caravan.

When we looked out of the car window the next morning all was changed. Sugar-cane fields waving attractively in the sunlight, big wheeled carts lumbering noisily along drawn by oxen or mules, lithe horsemen riding strong little ponies through thickets of dry scrub, had transformed the scene from the everlasting prairies of the pampas into the highlands of the northwest. The hills beyond the fields of cane were covered with a scrubby growth. To the north-west and north arose green mountains that seemed to be forested to their tops. Some of the trees were in bloom with brilliant yellow flowers.

The contrast between the dry, barren pampas and the green cane-fields of Tucuman is so striking that Argentine writers have been accustomed to speak of the latter in terms of the most extravagant praise. Even the well-travelled Sarmiento called it the "Eden of America," "where nature had displayed its greatest pomp!" As a matter of fact Tucuman is admirably situated in a very fertile and highly cultivated plain, and is the centre of the most important sugar-growing region in Argentina. In its immediate vicinity we counted a dozen tall chimneys of sugar factories.

We reached the city about ten o'clock.

It was founded about the time that Sir Walter Raleigh was looking for Eldorado. Here in 1816, the Argentine Congress passed their Declaration of Independence. Here Belgrano won a great victory over the Spanish armies that had descended from Peru to crush the Argentine patriots.

The Tucuman station, a large modern affair, was chiefly interesting because of the picturesque character of the luggage that was lying about the platforms. Chairs and cots, pots and pans, spring mattresses, and hen-coops, all bore evidence to the fact that this is still a young country into which new settlers are coming, and that the Railroad Company has the good sense to make it easy for people to travel with all their possessions. Everything was checked and went in the luggage-van, as a matter of course, instead of being handed over to "slow-freight" or rapacious express companies, as with us.

Most of the immigrants were Italians from Genoa and the north of Italy. A few came from Galicia, the home of Spain's most sturdy peasantry. Neither immigrants nor residents wore picturesque costumes. Even the Gauchos are dressed in civilized raiment and bear little resemblance to the South American Indian of our dreams. It is too progressive a country to allow its clothes to get in its way.

The facts relating to Buenos Aires and Argentina are at every one's elbow so it is all the more astonishing how ignorant the average American is regarding the great metropolis of the southern hemisphere. We are very fond of telling stories of our English cousins who imagine that our western states are overrun with wild Indians and desperadoes. And we think it inexcusable in them to judge from the frequent press reports of lynchings and "hold-ups" that we are an uncivilized, lawless people. Yet we judge the Argentino just as hastily. Not only are we quite ignorant of his material progress, we also frequently slander him for having an "unstable government." "Revolutions" or struggles for governmental control occur, it is true, but they do not amount to much and hardly deserve the exaggerated reports of them which are published abroad. In a country that has been bound together by such a network of railroads as Argentina, making it possible for the government in power to send its troops rapidly wheresoever it will, the habit of playing with revolutions is sure to die out. In the old days when transportation was slow and difficult, it was possible for a popular leader to gather a considerable band of followers and prepare to march on the capital before the government knew of his existence. Such uprisings, however, are necessarily the work of days or weeks, and it is becoming more and more difficult to bring them to a successful issue. As an evidence of the more stable condition of the government and as showing how Argentina has recovered from the setback which it got at the time of the failure of the Baring Brothers, it is well to note that in the ten years between 1895 and 1905, the foreign trade of Buenos Aires more than doubled, growing to more than half a billion dollars annually.

CHAPTER VI
THROUGH THE ARGENTINE HIGHLANDS

At Tucuman we left the broad gauge of the British-built Buenos Aires and Rosario R. R. for the metre gauge of the North Central Railway, an Argentine Government line, that runs to Jujuy and has recently been continued northward to La Quiaca, on the Bolivian frontier. The distance from Buenos Aires to La Quiaca is 1150 miles. Of this we had done 700 miles in the first twenty-four hours. The last 450 miles required another twenty-four hours, divided into two daylight periods, as sleeping-cars are not run on the North Central R. R. In this stretch the elevation rises from thirteen hundred feet to twelve thousand feet, and the journey lies entirely in the Argentine Highlands.

Our train was mixed passenger and freight. The locomotive was a "Baldwin" and the cars were made in Wilmington, Del. We had, besides, an excellent dining-car that seated sixteen people and provided a table d'hôte meal served in the usual Spanish style. The third-class passengers, however, patronized the enterprising women who sold flat loaves of bread, hard-boiled eggs, and native drinks at the stations where we stopped.

Not long after leaving Tucuman, we passed through a tunnel, the first one in eight hundred miles. Rather a different experience from my journey in Venezuela, from Caracas to Valencia, where in the course of an hour we passed through sixty-five tunnels, one every minute!

With many windings we climbed up into the hills. Grass became scarcer and cactus and mimosa trees more common. We passed a small flock of goats. Dust and sand came into the train in clouds. Occasionally we passed lofty whirlwinds, but none of them troubled us. The humidity to-day was very much less, being under forty per cent. The streams seemed to be very low. We saw a few locusts.

At many of the stations were carts drawn by mules harnessed three abreast, with a loose rope-tackle that is characteristic of this hilly region. The houses of some of the more well-to-do were built of corrugated iron and wood, but most were made of mud. As it was the dry season, the cots were usually out of doors.

The evidences of prosperity at Ruis de los Llanos consisted of new stucco buildings of attractive construction with arcades in front and courtyards in the interior, a modern application of old Spanish architectural ideas. Other buildings were nearing completion, to accommodate the bakers and grocers who supply the quebracho cutters. There are great forests of quebracho on the plains of the Gran Chaco to the east and northeast. The wood is extremely hard and very serviceable for railway-ties. Owing to the difficulty that is experienced in cutting it, it has earned for itself the sobriquet of "axe-breaker." It is the chief article of export from this region. The bark is shipped to tanneries as far away as California.

At Matan, another important station, there was a new hotel, the "Cosmopolita," a clean-looking Spanish inn, near the railway station. Near by lay huge logs of quebracho awaiting shipment. The hills were well wooded, and we saw a number of agave plants and mimosa trees. Firewood is shipped from here to the treeless Pampas. Here we noticed, for the first time, riding-boots of a curious fashion, so very corrugated that we dubbed them "concertinas." They are much in vogue also in southern Bolivia.

At Rio Piedras, where a dozen of our third-class passengers alighted with many baskets and bundles, we heard the familiar hum of a sawmill. Near the track were more quebracho logs. A burly passenger who had joined us at Tucuman, ready dressed and prepared for a long horseback ride, left us here. With a large broad-brimmed hat, loose white jumper, large baggy white cotton trousers, and "concertinas," he came very near being picturesque. Throwing over his shoulder a pair of cotton saddle-bags well stocked with interesting little bundles, he walked slowly away from the train with that curious shuffling gait common to those who spend most of their lives in the saddle.

Not far away we saw some newly arrived American farm machinery, a part of the largest item of Argentine imports from the United States.

During the course of the afternoon, we wound out of the hills far enough to be able to see far over the plains to the east. Here there was more vegetation and some corn growing. On the left were jagged hills and mountains. The temperature in the car about four o'clock was eighty-five degrees. Our altitude was about twenty-five hundred feet.

As we went north through hot, dusty valleys, climbing up into the foot-hills of the Andes, the faces of the loiterers at the stations lost the cosmopolitan aspect that they have in and about Buenos Aires. We saw more of the typical Gaucho who is descended from the aboriginal Indians of the Pampas and bold Spanish cattle-drivers. Tall in stature, with a robust frame and a swarthy complexion, he possesses great powers of endurance and is a difficult person to handle. His tendencies are much like those of the fast disappearing American "cow puncher," but he has the disadvantage of having inherited a contempt for manual labor and an excessive vanity which finds expression in silver spurs and brilliantly colored ponchos. His territory is rapidly being invaded by hard-working Italians, more desirable because more dependable.

Near Juramento the country grows more arid and desolate. A few scrubby mimosa trees, sheltering the white tents of railway engineers, offered but little welcome to intending settlers.

Just at dark we reached Guemes, where we were obliged to change cars. The through train from Tucuman goes west to Salta, the most important city of the vicinity. We arrived at Jujuy shortly after nine o'clock. A score of ancient vehicles were waiting to take us a mile up into the town to one of the three hotels. We went to the Bristol and found it quite comfortable according to Spanish-American ideas. That means that the toilet facilities were absent, that the room had a tile floor, and that there were beds and chairs.

In the morning we got up early enough to look at the town for a few minutes before leaving on the semi-weekly train for La Quiaca.

Jujuy was built by Spanish settlers a generation before the Pilgrims landed at Plymouth, and still preserves the white-walled, red-tiled-roof aspect of the old Spanish-American towns. Lying in a pleasant, well-watered plain, a trifle over four thousand feet above the sea, it is attractively surrounded by high hills. Beyond them, we caught glimpses of lofty barren mountains, the summits of the Andes. The near-by valleys were green, and there is some rainfall even in the dry time of the year. Although Jujuy produces a large amount of sub-tropical fruit, it really owes its importance to its strategical position on the old trade route to Bolivia. It is the last important town on the road because it is the last place that enjoys a salubrious situation. For centuries it has been the natural resting-place for overland travellers.

In fact, these northwestern highlands of Argentina, Jujuy, and Tucuman, were first settled by emigrants from the mountains of Upper Peru now called Bolivia, of which they form the southern extension. Their political and commercial relations were with Potosí and Lima rather than Buenos Aires. The great prosperity of the mining regions of the lofty plateau created a demand for provisions that could not be met by the possibilities of agriculture in the semi-arid irrigated valleys of southern Bolivia. Beef and other provisions could most easily be brought from the fertile valleys near Tucuman and Jujuy. The necessity for some better animal than the llama, to carry not only freight but also passengers, caused a demand for the horses and mules which, raised on the Argentine Pampas, were brought here to be put into shape for mountain travel, and were an important item in the early fairs.

When the railroad came, Jujuy was for many years the northern terminus. This only added to the importance of the town, and increased the reputation of its annual fair. But with the building of the continuation to La Quiaca, its importance is bound to decrease. However, it will always be a favorite resort for Bolivians seeking a refuge from the rigors of their Thibetan climate. We met many families in southern Bolivia who had at one time or another passed the winter season here.

Before leaving the Bristol we succeeded in getting eggs and coffee only with considerable difficulty as the train was due to leave at seven o'clock, and the average Spanish-American traveller is quite willing to start off on a long day's journey without even a cup of coffee if he can be sure of something substantial about ten or eleven o'clock.

When we arrived at the station, we found a scene of great confusion. The line had been running only a few months, and many of the intending passengers were not accustomed to the ways of railroads. An official, and his family of three, had spread himself over one half of the car, with bags, bird-cages, bundles, rolls, and potted plants. He filled so many seats with his impedimenta that several of the passengers had to stand up, although that did not worry him in the least. Had we known how much luggage belonged to him, we should have dumped it on the floor and had a more comfortable ride, but unfortunately we did not discover how greatly he had imposed on everybody until the end of the day.

From Jujuy the train climbs slowly through a valley toward a wonderful vista of great mountains. At 6000 feet the verdure disappeared, the grass became brown, and on the barren mountains a few sheep and goats were trying to pick up a living.

The railway had a hard time overcoming the difficulties of the first part of the way. The grade is so steep that for some distance a cog road was found to be necessary. In the first one hundred and fourteen miles, the line climbs up 8000 feet to an altitude of over 12,000 feet above sea-level.

Notwithstanding the newness of the road and the steepness of the grade, we carried with us an excellent little restaurant car that gave us two very good meals before we reached La Quiaca.

The cog railway begins at Leon at an altitude of 5300 feet and continues to Volcan, rising 1500 feet in a distance of eight miles. At Volcan there is supposed to be a mud volcano, but, as was pointed out some years ago by Mr. O'Driscoll in the "Geographical Journal," there is no volcano at all. It is simply a mud avalanche, that comes down after unusually heavy rains from the rapidly disintegrating hillside. Although not a volcano, it is nevertheless a difficult problem for the engineers. It has already completely submerged a mile or two of track more than once.

This is on the line of the proposed Pan-American railway from New York to Buenos Aires. With a sufficiently vivid imagination, one can picture a New Yorker of the year 1950 being detained here by a mud-slide which will have put the tracks over which he proposes to travel two or three feet under ground. It is to be hoped that he will not be obliged to stay at the local inn where Edmund Temple stopped on his journey from Buenos Aires to Potosí. Temple was aroused in the middle of the night by a noise under his bed as if of a struggle between two animals. To his astonishment (and to that of the reader of his charming volumes) he "discovered, by the light of the moon, a cat eating the head of a viper which she had just subdued: a common occurrence I was informed, and without any ill consequences to the cat, however venomous the snake!"

Some effort had been made to plant a few trees in the sandy, rocky soil around the station of Volcan, which is not far from the mud-slide. They seemed, however, to be having a hard time of it, although, at a ranch near by, quite a grove of eucalyptus trees had been successfully raised by means of irrigation. The mountains round about are very barren and gave evidence of being rapidly wasted away by erosion, their summits assuming many fantastic forms.

Twenty miles beyond Volcan is Maimará, where there was further evidence of irrigation in the valley, the trees and green fruits being in marked contrast to the barren hillsides.

As the road ascends, the country becomes more and more arid. Cactus is common. Sometimes it is used as a hedge; at other times, by being planted on the top of a mud-fence, it answers the same purpose as a barbed wire.

Great barren mountains on each side continue for mile after mile, making the scenery unspeakably dreary. Judging by the northward inclination of the cactus and the trees, the prevailing wind is from the south.

Some of the valley is irrigated, but there is little sign of life anywhere. Nothing grows without irrigation. In the days before the railway it was absolutely necessary to have alfalfa and other animal fodder grown near the post-houses that supplied travellers and freight-carriers with shelter at night. This business has, of course, fallen off very much in the past few months, yet just before reaching Humahuaca we stopped at Uquia, where enough hay is still raised to make it worth while to bale it and ship it north to the barren plateau beyond.

Late in the afternoon, we saw a group of llamas, but they are not at all common in this region.

At Tres Cruces, 1052 miles from Buenos Aires, we reached our highest elevation, something over 12,000 feet. It was a dreary spot with scarcely anything in sight except barren mountains, the two wire fences that everlastingly line the railroad tracks, and the mud-walled railroad station. The little "hotel" looked like an abandoned adobe dwelling in Arizona, and the region bore a striking resemblance to the unirrigated part of our new southwest. Erosion has cut the hillsides into interesting sections of shallow gulches and semi-cylindrical slopes. The only green things to be seen are occasional clumps of bushes like sage-brush.

From here to La Quiaca, sixty miles, we maintained about the same altitude, although La Quiaca itself is 500 feet lower than Tres Cruces. We had, in fact, surmounted the great plateau of the Andes. South of us lay the desert of Atacama; to the north the arid valleys of southern Bolivia and the Bolivian tableland. East of us, beyond many intervening ranges and the steep slopes of the eastern Andes, lay the Gran Chaco of Bolivia and the valley of the lower Pilcomayo with its wild Indian tribes and its tropical forests. To the west lay the still higher Andes of the great Cordillera, some of whose peaks rise at this point to an altitude of twenty thousand feet. Notwithstanding these interesting surroundings, the extreme bareness of this desolate region reacts on one's enthusiasm.

We reached La Quiaca just before nine o'clock. The railroad offices were still incomplete, as the line had only been opened to traffic for a month or two. The old town of La Quiaca, a small mud-walled affair two miles away from the railroad station, is destined soon to be deserted for the thriving young settlement that is springing up near the terminus of the railway. There are two "hotels." Ours, the 25 de Mayo, had only just been opened. In fact, its ex terior walls had not yet received their proper coat of whitewash and stucco.

All day long we had been travelling through an extremely sparsely populated region, so dry, high, and inhospitable as to dispel any idea that this railroad can rely upon it for much traffic. In fact, the line was built by the Argentine Government, not so much to open up this part of the Republic as to tap the mining region of southern Bolivia, with the idea of developing Argentina's foreign commerce by securing in Bolivia a good market for her food-stuffs and bringing back in return ore to be shipped to Europe from the ports of the Paraná.

An agreement was entered into between Argentina and Bolivia whereby Bolivia was to extend her system of national railways southeast from Oruro to Potosí and thence due south to Tupiza, fifty miles north of the Argentine boundary. The Argentinos on their part agreed to continue their railway north from Jujuy to Tupiza. By the time they reached La Quiaca, however, the English Company that owns the rich Oruro-Antofagasta line became alarmed lest such an arrangement as was proposed would interfere with their profits. By some means or other, the Bolivian government was persuaded to change its plans and decide to build the national railways so as to connect with the Antofagasta line rather than with the Argentine lines. This breach of faith on the part of the Bolivianos was naturally resented not only in Argentina but also by the southern Bolivianos themselves who would be much more benefited by hav ing good connections with Buenos Aires than with the Chilean seaboard.

As a result of this difficulty, the Argentinos, at the time of my visit, had not carried their railway beyond the frontier. This makes La Quiaca the outfitting point for mule-trains that now start here with merchandise destined for the cities of southern Bolivia.

A stage-line has been opened, running once a week to Tupiza, where it connects with stages for Uyuni on the Antofagasta line and Potosí. This stage-line was owned and operated by that same energetic Scotchman, Don Santiago Hutcheon, who used to run stages between La Paz and Oruro before the completion of the Bolivia Railway. By great good fortune, we found him in La Quiaca where he had arrived that day on one of his own stages.

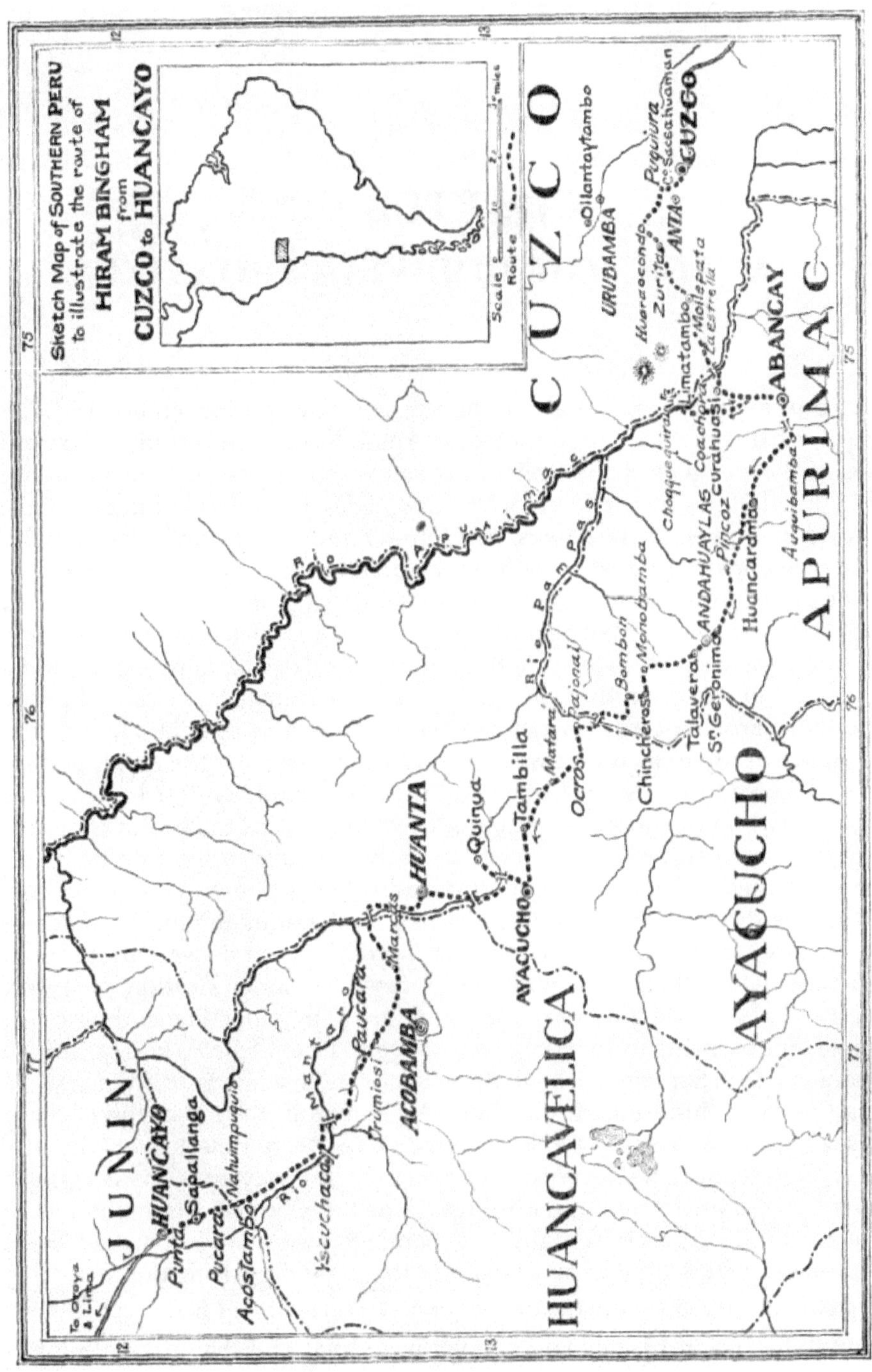

SOUTHERN PERU

CHAPTER VII
ACROSS THE BOLIVIAN FRONTIER

Soon after our arrival at La Quiaca, at 9 P.M. on November 15, 1908, we received a call from two rough-looking Anglo-Saxons who told us hair-raising stories of the dangers of the Bolivian roads where highway robbers driven out of the United States by the force of law and order and hounded to death all over the world by Pinkerton detectives, had found a pleasant resting-place in which to pursue their chosen occupation without let or hindrance. We found out afterwards that one of our informants was one of this same gang of robbers. Either he decided that we were disposed to regard his "pals" in a sufficiently lenient manner to make our presence in Bolivia immaterial to them, or else he came to the conclusion that we had nothing worth stealing, for we were allowed to proceed peaceably and without any annoyance wherever we journeyed in Bolivia. He put the case quite emphatically to us that it was necessary for them to make a living, that they were not allowed to do so peaceably in the States, that they desired only to be let alone and had no intention of troubling travellers except those that sought to get information against them. They relied entirely for their support on being able to overcome armed escorts accompanying loads of cash going to the mines to liquidate the monthly payroll. This they claimed was legitimate plunder taken in fair fight. The only individuals who had to suffer at their hands were those who took up the case against them. Having laid this down for our edification, he proceeded to tell us what a reckless lot they were and how famous had been their crimes, at the same time assuring us that they were all very decent fellows and quite pleasant companions. Don Santiago, who in his capacity as coach-master and stage-driver, has had to carry hundreds of thousands of dollars in cash over the unprotected Bolivian highways, assured us that he had never been molested by any of these highwaymen because he never troubled them in any way either by carrying arms or spreading information of their doings. If the Bolivian bandits are half as bad as they were painted to us that night, Don Santiago must lead a charmed life for he and his stages certainly offer an easy mark for any enterprising outlaw.

The view from our hotel the next morning across the sandy plaza of La Quiaca was anything but inspiring. The plateau is so high and dry that nothing grows here. Even the mountains, whose tops are really higher than our own far-famed Pike's Peak, look stunted like low sand-hills. Partly finished adobe houses, which were gradually meeting the demands of the newly-born commercial life of La Quiaca add to the forlorn and desolate appearance of everything. There was nothing to make us wish to stay any longer in Argentina, and we eagerly welcomed Don Santiago and his eight-mule team that

OUR COACH LEAVING THE HOTEL AT LA QUIACA

rattled up to the door a few minutes after six o'clock.

A quarter of a mile north of the town we crossed the frontier and entered Bolivia. For the next four hours there was little in the landscape to relieve the monotony of the journey. As those who are familiar with stage travel know to their cost, bumping over rough roads of stone or sand, in a cloud of dust with nothing to see on either side except a brown, treeless, rolling plateau, is not exciting. Nevertheless the process of keeping eight mules on the go, up hill and down hill, is never absolutely devoid of interest. As it was quite impossible for the driver to reach the foremost mules with his long whip, he employed a strong-lunged boy to race alongside of the mules, pelt them with stones, curse them in his worst Spanish, and frighten them into frantic activity with the lash of a short-handled whip which he laid on with no delicate hand. The mules became so afraid of his mad rushes that when they heard him coming they bolted in the opposite direction, sometimes pulling the stage-coach a rod or two off the road.

In a rarefied atmosphere that would almost kill a foreigner who should try to run any distance, the Indian boy only found it necessary to take short rests on the running-board of the coach, and even then he had breath enough left to keep up shrill whistling and loud shouting so as to make the mules remember his presence. If he stopped this continuous performance he heard from the driver in no uncertain language. The result was that, notwithstanding the primitive cart-track, the stage was able to make the sixty miles between La Quiaca and Tupiza in twelve hours. To be sure, there are two changes of mules and the luggage is carried on a separate wagon. But the road is as bad as it possibly can be. So much of it is in the bed of a stream, the coaches can only run in the dry season, May to November. In the rainy season the road disappears under swollen rivers and resort has to be had to saddle and pack animals.

In this extremely arid region the business of feeding the mules is a most difficult one. The rainfall is very slight. It is only by irrigation that fodder will grow at all. The ground is not sterile but it is so dry and parched that it does not look as if it would ever grow anything. The Indians in the vicinity are Quichuas, who speak the same language as did their former masters, the Incas. They are a patient race with little ambition and few wants. This does not prevent them, however, from charging all the traffic will bear when any one desires to purchase alfalfa or barley straw for his mules. Don Santiago told me that he had once been obliged to pay as high as forty dollars, gold, for enough fodder to give an eight-mule team a proper luncheon. Needless to say, transportation is expensive. The coach-fare from La Quiaca to Tupiza was ten dollars, about sixteen cents a mile. A charge of two cents a pound is made for luggage. None is carried free.

Our first stop was at Mojo, to change mules and eat a "breakfast" which consisted of the customary highly-spiced mutton and potatoes. We were not "favored by the addition of an excellent roasted guinea pig" as was Edmond Temple when he stopped here in 1826. Yet guinea-pigs are still common hereabouts and we saw several on the road.

Mojo is a village of four hundred inhabitants. There is a small branch office of the Bolivian customs service here which is supposed to look after travellers and their baggage. The principal custom house for southern Bolivia is at Tupiza, a much more agreeable spot for the residence of the officials and a natural distributing point for the region.

A short distance from Mojo we began an abrupt descent. In one place the hill was too steep to permit the road to make a proper turn, so we all had to get out and help lift the stage-coach around a "switch back." After this tortuous zigzag we came out on a broad plain over which we passed without difficulty to the banks of the river Suipacha.

The water was low and the cart-track attempted to steer a straight course up stream. But as the shrunken current meandered over the sandy river-bed, we were obliged to ford it every three or four minutes. This entailed constant difficulties, for the leading mules would invariably stop to walk as soon as they entered the water, while the others trotted briskly in and tangled up the whole team. Perhaps the fault was mine, for I was having my first experience in driving an eight-in-hand, and the hard-mouthed mules took particular delight in giving me a bad time. Notwithstanding our difficulties, we reached Suipacha on time, and stopped to change mules.

This valley was the scene of one of the earliest victories of the patriots in 1810 at the beginning of the wars of independence. It will be remembered that after the glorious 25th of May, recently celebrated in Buenos Aires, the Argentinos attempted to free the province of Upper Peru from Spanish control. The result of the victory of Suipacha was to cause the Bolivians to rise and join the Argentinos against their oppressors. The patriot army marched joyously northward across the plateau, although the Argentinos suffered greatly from the cold and the high altitude. When they reached the southern end of Lake Titicaca, the Spanish army, augmented by hundreds of obedient Quichuas, attacked the patriots and practically annihilated them.

Suipacha itself, situated on a slight elevation above the banks of the river, looks like all the other small villages of this arid region. Plenty of sand and stones, a few mud-walled hovels, some thorny scrub, here and there an irrigation ditch and a green field, and on every side barren mountains. A favorite form of fence here is a wall of adobe blocks, adorned with cactus or thorny mimosa branches.

Suipacha is said to have six hundred inhabitants but it did not seem to be any larger than Mojo. From here a road goes east to the important city of Tarija, a pleasant, fertile town in southeastern Bolivia that enjoys a charming climate, and has often served as a city of refuge for defeated Argentine politicians who are glad enough to escape to such a land of corn and wine after unsuccessful revolutions on the dreary pampas.

The road to Tupiza took us northwest, and continued to follow the bed of the Suipacha or Estarca,

THE "ANGOSTA DE TUPIZA"

and one of its tributaries. In the valley were several farms or fincas as they are called here, where small crops are raised by irrigation. Half-way from Suipacha to Tupiza we passed through a magnificent rocky gateway called the Angosta de Tupiza. Cliffs five hundred feet high rise abruptly on each side of the river, leaving barely room enough for the road even in dry weather. For a distance of seventy feet, the width is less than thirty feet. Beyond the gate the mountains form a spacious amphitheatre. During the rainy season, from November to March, it is frequently impossible to pass through this gorge, even on good saddle-mules. Fortunately for us, the rains had not yet begun, and we had no difficulty.

We reached Tupiza, a town of about two thousand inhabitants, just at six o'clock. It is only ten thousand feet above sea-level, nearly two thousand feet lower than La Quiaca, and is prettily situated in a plain less than a mile in width, that in this region may fairly be called fertile, so great is the contrast with the surrounding desert. Good use has been made of the water in the little stream, and there are many cultivated fields and trees in the vicinity.

The plaza is quite an oasis in the wilderness. It is carefully cultivated and the shrubbery and willow trees make it a delightful spot. Around the plaza are a few kerosene oil street-lamps on top of wooden poles set in stone foundations. The white tower of a new church rises above the trees and makes a good landmark. Near by is the large two-story warehouse belonging to the Bolivian government and used as a post-office and custom house.

In the early '80's, before the construction of the Antofagasta railway, most of the commerce of Southern Bolivia passed through Tupiza and the custom house had more importance than it has now. To-day it has less than a tenth of its former business. With the completion of the railway to La Quiaca and its contemplated projection to Tupiza, however, the local revenue business is bound to increase.

Even at the time of my visit (November, 1908), the street in front of the custom house was blocked by scores of bales and boxes recently arrived from La Quiaca and awaiting examination prior to being shipped north to Potosí on the backs of mules.

On the opposite side of the plaza was a branch of the National Bank of Bolivia. Here we found that the Bolivian dollar or peso is worth about forty cents in our money.

The common currency consists of banknotes ranging from one to twenty pesos in value. These depend entirely for their value upon the solvency of the bank of issue. Several banks have failed, and the Indians are very particular what bills they accept. They dislike the bills of banks that have no agencies in the vicinity and prefer the bills of the National Bank of Francisco Argondaño.

The nickel subsidiary coinage is usually genuine and is in great demand, but the smaller silver coins are frequently either counterfeit or so badly made that they do not ring true and are not accepted by the Indians with whom one has most to do on the road. Consequently it is the common practice to tear bills in two when change cannot be made in any other way. The result is that perfect bills are growing scarce and the expense of issuing new ones is being felt by the banks. Several times when cashing checks at branches of these banks, I was paid entirely in half bills. They are accepted in almost all parts of Bolivia but are at a discount in La Paz and are not received at all in some localities.

We are told that the scarcity of subsidiary coinage, and the relative frequency of counterfeit money, is due to the native habit of burying all coins of real value lest they fall into the hands of unscrupulous officials and rapacious soldiers. Since time immemorial, enormous quantities of articles made of the precious metals have been buried by the Indians.

Tupiza was the scene in 1819 of one of those ineffectual skirmishes in which the unaided Bolivian patriots endeavored to secure their independence. In fact, this old trade-route from the Pampas to Potosí was the scene of numerous engagements during the Wars of Independence.

There are two hotels in Tupiza, one of them being the headquarters of that section of the Bolivian army which is stationed here to guard the frontier. The other is more commonly resorted to by travellers. Our inn, the Grand Hotel Terminus, a long, low building once white-washed, with a courtyard paved with cobblestones and a few bedrooms opening into the court, was run by an amiable rascal who I believe claimed to be an Austrian. However that may be, he belonged to the type that believes in charging foreigners double the regular tariff. "For one roast fowl, $2.00, a bottle of vichy, $1.25, one bottle of German beer, $1.00, half pint of Appolinaris, $.40." We were not able to get any discount. Instead of fighting our own battles we foolishly referred the matter to Don Santiago who lives at the hotel, has his office here, and depends upon the hotel proprietor for a number of favors. Our request naturally put him in an embarrassing situation, and all he could say was that the charges seemed to him to be regular. The proprietor appeared to be drunk most of the time, but he was not too drunk to charge up all drinks to his American guests.

There is a club here which was not in a very prosperous condition at the time of my visit. This may have been due to a patriotic celebration that had taken place a fortnight before. At that time a little poetical drama, reminiscent of the first conflict for independence in 1810, was played in the club-rooms. The drama, written by a local poet, was dedicated to Señor Aramayo, the Mæcenas of Tupiza, a member of the wealthiest family of southern Bolivia, and the owner of several rich silver mines and a large importing warehouse.

The shops of Tupiza were not brilliantly lighted although they contained quite an assortment of articles of European origin. The trade which they appeal to is that of the mule-drivers, the arrieros, who congregate here while their cargoes are being inspected by the revenue officers. The Indians of the vicinity, whose money comes chiefly from the product of their irrigation ditches, have little to spend.

Tupiza boasts two newspapers; one of them a biweekly, now in its third year, and the other a literary

FANTASTIC PINNACLES IN THE VALLEYS NORTH OF TUPIZA

weekly that had recently been started by the author of the poetical drama just alluded to. The weekly refers to the celebration in most flattering terms. "Undoubtedly social life in Tupiza had increased so far that it is high time to commence to notice its faults and deficiencies. These could easily be removed with proper enthusiasm and good will. Tupiza is a centre of social culture, but unfortunately it is not yet able to appreciate such worthy theatrical spectacles as have recently taken place!"

CHAPTER VIII
TUPIZA TO COTAGAITA

WE found that the Bolivian government had recently subsidized a week-ly stage line from Tupiza to Uyuni on the Antofagasta railway and another from Tupiza to Potosí, our next objective point. The fare to Potosí is twenty-two dollars, and the journey takes only four days. But we had enough of being shaken to pieces in a stage-coach, and decided we could see the country better and be more inde-pendent if we used saddle mules.

Two weeks before our arrival a couple of bandits, one of whom had been hunt-ed out of Arizona by Pinkerton detectives, had held up a cart containing twenty thousand dollars, on its way to pay off the laborers in a large mine. The owners, wealthy Bolivians, immediately offered a large reward for the capture of the ban-dits, dead or alive, notwithstanding that the robbers and their friends, of whom there seemed to be a score or more, let it be carefully understood that they would take a definite revenge for any lives that might be lost in pursuit of the highway-men. This did not deter the mine owners, however, and a party of fifty Bolivian soldiers went on the trail of the robbers, who were found lunching in an Indian hut. They had carelessly left their mules and rifles several yards away from the door of the hut and were unable to escape. After a fight, in which three or four of the soldiers were killed and as many more wounded, the thatch roof of the hut was set on fire and the bandits forced out into the open where they finally fell, each with half a dozen bullets in his body. Their mules were captured and sold to Don Santiago who let me have one of them for my journey. He turned out to be a wonderfully fine saddle mule. When his former owner had had the benefit of his fleet legs and his splendid lungs, there was no question of his being caught by the Bolivian soldiery.

In that part of the Andes where one is following the usual trade-routes, there are four modes of travelling. One may purchase one's own animals, employ ser-vants to attend to them, and sell them for a song at the end of the journey. This is the most expensive, the most satisfactory, and the surest method of travel, pro-vided always that one succeeds in getting a reliable, well-recommended arriero. A careless arriero will soon drive you to despair and allow your mules to get into a state of semi-starvation and sore back that will speedily destroy their usefulness. The second method is to hire a professional carrier who, for a stipulated sum of money, will provide you with animals, go along with them, feed and care for them, and get you to your destination as speedily as possible. If your sole object is speed, this method is even surer than the first, for owing to the high price of fodder in the post-houses, the contractor may be relied upon to push the caravan forward as speedily as possible. The third method is by far the least expensive, the most troublesome, and the least certain. This is to depend on the mules that are supposed to be in readiness for travellers at the post-houses. We frequently amused ourselves on our journey by imagining what we could possibly have done had we attempted to rely on this last method. Repeatedly we reached post-houses where there was not a mule to be seen, or where the two or three that were there, were drearily hanging their melancholy heads in the corral, so worn out and broken down as to convince us of their inability to carry even an ordinary load at anything faster than a slow walk. The traveller who trusts to post-house mules rarely remembers much of the scenery or the nature of the country. His chief impression is that of unfortunate mules continually being beaten in order to reach the next post before dark. The fourth method, and the one we decided to adopt, is to hire from a reputable contractor a number of his best mules and one of his most trusted arrieros at so much per day. In this way, you are not hurried faster than you want to go, the mules are sure to be well cared for, and the discomforts of mountain travel are reduced to a minimum. Except on a long journey, it is not as expensive as buying one's own animals and is less risky.

Thanks to the energy of Don Santiago, the necessary mules and provisions were ready in two days. On his suggestion, we took with us as arriero, one Mac, a wandering Scotchman who had seen service in the Boer War, had drifted thence to Argentina, and was now trying his luck in southern Bolivia. He seemed just the sort of person to make a good orderly,

A QUICHUA FAMILY GOING TO PLOW

and we thought we were quite fortunate in securing his services. Relying on his past experience, we told him to purchase such provisions as were necessary for the next five days. He proceeded to purchase four dozen hard-boiled eggs and three roast fowls. These he packed carelessly in my leather saddle-bags, together with a bottle of Eno's fruit salts of which he was very fond. The expected happened. The eggs were reduced to an unrecognizable mass, the bottle of fruit salts was broken and the contents well rubbed into the chicken, so that our fare for the next two or three days was not much above the ordinary.

We left Tupiza on a bright, clear morning and rode northward through a semi-arid region where we were continually reminded of Utah and southern Colorado. For two leagues we saw no house and met no one. The floor of the valley was broad and flat, covered with sand and pebbles, and occasionally intersected by small irrigating ditches. Almost the only green things were cactus and mimosa trees. Barren hills that appear to be crumbling rapidly away rose abruptly on each side. In some places, the eroded hillside took the form of chimneys, ruined factories, or even forts. In others erosion had produced fantastic pinnacles, and often the buttressed hills looked very much like cathedrals.

About nine o'clock we met a Quichua family, the wife carrying the baby and spinning, the man carrying his wooden plough on his shoulder and driving his oxen to an irrigated field where he proposed to do his spring ploughing. His wife had on as many gaudy-colored petticoats as she could afford. Such is the fashion of the country.

Near one of the irrigating ditches under the shadow of the buttressed walls of the cañon, we came upon a hundred mules. Some of them were carrying huge packing-cases, large enough to hold the entire body of the patient mule, provided of course that it were properly cut up and the extremities shortened. In general the pack-mules were fine, large animals, well able to carry their three-hundred-pound loads. With such a caravan as this go a dozen arrieros who rise each day three hours before dawn and commence the everlasting task of saddling and loading. When this is done, the men eat a hearty breakfast, prepared in the meantime by one of their number, and then start out for an eight-hour march. About five o'clock in the afternoon, or earlier, if they have by that time reached a suitable camping-place, the caravan stops and unloading begins, which is finished barely in time to give the men a few hours of slumber before the whole process has to be repeated.

Fortunately, most of these cases of merchandise were packed in Germany where they know how to meet the exigencies of South American mountain travel, and although the great wooden boxes were banged against projecting rocks by the roadside and often allowed to fall with a crash when the saddle-ropes were untied at the end of the day, the contents were practically sure to reach their destination in good condition.

At noon we came to a group of freshly white-washed adobe farm buildings, the property of an absentee landlord. Here we were able to purchase green fodder for the mules, and luncheon, in the shape of very hot soup and tea, for ourselves. In one of the buildings was a district school with six or eight pupils, the scholars evincing their studiousness by learning their lessons out loud. The resultant noise would considerably jar on the ear of a highly strung New England "schoolmarm," but the good-natured Bolivian teacher did not know that he had any nerves, and only wanted to be sure that all his pupils were busy.

After lunch our road continued up the same arid valley past flocks of goats that strove to get a living from the low-hanging branches of the mimosa trees. Some of the more adventurous had even gone up into the trees to secure a meal.

In the middle of the afternoon, we climbed out of one valley and looked down into another. From the pass we had a fine view of the valley through which we had come. The prevailing color was brown with here and there a touch of dusty green. All around there was a confusion of barren hills and arid mountains without a single evidence of human habitation. The only sign of life was the long line of the mule caravan which we had passed earlier in the day. The country is so unfitted for the habitation of man that the general effect of this and of most of the scenery in southern Bolivia is oppressive and dispiriting.

Shortly before sunset, however, we came to a beautiful spring called the "Eye of the Water," which bubbled up by the roadside and flowed off into carefully guarded irrigating ditches. As was to be expected, there was a small Indian village in the vicinity. The villagers were Quichuas, wearing small felt hats, scanty shirts, and short loose pantaloons made of what seemed to be homespun cloth. It was rather attractive in appearance, and as it had the romantic flavor of being made here by the Indians, we were inclined to purchase some until we discovered that it was only "imitation" and was made in great quantities in Manchester, England. These Quichuas are a humble folk, excessively polite to each other, doffing their hats whenever they meet. Both men and women wore their hair in long braids down their backs.

The little village sprawled up the side of the cañon just out of reach of the floods which occasionally pour through this valley in the rainy season. In one of the huts a kind of spring carnival was being celebrated with a reasonable amount of drinking. Solemn singing and a monotonous tom-tomming of a primitive drum were the only signs of gaiety except a few bright flowers which they had gathered somewhere and put in their hair. As no rain was to be expected and the village had the usual component of filth and insects, we set up our folding cots in the dry bed of the stream. The elevation was about ten thousand feet. The stars were very brilliant. The night was cool, the minimum temperature being 47°F., a drop of forty degrees from the afternoon's maximum.

THE VALLEY THROUGH WHICH WE HAD COME

The next morning, after a breakfast of cold chicken and Eno's fruit salts, all that our Boer War veteran could provide for our comfort, we pushed up the valley, and before long reached Totora, a typical Bolivian poste or tambo. It consisted of a small inclosure surrounded by half a dozen low mud-huts without windows. In one of these was kept alfalfa fodder to be sold to passing travellers. In another lived the keeper of the poste and his family. Here also was a fire from which one had the right to demand hot water, the only thing furnished for the comfort of humans. In another, two or three well-baked mounds of earth, flattened on top, were intended for beds. A roof, an earth floor, and a wooden door were the only other conveniences at the disposition of travellers.

These postes, more or less dirty and uncomfortable, may usually be found on the well-travelled roads in southern Bolivia at a distance varying from fifteen to twenty-five miles from each other. They are not picturesque, but after some little experience in travelling in that desolate region, one learns to welcome the little collection of mud-huts, with possibly a green spot or two of alfalfa, as a perfect haven of rest. To be sure, the only thing to eat is the food you bring with you, but you may be always certain of having hot water, and your arriero (unless he happens to be a veteran of the Boer War) will bring you a cup of excellent tea within twenty minutes after your arrival.

The road from Totora continued to be the rocky floor of a valley in which from time to time little streams of water or irrigation ditches appeared, only to lose themselves in fields of alfalfa or quinoa. During the dry season carts attempt to use this road, and we overtook a dozen of them on their way north. Each cart was drawn by six mules driven three abreast by a driver who rode postillion on the nigh mule nearest the cart. Before noon we climbed out of this valley and descended into a rocky, sandy plain through which flowed the river Cotagaita on its way eastward to join the great Pilcomayo. At this time of the year, the latter part of November, the river is a broad, shallow stream, easily fordable. On sandy bars left dry by the receding waters were camped caravans of pack-mules and carts. Beyond them lay the little town of Cotagaita, where the Argentine patriots were badly defeated in 1816. This place is, in a sense, the crossroads of southern Bolivia and is one of the main stations of Don Santiago's stage-lines. Uyuni, on the Antofagasta railway, is one hundred and fifteen miles west of here, three or four days by stage. The mines of Potosí are nearly the same distance north. Camargo, the capital of the province of Cinti, is a few days due east, while Tupiza is fifty-four miles due south. There are several routes from Tupiza to Uyuni but the most important and the only one practicable for coaches is by way of Cotagaita. The road is new and said to be very uncomfortable. There is not much to interest the traveller, except a few mines. Not far away is Chorolque, a famous silver mine, at an altitude of over seventeen thousand feet.

The town of Cotagaita is an old Spanish settle ment with the customary plaza, a few trees, a fountain in the centre and a church on one side; one story white-washed houses built of baked mud, the usual narrow streets crossing each other at right angles, their stone paving sloping toward the centre where a ditch does duty as a sewer; a few Indians and a few shops to minister to their wants. There are said to be twelve hundred inhabitants but I doubt it. The elevation is slightly lower than Tupiza.

We left Cotagaita after lunch, hoping to make the tambo at Escara before dark, but we were destined to disappointment. Mac, our Scotch arriero, had decided that the pack-mules, which Don Santiago selected for us at Tupiza, were not good enough to stand the march to Potosí, so he requested the coach agent here to give us two better animals. The latter allowed our veteran to go into the corral and take any mules he pleased. Rich in knowledge of the Boer War, but poor in experience with Bolivian mules, he picked out two strong-looking beasts that had been driven in the stage-coach but had never carried a pack in their lives. After being blindfold-ed they were saddled, with some difficulty, and we were about to start when it was discovered that one of them lacked a shoe on its nigh hind-foot. The blacksmith, a half-drunk, strongly built Indian, was summoned. He brought a new shoe, a few nails, and a hammer out into the street. The blindfolded mule was held by Mac while an Indian tied the foot that was to be shod securely to the mule's tail. Then the blacksmith went to work. No attempt was made to fit the shoe, and when the second nail was driven, the mule kicked and struggled so violently as to throw itself and all three men in a heap in the middle of the road. Finally, after much tribulation, the shoe was securely fastened, and amid the cheers of the populace, we started briskly off for Potosí.

The new pack-mules, lacking all road sense and missing the bridle, promptly ran away. One of them was secured without much difficulty, but the other one went up the hillside through a grove of young mimosa trees which attempted to detain the load with their thorny branches. They only succeeded in partly dislodg-ing it, however, and the mule continued his headlong career until his load turned completely under him, tripped him up, and ended by rolling him down-hill. Fortunately the dunnage bags were new and no great harm was done. Mac insisted that he could drive this mule as well as any other—which may have been true—so the poor coach-mule was reloaded. Then four of us tried for over an hour to make the two wretched animals carry their packs properly and stick to the road as pack-animals should. But they declined to enter our service, and we were obliged to send them back to Cotagaita, minus their loads. Meanwhile the two mules which Mac had so thoughtfully discarded at lunch time were reengaged. The exhibition was useful, for it showed us that Mac knew even less about saddling pack-animals than we did and was perfectly useless in an emergency. Fortunately, an excellent fellow, a brother of Don Santiago, became our deus ex machina, helped us out of our difficulty, and promised to join us the next morning with a new arriero. By hard riding we arrived at the little tambo of Escara an hour after dark and had some difficulty in securing admittance. No one has any business to travel at night in this country, unless bent on mischief.

CHAPTER IX
ESCARA TO LAJA TAMBO

W_E got up early enough the next morning to witness a phase of Bolivian life which we had heard of but had not as yet seen. An officer and two soldiers of the Bolivian army, travelling southward, had spent the night at Escara and desired to proceed promptly. The postes are subsidized by the Government on the understanding that all travelling government officials shall be furnished with mules and a man. Each poste has three or four guides called postillons, connected with it. This morning things did not move fast enough to suit the officer. The mules were not ready when he wanted to start and the meek Quichua postillon was offering an explanation. In the midst of it, the officer lost his temper, and taking his strong riding-whip, commenced to lash the poor half-clad Indian across the face and shoulders. The latter stood it for a few minutes stolidly and then commenced to back off, followed by the officer who continued to lay on the blows as fast as possible. At length the postillon turned to run and the officer pursued him, beating him and cursing him until out of breath. It was a sickening sight, but the strangest part of all was the absolute meekness with which the Indian took his beating. There was not the slightest sign of resentment or even annoyance. The strokes of the whip made the blood start and trickle down his face and sides, but he gave no evidence of feeling it.

Later in the day at Quirve, another poste, we witnessed a similar exhibition, only in this case the Indian did not even run away. The son of the proprietor, a great hulking brute, six feet tall and powerfully built, found fault with one of the postillons for some trifling mistake and beat him across the face and chest with a rawhide thong until the blood flowed freely. Like the other Indian, his face remained perfectly stolid, and he showed no signs of anger or irritation.

We had been furious with the officer in the morning and this exhibition was even more trying. Yet the Bolivianos thought nothing of it. As Mr. Bryce has so ably put it: "One must have lived among a weaker race in order to realize the kind of irritation which its defects produce in those who deal with it, and how temper and self-control are strained in resisting temptations to harsh or arbitrary action. It needs something more than the virtue of a philosopher—it needs the tenderness of a saint to preserve the same courtesy and respect towards the members of a backward race as are naturally extended to equals." There is no doubt about the Quichuas being a backward race.

From the earliest historical times these poor Indians have virtually been slaves. Bred up to look upon subjection as their natural lot, they bear it as the dispensation of Providence. The Incas treated them well, so far as we can judge, and took pains to see that the irrigation works, the foot-paths over the mountains, the suspension bridges over the raging torrents and tambos for the convenience of travellers, should all be kept in good condition. The gold-hunting Spanish conquistadores, on the other hand, had no interest in the servile Quichuas further than to secure their services as forced laborers in the mines. The modern Bolivianos have done little to improve their condition.

After seeing these two Indians meekly take such severe beatings, I found it easier to understand why Pizarro had been able to conquer the Empire of Peru with a handful of determined Spanish soldiers, and why the unfortunate Tupac Amaru could make so little headway in 1781 when he attempted to rouse the Indians to revolt against Spanish tyranny. Although he had sixty thousand men under him, the Spanish general easily defeated him with barely twenty thousand, of whom only a few hundred were Spaniards, the majority being friendly Indians.

How much the extremely severe conditions of life that prevail on this arid plateau have had to do in breaking the spirit of the race is a question. It is a generally accepted fact that a race who are dependent for their living on irrigating ditches, can easily be conquered. All that the invading army has to do is to destroy the dams, ruin the crops, and force the inhabitants to face starvation.

The Quichua shows few of the traits which we ordinarily connect with mountaineers. His country is too forlorn to give him an easy living or much time for thought. He is half starved nearly all the time. His only comfort comes from chewing coca leaves. Coca is the plant from which we extract cocaine. It is said that the Quichua can go for days without food, provided he has a good supply of coca. It would be extremely interesting to determine the effect on his intelligence of this cocaine habit, which seems to be centuries old. If a man can stand up and take severe punishment for trivial offences without getting angry, showing vexation, or apparently without bearing any grudge against his oppressor, there must be something constitutionally wrong with him. I believe that the coca habit is answerable for a large part of this very unsatisfactory state of affairs. Coca has deadened his sensibilities to a degree that passes comprehension. It has made him stupid, willing to submit to almost any injury, lacking in all ambition, caring for almost none of the things which we consider the natural desires of the human heart.

In travelling through Bolivia and Peru, I found it repeatedly to be the case that the Quichua does not care to sell for money either food or lodging. Presents of coca leaves and tobacco are acceptable. A liberal offer of money rarely moves him, although it would be possible for him to purchase with it many articles of necessity or comfort in near-by towns. As a rule he prefers neither to rent his animal, nor sell you cheese or eggs, or anything else. The first Quichua words one learns, and the answer which one most commonly receives to all questions as to the existence of the necessaries of life, is "mana canca," "there is none."

This condition of affairs is not new. When Temple travelled through Bolivia in 1825, he was struck by the prevailing "no hay nada" (there is nothing at all). Poverty, want, misery, and negligence are the story that is told by the melancholy phrase. The truth is, the Quichua not only has no ambition, he has long ago ceased to care whether you or he or anybody else has more than just barely enough to keep body and soul together.

Needless to say, the Quichuas have no concern with the politics of Bolivia, although they constitute a large majority of the inhabitants.

From Escara our road continued to follow a semi-arid valley. We passed a caravan of mule-carts bound for Potosí and Sucre. In one of the carts was an up-right piano; in another, pieces of mining machinery, while still others contained large cast-iron pipes destined for Sucre's new waterworks. Nearly all of the carts carried bales of Argentine hay as this region is so arid that it is extremely difficult to secure any fodder for the animals, and the barley or alfalfa, when procurable, is often too expensive.

The weather continued to be fine. After a hot, dusty ride of twenty miles, we stopped at the poste of Quirve.

Just before reaching Quirve, we crossed the Tumusla River, the site of the last battle of the Bolivian wars of independence. After Sucre's great victory at Aya-cucho, in 1824, the only Spanish troops which remained unconquered in all South America were the garrison of Callao and a small band under General Ollaneta in southern Bolivia. His men were badly disaffected by the news of the battle of Ayacucho, and an officer who commanded a small garrison at this strategic point, came out openly for the patriotic cause. Ollaneta tried in vain to suppress the re-volt. The result was a battle here on the first of April, 1825, in which the Spanish general was defeated and slain. The garrison of Callao held out for a few months longer, but this was the end of active warfare.

We found the tambo of Quirve to be of the most primitive sort, not even af-fording shelter for man or beast. The weekly Potosí stage-coach came in from the north about six o'clock carrying one passenger. He soon spread his bed under the wagon and made himself comfortable for the night. The luggage from Potosí was shipped on pack-animals and was in charge of an Argentine Gaucho named Fer-min Chaile. This man we took in exchange for Mac, whom we were glad enough to get rid of. Fermin, the Gaucho, tall and gaunt, round-shouldered and bow-legged, his dark Mongolian-like features crowned by a mop of coarse, black hair, proved to be a god-send. His loose-fitting suit of brown corduroys, far better raiment than most arrieros can afford, bore witness to the fact that he was sober, industrious, and trustworthy. No one ever had a better muleteer. Like Rafael Rivas, the faithful Venezuelan peon who had guided my cart across the Llanos in 1907, he took excel-lent care of the mules, yet drove them almost to the limit of their endurance, was devoted to us, and proved to be reliable and attentive. He was a plainsman, as dif-ferent in spirit and achieve ment from the wretched mountaineers through whose country we were passing, as though he had belonged to a different continent.

As we continued northward from Quirve, the valley grew narrower and our road continued to be in the dry river course. All the water that was visible was collected in little ditches and conducted along the hillsides fifteen or twenty feet above the bed of the stream. On some of the hillsides of this valley are terraces or andines where maize, quinoa, potatoes, and even grapes are made to grow, with much painstaking labor. These terraces, common enough farther north, were the first we had seen. The staple food of the Indians is chuno, a small potato that has been put through a freezing process until its natural flavor is completely lost. One of the principal dishes at this time of the year is the fruit of the cactus. Everybody seems to be very fond of the broad-leaved edible species, a thornless variety of which we are developing in Arizona and New Mexico.

Farther up the valley I was struck by the ingenuity which had been exercised in carrying the irrigation ditches along the side of precipitous cliffs. Numerous little tunnels, connected by small viaducts, enabled a tiny stream of water to travel three or four miles until it reached a level space sufficiently above highwater mark to warrant the planting of a small field. The only animals to be seen beside mules and horses, goats, pigs, dogs, and a very few birds, were the little wild guinea-pigs of a color closely resembling the everlasting brown hills. I was surprised not to see any llamas.

Soon after leaving Quirve, we came to the little village of Toropalca, in every way as brown and dusty as the guinea-pigs. In fact, it melted into the landscape as perfectly as they did.

About noon we reached another hillside village, Saropalca, its houses placed so closely one above another on the steep slope as to give the appearance of a giant stairway. We climbed up through the irregular lanes of the little village, until we found a wretched little tambo where we bought a few bundles of alfalfa and a bowl of soup.

Whenever we could secure sufficient alfalfa for the mules and a bowl of hot chupe for ourselves in addition to the customary pot of hot water for our tea, we considered ourselves most fortunate and were willing to admit that the poste was well provided with "all the necessaries of life." Chupe is a kind of stew or thick soup consisting of frozen potatoes and tough mutton or llama meat. In its natural state, its taste is disagreeable enough, but when it is served to the liking of the natives it is seasoned so highly with red pepper as to be far too fiery for foreign palates.

In the course of the afternoon, the valley narrowed to a gorge in which we passed more heavily-laden mule-carts making their way along with the utmost difficulty. Beyond the gorge we found sulphur springs and some banks of sulphur. One of the hot springs gushed up close by the roadside. "El Lazarillo," the eighteenth century Baedeker, says there was once a "modest thermal establishment" here, intended to attract bathers from Potosí.

At the end of the day we reached Caisa, after having made nearly forty miles since morning. Caisa is an old Spanish town and looks like all the rest. One-story houses, narrow streets, badly paved, a city block left open for a plaza, on one side of it a church and the house of the priest, on the other three sides, a few shops where we bought newly-baked hot bread, beer, cheese, and candles. The tambo was called "La Libertad" and bore the legend "Muy barato" (very cheap). We surmised this meant that the proprietor would charge all the traffic would bear; and such proved to be the case. In fact, we had a very disagreeable dispute with the landlady the next morning. Fermin indignantly declared she had tripled the usual prices.

At Caisa the road from Argentina to Sucre branches off to the right, going due north to Puna and thence to Yotala, where it joins the road from Potosí to Sucre.

Leaving Caisa on November 22, we went north-west and soon had our first glimpse of a snow-clad Bolivian mountain. The snow was not very deep, however, as it had fallen during the night, and before noon it was all gone. Our road crossed several ridges and then descended into a partly cultivated valley near an old silver mine and a smelter called Cuchu Ingenio. The road here was unusually good. Even in 1773 "The Blind Man's Guide" says it was a "camino de Trote, y Galope."

As we ascended a gorge, I was attracted by a little waterfall of crystal clearness that came tumbling down from the heights above, and was tempted to

OUR FIRST GLIMPSE OF A SNOW-CLAD BOLIVIAN MOUNTAIN

take a hearty drink of the delicious cool liquid. A Boliviano from Tupiza, who was travelling with us for company, warned me against such a rash act as drinking cold water at this altitude. I had noticed that no one in this region ever touches cold water, and I thought the universal prejudice against it was founded on a natural preference for alcohol. So I laughingly enjoyed my cup of cold water and assured him that there could be no harm in it. An hour later we reached Laja Tambo, a wretched little poste, standing alone on the edge of a tableland twenty miles from Potosí. The altitude was about thirteen thousand feet. The sun had been very warm, and soon after alighting on the rough stone pavement of the inn yard, I arranged the thermometers so as to test the difference in temperature between sun and shade. The temperature in the sun at noon was 85° F. In the shade it was 48° F.

Scarcely had I taken the readings when I began to feel chilly. Hot tea followed by hot soup and still hotter brandy and water failed to warm me, notwithstanding the fact that I had unpacked my bag and put on two heavy sweaters. A wretched sense of dizziness and of longing to get warm made me lie down on the warm stones of the courtyard. I grew rapidly worse, and was soon experiencing the common symptoms of soroche, puna, or mountain sickness. The combination of vomiting, diarrhœa, and chills was bad enough, but the prospect of being ill in this desolate poste, twenty miles from the nearest doctor, with nothing better than the usual accessories of a Bolivian tambo, was infinitely worse. Somehow or other, I man aged to persuade Fermin to saddle and load the animals and put me on my mule, where I was determined to stay until we should reach Potosí.

The last thing to do before leaving the tambo was to pay the bill, and this I proceeded to do in the Bolivian paper currency which I had purchased in Tupiza. Alas, one of the bills was on a bank situated two hundred and fifty miles away in La Paz, a bank, in fact, in which the postillon did not have much confidence. The idea of having a servile Quichua postillon decline to receive good money was extremely irritating, and I tried my best, notwithstanding my soroche, to force him to take it. He persisted and I was obliged to find another bill in my wallet. I suppose my hand trembled a little with chill or excitement and in taking out the bill I partly tore it.

This would not have mattered had the tear been in the middle, but it was near-er one end than the other and the Indian refused to accept it. I had no other small bills and was at a loss to know what to do. In the meantime, Fermin and the pack-mules had left the inclosure of the tambo and started for Potosí while Mr. Smith was just outside of the gate waiting for me. So I rolled up the sound bill which the Indian had declined to receive, gave it to him, and while he was investigating it, made a dash for the road. He was too quick for me, however, and gripped my bridle. Exasperated beyond measure, I rode him against the wall of the tambo and made him let go long enough to allow me to escape. It seemed on the whole a law-less performance, although the bank-note was perfectly good. I fully expected that he would follow us with stones or something worse, but as he was only a Quichua he accepted the inevitable and we saw no more of him.

In the face of a bitterly cold wind we crossed the twenty-mile plateau that lies between Laja Tambo and the famous city of Potosí. On the plain were herds of llamas feeding, but these did not interest us as much as the conical hill ahead. It was the Cerro of Potosí, the hill that for two hundred and fifty years, was the mar-vel of the world. No tale of the Arabian Nights, no dream of Midas, ever equalled the riches that flowed from this romantic cone. Two billion ounces of silver is the record of its output and the tale is not yet told.

Rounding the eastern shoulder of the mountain, we passed several large smelters, some of them abandoned. Near by are the ruins of an edifice said to have been built by the Spaniards to confine the poor Indians whom they brought here by the thousands to work in the mines. The road descends a little valley and runs for a mile, past the ruins of hundreds of buildings. In the eighteenth century, Potosí boasted a population of over one hundred and fifty thousand. Now there are scarcely fifteen thousand. The part of the city that is still standing is near the ancient plaza, the mint, and the market-place.

Our caravan clattered noisily down the steep, stony streets until we reached the doors of the Hotel Colon where an attentive Austrian landlord made us welcome, notwithstanding the fact that one of the party was evidently quite ill. I could not help wondering whether an American hotel-keeper would have been so willing to receive a sick man as this benighted citizen of Potosí. The paved courtyard was small, but the rooms on the second floor were commodious and so much better than the unspeakably forlorn adobe walls of Laja Tambo, that I felt quite willing to retire from active exploration for a day or two. Fortunately, I fell into the hands of a well-trained Bolivian physician, who knew exactly what to do, and with his aid, and the kind nursing of Fermin and Mr. Smith, I was soon on my feet again.

CHAPTER X
POTOSÍ

WE had not been in Potosí many hours before we realized that it was a most fascinating place with an atmosphere all its own. By the time we had been here a week we were ready to agree with those who call it the most interesting city in South America.

The prestige of its former wealth, the evidence on every side of former Spanish magnificence, the picturesquely clad Indians and the troops of graceful, inquisitive llamas in the streets, aroused to the utmost our curiosity and interest.

Our first duty was to call on the Prefect who had been expecting our arrival and was most kind during our entire stay. A Bolivian prefect has almost unlimited power in his department and is directly responsible to the President. His orders are carried out by the sub-prefect who is also chief of police and has a small body of soldiers under his immediate control.

We found the Government House, or Prefectura, to be a fine old building dating back to colonial days. Probably the most interesting person that has ever occupied it was General William Miller, that picturesque British veteran who fought valiantly through all the Peruvian Wars of Independence, re ceiving so many wounds that he was said to have been "honeycombed with bullets." At the end of the wars he was appointed Prefect of Potosí, and it was during his incumbency that the great liberator Simon Bolivar made his visit. There is a vivid description of it in Miller's "Memoirs." When Bolivar arrived in sight of the far-famed mountain, the flags of Peru, Buenos Aires, Chile, and Colombia were unfurled on its summit. As he entered the town, twenty-one petards were exploded on the peak, an aërial salute "that had a very singular and imposing effect." "Upon alighting at the Government House, under a grand triumphal arch, decorated with flags, the reception of His Excellency was according to the Hispanic-American taste. Two children, dressed as angels, were let down from the arch as he approached, and each pronounced a short oration! Upon entering the grand saloon, six handsome women, representing the fair sex of Potosí, hailed the arrival of His Excellency, crowned him with a wreath of laurel, and strewed flowers, which had been brought from a great distance for the occasion." This was followed by seven weeks of bull-fights, grand dinners, balls, fireworks, illuminations, and other signs of public rejoicing, which would seem to have surfeited even a person so fond of pomp and adulation as the great liberator.

Opposite the Government House, on the east side of the plaza, is a curious many-arched arcade which incloses a new plaza, the work of an ambitious prefect. The tall column surmounted by a statue, that stands as the only ornament in the new plaza, once stood in the centre of the old, but was moved to its new position by the Prefect who decided that his work would be incomplete unless properly graced by a monument.

On a corner of the new plaza is Potosí's only bookshop. Judging by the stock in trade, the principal customers are school children and lawyers. The book trade was dull when we were there, but considerable interest was shown in other departments of the store where toys and picture post cards were on sale.

Near by is the "University" where second-rate secondary instruction is given to poor little boys who sit on damp adobe seats in badly-lighted, foul-smelling rooms. It was once a convent, but the church connected with it has long since been transformed into a theatre. The only attractive thing about the "University" is the charming old convent garden where rare old flowers still try to bloom.

Opposite the "University" is the club. Here there are billiard tables (it is really remarkable how many billiard tables one finds scattered all over South America, even in the most inaccessible places) and a bar. The custom of serving a little felt mat with each drink is resorted to, and when a member chooses to stand treat, he goes about and gathers up all the mats in sight and takes them to the bar where he cashes them with his own money, or some that he has recently won. The bar was well patronized. And no one is to blame but the climate, which is the worst in South America.

Although Potosí is in the Tropics, the highest re corded temperature here in the shade on the hottest day ever known, was 59° F. The city is nearly thirteen thousand five hundred feet above the sea, almost as high as Pike's Peak. Every afternoon cold winds sweep down through the streets striking a chill into one's very marrow. A temperature of 22° F. is not unknown, yet none of the houses have stoves or any appliances (except soup) for warming their shivering inhabitants. As the prevailing temperature indoors is below 50° F., almost every one wears coats and hats in the house as much as outdoors, or even more so, for a brisk walk of a block or two at this altitude makes one quite warm, and in the middle of the day the sun is hot.

Wherever we wandered in this fascinating city, our eyes continually turned southward to the Cerro, the beautifully colored cone that raises itself fifteen hundred feet above the city. It is impossible to describe adequately the beauty of its colors and the marvellous way in which they change as the sun sinks behind the western Andes. I hope that some day a great painter will come here and put on canvas the marvellous hues of this world-renowned hill. Pink, purple, lavender, brown, gray, and yellow streaks make it look as though the gods, having finished painting the universe, had used this as a dumping-ground for their surplus pigments. In reality, the hand of man has had much to do with its present variegated aspect, for he has been busily engaged during the past three hundred years in turning the hill inside out. Much of the most beautifully colored material has been painfully brought out from

VIEW OF THE CERRO FROM THE ROOF OF THE MINT

the very heart of the hill through long tunnels, in man's effort to get at the rich veins of silver and tin which lie within.

The discovery of silver at Potosí was made by a llama driver about the middle of the sixteenth century. It was soon found that the mountain was traversed by veins of extremely rich ore. After the gold of the Incas had been gathered up and disposed of, Potosí became the most important part of all the Spanish possessions in America. At the beginning of the seventeenth century, when New York and Boston were still undreamed of, Potosí was already a large and extremely wealthy city. It attracted the presence of hundreds of Spanish adventurers including many grandees. In short it had taken on all the signs of luxury that are common to big mining camps. Grandees in sumptuous apparel rode gayly caparisoned horses up and down the stony streets, bowing graciously to charming ladies dressed in the most costly attire that newly-gotten wealth could procure. On feast days, and particularly on great national holidays, like the King's birthday, elaborate and expensive entertainments were given.

If it were not for the great expanse of ruins and the very large number of churches, it would be difficult to realize to-day that for over a century this was the largest city in the Western Hemisphere. The routes which led to the Bolivian plateau became the greatest thoroughfares in America. Money flowed more freely than water. In fact, the Spaniards found great difficulty during the dry season in supplying the city with sufficient water to use in washing the ore and in meeting the ordinary needs of a large population. Consequently, they went up into the hills above the city and built, at great expense, a score of dams to hold back the water that fell during the rainy season and preserve it for the dry.

Immediately following the Wars of Independence and the consequent opening of the country to foreign capital, a wild mining fever set in among London capitalists. Greedy and ignorant directors took advantage of the cupidity of the British public to enrich themselves, while incidentally working the mines of Potosí with disproportionately expensive establishments. So eager was the public to take stock in Potosí that shares which at the outset were quoted at 75 or 80, rose incredibly in the short space of six weeks. Some of them went up above 5000. As was to be expected, this speculative fever was followed by a panic which ruined not only the stockholders but those unfortunates like Edmund Temple, who had gone to Potosí in the employ of one of the wildcat companies, and those South Americans that had honored their drafts on London.

Then followed a long period of stagnation. But as railroads came nearer and cart-roads began to multiply, transportation became cheaper and new enterprises sprang up.

Any one is at liberty to secure a license from the proper authorities to dig a mine in the side of the mountain, provided he does not interfere with the property of someone else. The records show that since the Cerro was first discovered licenses have been issued for over five thousand mines. It is easy to imagine what a vast underground labyrinth exists beneath those many-colored slopes. Most of the openings, however, have been closed by avalanches of refuse from mines higher up the hill.

One day I was invited to visit several new mines that had recently been opened by a Chilean Company. In one mine, at an altitude of about fifteen thousand feet, I undertook to crawl into the depths for five hundred yards in order to see a new vein of silver ore that had recently been encountered. The exertion of getting in and out again at that altitude was terrific, yet the miners did not appear to feel it. They wear thick knitted caps which save their heads from the bumps and shield them from falling rocks. Their knees are protected by strong leather caps. Their feet they bind in huge moccasins. Those that carry out the ore frequently wear leather aprons tied on their backs. The workmen are a sordid, rough-looking lot who earn and deserve very good wages. Sometime ago when tin was higher than it is now, a large number of new mines were opened and unheard-of prices were paid for labor. Now that the price of tin has fallen, it is extremely difficult to get the Indians to accept a lower scale of wages. Consequently, most of the new mines have had to be closed.

In the old days, the tin was discarded as the eager Spanish miners thought only of the silver. But now the richer veins of silver have become exhausted, and although some are being worked, most of the activity is confined to the tin ore. At the top of the cone there is an immense quantity of it; the only diffi culty is how to get it down to the smelters in the valley between the hill and the city.

In this valley runs a small stream of water that comes from the hill reservoirs. Attracted by its presence, most of the smelters have located themselves on one side or the other of the little gorge. There are innumerable small ingenios worked by the Indians in a very primitive fashion. Some of them are scarcely more than a family affair. Besides these there are twenty-eight large smelters, and all of them devoted more to tin than to silver. Not one of these is owned by a Bolivian. A few belong to English capitalists, more to Chileans, and the largest of all to a Frenchman who has constructed an aërial railway to bring the ore from high up on the mountainside to his furnaces. The never ending line of iron buckets adds a curiously modern note to the ruins over which they pass. Ore is also brought down on the backs of donkeys and llamas. The workmen are mostly Quichuas. Some of them are evidently not city bred, for they dress with the same pigtails and small clothes that they wore when Spanish conquistadores forced them to take the precious metal out of the hill without any thought of reward other than the fact that they were likely to die sooner and reach heaven earlier than if they stayed quietly at home. The product of this smelter is shipped both as pure tin in ingots and also as highly concentrated and refined ore.

The most picturesque feature of the valley was a small chimney smoking lustily away all by itself, high up on the opposite hillside, like a young volcano with a smoke stack. In order to get a good draft for

THE CERRO OF POTOSÍ FROM THE SPANISH RESERVOIRS

AN ANCIENT QUICHUA ORE CRUSHER

the blast furnaces, the smoke is conducted across the stream on a stone viaduct, enters the hill by a tunnel, and ascends a vertical shaft for one hundred and fifty feet to the chimney which then carries it thirty feet further up into the air. The tunnel does just as good work in the way of producing a draft as though it were a modern brick chimney, two hundred feet high, but the effect is uncanny, to say the least.

We found among the boarders at the Hotel Colon a group of young Peruvian and Chilean mining engineers who were very congenial. They made the best of their voluntary exile, and although none of them enjoyed the fearful climatic conditions, they managed to make their surroundings quite tolerable with hard work, cheerful conversation, birthday dinners, and social calls.

The courtyard of the hotel was a fine example of the prevailing mixture of old and new. The roof was covered with beautiful large red tiles whose weight had crushed down the rafters in places so as to produce a wavy effect. Meanwhile the shaky old balcony that ran around the court connecting the rooms on the second floor, was sheltered from the rain by strips of corrugated iron! The fine old stone-paved patio was marred by a vile wainscoting painted in imitation of cheap oil-cloth. In one corner stood a little old-fashioned stove where arrieros, who need to make an early start, cook their tea without disturbing the hotel servants. An archway running under the best bedrooms of the second floor, led out to the street. Another archway led in to the filth of the backyard where, amid indescribable scenes and smells, six-course dinners were prepared for our consumption. It was a miracle that we did not get every disease in the calendar.

Opposite the hotel was a fine old building with a wonderfully carved stone gateway and attractive iron balconies jutting out with stone supports from each second-story window. It is now the residence and warehouse of one of the largest importers in Bolivia. Once it was the abode of a Spanish marquis. The exquisitely finished exterior bears witness to the good taste of its builder and the riches and extravagance that once ran riot in Potosí.

So also do the beautiful towers, all that are left standing of the Jesuit church. The church itself has disappeared, but the solidly constructed, exquisitely carved stone towers remain as silent witnesses to the power of that Christian order that did most to advance the cause of civilization in South America.

Unquestionably the most picturesque part of Potosí is the market-place and the streets in its immediate vicinity. Hither come the miners and their families to spend their hard-earned wages. Here can be purchased all the native articles of luxury: coca, chupe, frozen potatoes, parched corn, and chicha (native hard cider made from anything that happens to be handy). The streets are lined with small merchants who stack their wares on the sidewalk against the walls of the build-ings. There are no carriages and few horseback riders, so that one does not mind being crowded off the sidewalks by the picturesque booths of the Quichua mer-chants.

In the streets flocks of llamas driven by gayly-dressed Indians add a rare fla-vor not easily forgotten. The llamas move noiselessly only making little grunts of private conversation among themselves; quite haughty, yet so timid withal, they are easily guided in droves of fifty by a couple of diminutive Indians.

To see these ridiculous animals stalking slowly along, looking inquisitively at everyone, continually reminded me of Oliver Herford's verses about that person in Boston who

> "Looked about him with that air
> Of supercilious despair
> That very stuck-up people wear
> At some society affair
> When no one in their set is there."

In the immediate vicinity of the market-place every available inch on each side of the street is used by the small tradesmen. They are allowed to erect canopies to protect their goods from the sun and rain, and the general effect is not unlike a street in Cairo. On one corner are piled up bolts of foreign cloth, their owners squatting on the sidewalk in front of them. On another corner, leaning against the white-washed walls of a building, is a native drug store. The different herbs and medicines exposed for sale in the little cloth bags are cleverly stacked up so as to show their contents without allowing the medicines to mix. The most conspicuous article offered for sale is coca, which is more to the Quichua than tobacco is to the rest of mankind.

The market-place itself is roughly paved with ir regular stone blocks and is surrounded by arcades where are the more perishable European goods. The ven-dors of Indian merchandise squat on the stones wherever they can find a place and spread out before them their wares, whether they consist of eggs or pottery, potatoes or sandals.

It is the custom to arrange the corn and potatoes in little piles, each pile being worth a real, about four cents in our money, the standard of value in the market-place. Under umbrella-like shelters are gathered the purveyors of food and drink, their steaming cauldrons of chupe surrounded by squatting Indians who can thus get warmed and fed at the same time.

The Quichua garments are of every possible hue, although red predominates. The women dress in innumerable petticoats of many-colored materials and wear warm, heavy, colored shawls, brought together over the shoulders and secured with two large pins, occasionally of handsome workmanship, but more often in the shape of spoons. Generally they are content with uninteresting felt hats, but now and then one will have a specimen of a different design, the principal material of which is black velveteen, ornamented with red worsted and colored beads. On their feet the women usually wear the simplest kind of rawhide sandals, although when they can afford it, they affect an extraordinary footgear, a sandal with a French heel an inch and a half high, and shod with a leather device resembling a horse shoe.

Near the market-place is an interesting old church, its twin towers still in good repair. Services are rarely held here, and it was with some difficulty that

THE MARKET-PLACE OF POTOSÍ

we succeeded in finding the sexton, who finally brought a large key and allowed us to see the historical pictures that hang on the walls of two of the chapels. They are of considerable interest and appeared to date from the sixteenth century. We commented on the fact that a large painting had recently been removed and were regaled with a story of how a foreign millionaire had bribed some prelate or other to sell him the treasured relic!

In the eighteenth century Potosí boasted of sixty churches but of these consid-

erably more than half are now in ruins. The ruined portion of the city lies princi-
pally to the east and south. A few strongly built churches or church towers are still
standing amid the remains of buildings that have tumbled down in heaps.

Several of the old convents and monasteries, however, are still in a flourishing
condition. To us the chief interest consisted of their collections of fine old paintings
and their beautiful flowers. Nothing was more refreshing in this mountainous desert than to walk in their lovely green gardens.

The principal object of interest in the city, however, is the Casa Nacional de
Moneda, the great mint, which was begun in colonial days to receive the plunder
that the Spaniards took out of the hill by means of the forced labor of their Indian
slaves. It covers two city blocks, and is really a collection of buildings covered by
a massive roof and surrounded by a high wall with only one entrance. The front is
striking. At regular intervals along the roof are little stone ornaments like funeral
urns. The few windows are carefully guarded with iron bars. On either side of the
elaborately decorated façade of the two-storied portal are wooden balconies over
which projects the heavily timbered roof covered with large red tiles.

As one enters the great building from the street and passes between heavy
doors into a large courtyard, the first thing that attracts one's attention is an enormous face, four feet in diameter, which looks down at the intruder from over an
archway that leads to a second courtyard. The gigantic face has a malicious grin
yet bears a distinct resemblance to Bacchus. Who put it here and what it signifies
does not seem to be known. Suffice it to say that many of the Quichuas before starting on a journey, come to this courtyard and make obeisance to the face, throwing
down in front of it a quid of coca leaves just as they used to do to the rising sun in
the time of the Incas.

The courtyard is surrounded by an arcade with massive arches over which
runs the carved wooden balustrade of the second-story balcony. In the second
patio, which is also paved with cut stones, a tiny narrow-gauge railway is used to
carry silver ingots from the treasure-room to the stamping-machines. In one of the
buildings is a physics laboratory. In another a little gymnasium. In still a third, a
collection of minerals. All of which are evidences that here are the beginnings of
a school of mines that is being built up under the able direction of an intelligent
young Bolivian engineer who received his training at Notre Dame University in
the United States. In one old building are still standing the great wooden machines
that were formerly used in the process of hammering out the silver. In a large
room on the second floor of another building are kept the vellum-bound records
of the mint and all the dies which have been used for the past two hundred years.
According to the records, the value of the silver taken from here in the colonial
days amounted to about one billion dollars. Most of the stamping was done by
hand. The Bolivian government has cleared out two or three of the buildings and
installed modern machinery, imported from the United States.

One of the most remarkable features of the mint is the size and condition of
the huge timbers that support the roof. They are as sound to-day as they were two
hundred years ago when, with infinite labor, they were brought across the moun-

tains from the distant forests of the Chaco.

The roof is surmounted by a number of small sentry-boxes which are connected by little paths and stairways that lead to all parts of the structure. In the old days, it was necessary not only to protect the "money-house" against possible attacks from without, but to make sure that the Indians, who were assigned to work in the mint, did not escape from the attics where they slept at night.

I crawled through several of these attics where not even an underfed Indian could stand upright. The roof was scarcely four feet above the floor. In the corners were rude fireplaces where they may have cooked their chupe, with dried llama dung as their only fuel. The rooms were dark, even in midday. The tiny peek-holes that served as windows admitted scarcely any light. Altogether it was as wretched a dormitory as could possibly be imagined.

The view from the roof was most interesting. The romantic cone of the mountain-of-silver rises to the south beyond the graceful towers of the cathedral. East of it are the hills where the Spaniards built their famous reservoirs. Further east are higher hills which have been the scene of several bloody encounters in the unprofitable civil wars that have devastated Bolivia. Here on the battle-field of Kari Kari, several hundred unfortunate Indians, fighting for revolutionary leaders with whose selfish aims they had little sympathy, fell victims to the unfortunate habit of appealing to arms instead of ballots.

North of us, in the foreground, is the picturesque market-place, while northwest, in the distance, the old trail for Oruro and Lima winds away through the barren hills. To the west the far extending vista discloses a wilderness of variegated hills and mountain ranges. While all around, the quaint old arched roofs, rolling like giant swells of the Pacific, are surrounded by the narrow streets, the red-tiled houses, and the ruinous towers of the ancient city.

GREENER AND MORE POPULOUS VALLEYS

CHAPTER XI
SUCRE THE DE JURE CAPITAL OF BOLIVIA

Potosí was an irresistible attraction to thousands, but the dreadful climate, the high altitude, the cold winds, and the chilling rains drove away those who could afford it to the more hospitable valleys a few days' journey eastward where, with an abundant water-supply at an elevation of eight thousand feet, charming villas sprang up surrounded by attractive plantations, the present suburbs of Sucre.

A fairly good coach road has recently been completed, and a weekly stage carries mail and passengers between the two cities. We preferred, however, to continue on our saddle mules and followed the older route. The new road is a hundred miles long. The old trail is only seventy-five. With good animals it need take but two days. We were in no hurry, however, and decided to do it in three.

The valleys through which our road descended, at first arid and desolate, gradually became greener and more populous. The views were often very fine and extensive and we saw a few snow-covered mountains. In the middle of winter, that is June and July, the snow frequently covers everything. Now, on the 29th of November, the prevailing color was a tawny brown.

On the road we met long strings of llamas, donkeys, and mules laden with every conceivable shape of basket, bag, and bundle bringing from the fertile valleys to the eastward, potatoes, maize, wine, green vegetables and fruits, the produce that feeds Potosí.

Further evidence of the extent of this traffic and the number of arrieros that continually pass over this road is the frequency of little chicherias, wretched little huts built of stone and mud, baked in the sun, and thatched with grass or bushes, where "chicha" can be bought for a penny a gourd.

On the bare ground in front of one of them a woman had pegged down the framework of a hand loom and was beginning to weave a poncho. Near her the family dinner of chupe was simmering away in a huge earthen-ware pot, supported on three stones, over a tiny fire of thorns and llama dung. Other picturesque jars filled with chicha awaited her customers.

We lunched at what Baedeker would call "a primitive thermal establishment," a favorite weekend resort for German clerks in the importing houses of Potosí. A swimming-pool that affords opportunity to luxuriate in the warm sulphur water attracts many visitors, as it is practically the only place in southern Bolivia where one can get a hot tub bath.

The proprietor of the Baths, a type of Englishman that in the Pacific Ocean is called a "beach comber," was an amusing old vagabond who made a great fuss ordering his half-starved Indians to prepare us a suitable meal. Our expectations were aroused to a high pitch by his enthusiasm, but the quality of the food was not any better than that of

THE PICTURESQUE OLD CHURCH OF BARTOLO

the ordinary native inn. There was one very marked difference, however. We were not met by any declaration of "no hay nada."

Our second stopping-place was Bartolo, a small town of a thousand inhabitants, chiefly Quichua Indians, and a picturesque old church surrounded by a wall made of stone arches. We arrived on a Sunday evening and found the tambo already so full of travellers that there was no room for us or our beasts. The Prefect of Potosí had given us a circular letter requesting the masters of all the post-houses on our route to accord us "every facility for our journey." We soon found the letter to be of little avail, for when there was any difficulty such as lack of accommodation or of fodder we were invariably informed that the master of the poste was away attending to some business in another village. As our letter, however, included also the governors of towns, we now asked to be directed to the house of the Gobernador of Bartolo and found that worthy gentleman bidding good-bye to some Sunday visitors with whom he had been partaking freely of brandy and chicha. He was at first inclined to be insolent, and although he had a comparatively large house, declared that he had no room for us and that we must return to the inn. As the situation approached that point where it was becoming necessary to use force in order to secure shelter for the night, an obliging guest, who had possession of the largest room in the inn, learning from Fermin, the Gaucho, that we were delegados, offered us the use of his quarters while he sought accommodation among his acquaintances in the town.

In the meantime, the family of the tipsy governor had sobered him up enough to make him realize that he had shown discourtesy to the bearer of a government passport and he came to the inn with profuse offers of entertainment which we unfortunately could not accept.

We left Bartolo early the next morning. The dust had been laid by thunder-showers in the night and the crisp mountain air was most refreshing. Occasionally we passed the ruins of a rude stone cairn erected in colonial days to measure the leagues between Sucre and Potosí. Fermin had never been beyond Potosí, so we were obliged to fall back upon the service of guides or postillons from here on. They cannot be taken farther than from one poste to another, generally six leagues or twenty miles. They receive a regular tariff of four cents per league, and a small gratuity besides.

For this munificent sum of a little over a cent a mile, they are supposed to assist in catching and saddling the animals, to hold the packs while they are being loaded, and then to run beside the trotting pack-animals, ready to help if the loads become loosened, constantly at hand, a willing slave to the arriero and a guide to the traveller. Generally lightly clad with the regulation Quichua small clothes, that look as though made of meal-sacks, they march or lope along cheerily, now and then blowing lustily on an ox-horn, which they carry slung over the shoulder as a badge of their position.

The postillons will not budge unless their tariff is paid in advance, for they have learned through cen turies of experience that while the traveller with a stout whip, mounted on a good animal, with the authority of the government at his back, can force them to go the required distance after the fee has been paid, they have no means whatever of forcing him to pay after he has arrived at his destination and has no further need of their services. The first postilion we had, recognizing the fact that our arriero was a stranger in this part of the country and that we were foreigners, ran far ahead of the little caravan, and would have disappeared among the thorny shrubs of the arid hillside had we not galloped after him and threateningly ordered him to return to his post at the heels of the mules. The next one proved to be a good fellow and did his work well, notwithstanding the dust which was his portion during most of the day.

This morning we passed a field in which alpacas that looked like overgrown woolly dogs were feeding. As the sparse foliage increased, we met numerous flocks of sheep watched over by diminutive children in shawls and ponchos who ran away and hid behind rocks when they saw us coming.

About the middle of the morning we came to the edge of a plateau and enjoyed a wonderful view of fertile valleys, whose waters flow rapidly down to the

Pilcomayo. It seemed difficult to realize that a Bolivian landscape could have any other color than brown. Our descent was now rapid, and the temperature grew warmer except when we encountered a small hail-storm.

After passing the scene of a battle in the unsuc cessful revolution of General Camacho, a militant politician with whom Bolivia had considerable difficulty in the '90's, we stopped for lunch at a tumbled-down hostelry called Quebrada Honda, in honor of a deep little valley whose steep sides rise abruptly from a roaring mountain torrent. Squatting on the ground in front of the tambo was a Quichua woman weaving a bright-colored poncho.

In the afternoon we passed some primitive dwellings which consisted of huge flat boulders under which excavations had been made leaving them partially supported by piles of stones at the corners. The method did not seem to have proved successful, for in most cases, the roof, too heavy for the supports, was lying on the ground.

About five o'clock we arrived at the poste of Pampa Tambo. We found a postilion in charge; the "master of the poste was absent" as usual. The postilion decided to charge us three times the regular rate for forage and Fermin protested vigorously, but in vain. Although it was a matter of only a dollar or so, I decided to see whether my letter from the Prefect of Potosí would make any difference with his attitude toward us. The sight of the official seal, and an emphatic threat that he would get himself into trouble if he persisted in his outrageous demands, gradually brought him to lower the price until it came within two or three cents of the regular tariff.

Hardly had we settled the dispute when a violent thunder-storm came up. This was the last day of November and the rainy season was beginning. From now on we had showers nearly every afternoon.

A PASTURE FOR SHEEP AND ALPACAS

A QUICHUA WOMAN WEAVING AT QUEBRADA HONDA

In the evening a party of foreigners arrived, consisting of a wealthy Franco-Boliviano and his two sons who were on their way home from Paris. They amused us by their elaborate preparations to supply themselves with drinks and edibles. Little alcohol stoves were kept busy making hot toddy, and drinks without number soon produced a very drowsy party.

We got an early start the next morning and, in an hour after leaving Pampa Tambo, came in sight of the great river Pilcomayo which is associated with the tragic death of the French explorer, Creveaux. The Pilcomayo rises west of Potosí, receives the turbid waters that have passed through Potosí's smelters, flows east and then southeast towards Paraguay, finally joining the Paraguay River just above Asuncion. Were it not for the gigantic morass, the Estero Patino, which interrupts its course for about fifty miles, it would serve as a convenient means of communication between the mining region of Bolivia and the Rio de la Plata. Most of its course is through the Gran Chaco, a debateable land that has been only partly explored.

East of the Andes, where the affluents of the Pilcomayo are almost interlaced with those of the Mamoré, in the watershed between the basins of the Amazon and the Paraná, lies a region of rich tropical forests with possibilities of development that appeal very strongly to far-sighted Bolivianos. The conditions are tropical, the soil is fertile, and there is an abundance of rain. There are, however, in this region, many tribes of wild Indians of whom little is known and who have shown no desire to encour age the advent of strangers. Transportation is exceedingly difficult.

We found that a suspension bridge had been built across the Pilcomayo at its narrowest and deepest point, but owing to the tardiness of the wet season, we were able to ford the stream lower down and save a détour of several miles. After crossing the river we rode up a dry gulch in which an attempt at cultivation by means of irrigating ditches was producing both pomegranates and peaches.

An hour's ride beyond the river brought us to Calera, a little hamlet of Indian huts with a very primitive tambo. We had counted on resting here during the middle of the day, but there was absolutely nothing to be had either for man or beast. We could have unloaded and unpacked our own supplies, but there is no point in eating when your mules cannot eat, and so we pushed on, twelve miles further, to the town of Yotala. Our path crossed a low range of barren hills and then descended a thousand feet or more by a steep, winding path to the river Cachimayo which we forded without difficulty. In this little valley we found many attractive plantations, the fincas or country houses of the wealthy residents of Sucre. Extensive irrigation has transformed the bed of the valley into what seems like a veritable paradise, so great is its contrast with the barren region around about.

Yotala is an old Spanish town, much more dead than alive. There was an inn, misnamed a "restaurant," where there was nothing to be had in the way of food for any of us. Fermin finally succeeded in finding a poor widow who had a little fodder for sale and was willing to let the mules eat it in her back yard. As for ourselves, we had to fall back as usual on canned goods, just as though this were an isolated poste, twenty miles from anywhere, instead of being a town of several thousand inhabitants. We spread out our little lunch on the stones of the plaza under two trees.

As it was noon, and the sky cloudless, the sun shone with considerable ferocity. Presently a slovenly official with an expression on his face that said plainly he was not quite sure whether we were distinguished travellers who ought to be looked after or only vagabonds who should be driven off, came and inquired if we were French merchants. On receiving a negative reply he seemed rather relieved and withdrew to the shade of his own house. Of course if we had whispered the magic words "delegados de los Estados Unidos," all would have been different.

After the mules had had a rest we covered the remaining six miles to Sucre, passing on the way a number of large fincas. One of them seemed to bear a distant resemblance to a pleasure park. Statues of men and animals, summer houses, pagodas, and a small intramural railway whose imitation locomotive was a small automobile in disguise, lent the place a festive air which was increased by one or two minarets and other fantastic towers. We learned afterwards that this was La Glorieta, the seat of the Prince and Princess of Glorieta. The story, as told us by a pleasant old lady in Sucre, is as follows:—

It seems that the head of the richest family in Bolivia, who is also the leading banker of Sucre, wearying of republican simplicity, decided to make a large donation to the Pope. Soon afterwards his great generosity was rewarded with the title of "Prince of Glorieta." Unfortunately, our presence in this part of the world was not properly made known to this Bolivian royal house and I am unable to give an adequate description of the beauties of Glorieta. They have, however, been published by the owners in a pamphlet, and from all that I could hear, Glorieta has a distant resemblance to Coney Island.

After passing Glorieta, we crossed a small cañon, climbed the sides of a deep gorge, and suddenly found ourselves at the city gates.

Sucre has a population of twenty thousand souls, including fifty negroes, and two or three hundred foreigners, a large number of whom are Spaniards engaged in mercantile business. There are two or three hotels here, and we were in some doubt as to which might offer the best welcome. After a vain effort to locate the Prefect and get his advice, we decided to go to the Hotel Colon where we found large comfortable rooms on the second floor, facing the plaza. The proprietor was most polite and attentive. The only fault that we had to find with him was his continual spitting. The fact that there were no cuspidors and that he was ruining his own carpet did not deter him in the least. Perhaps he had rented the furnishings.

It is superfluous to speak of the filth of the kitchen

THE GREAT RIVER PILCOMAYO

OUR HOTEL IN SUCRE

through which we had to pass to reach the back yard. It differed from others only in the large number of guinea-pigs that swarmed everywhere. They helped to make the bill-of-fare more interesting.

Sucre owes its importance to its comparatively pleasant climate. The average temperature is 56° F. Bolivianos, accustomed as they are to one of the worst climates in the world, say that Sucre has "the finest climate in existence," which means, being translated, that it is fairly tolerable. Nevertheless, we found it very agreeable to be down at this lower elevation, and we could scarcely sympathize with Castelnau, who, coming up from the eastern plains in 1845, thought Sucre very "triste." He and his associates had been for many months in the warm regions of Brazil and found it difficult "to resist the cold and the effects of the altitude." Most of them suffered severely from soroche although few people now-a-days think of being troubled at an altitude of anything less than twelve thousand feet and Sucre is only a little over nine thousand.

If the miners had felt as Castelnau did, the old Indian city of Chuquisaca would never have become the social and literary capital of upper Peru. Its name was changed to La Plata in recognition of the stream of silver that flowed to it from Potosí. Here resided an important bishop who looked after the souls of countless thousands of Indians scattered up and down the Bolivian plateau and in the tangled jungles east of the Andes. The citizens of Chuquisaca, or La Plata, acquired before long a reputation for wealth and intelligence which spread far and wide. They called their city the "Athens of Peru" and they established here a university where students still come to study law and medicine.

After the great battle of Ayacucho in December, 1824, when General Sucre won the memorable victory that defeated the last Spanish army in South America, Upper Peru was erected into an independent Republic, taking its name from the great General Bolivar and giving to its capital city the name of its first president.

President Sucre was living at the capital when Edmond Temple came here in 1826. That entertaining writer describes him as tall and thin with mild, prepossessing manners and diffident address. Temple had lived in Bolivia for nearly a year and was moved to say that General Sucre was the best choice that could have been made to fill "the arduous, troublesome, and thankless office of Supreme Chief of the new republic of Bolivia." Temple attended a session of Congress where he was unfavorably impressed by the custom of remaining seated during the whole debate and by the constant practice of spitting, "which is a breach of decorum which no Englishman can patiently witness!" The innkeeper must have been a descendant of a Congressman.

As long as Congress sat here the representatives came mostly from this region and were naturally influenced by the aristocratic society of the capital. The wealthy politicians of Sucre succeeded in diverting a large part of the national revenues to beautifying their city, building extravagant public works, and neglecting the just claims of La Paz. La Paz, far more populous, and enjoying a much more important situation commercially, was overlooked. Little of the public revenue found its way thither. The result was a revolution in which La Paz emphatically proclaimed its desire to share in the distribution of the public moneys and public offices. The then President gathered the Government forces together in Sucre and proceeded to march on the rebellious metropolis. He was defeated not far from La Paz with great losses, and the war-like Aymarás of La Paz followed up the victory with orgies of a disgusting and barbaric if not cannibalistic character. The result was that while Sucre retained the Supreme Court and the title of Capital, La Paz became the actual seat of government, and few foreign diplomats have ever undertaken the five days of hard travel which separates Sucre from Challapata, the nearest railway station.

Nevertheless the wealthiest people in Bolivia live in Sucre. They are very aristocratic and extremely exclusive, and they feel very superior to the citizens of La Paz although that place is really much more important than Sucre. The great land-owners have established here the headquarters of the most important banks in the country.

At the largest of all, the Banco Nacional de Bolivia, I drew some money on my letter of credit. Among the coins which I trustfully accepted were seven or eight that proved to be bad. The Indians always ring a coin before accepting it. The result was I found myself the victim of a clever bank cashier. The coins were probably not counterfeit. The Bolivian government has not been above issuing "silver" coins, particularly "half pesos," that contain so much "alloy" as to be valueless.

These debased half dollars have long been a subject of annoyance not only to travellers but to the neighboring Peruvians. Sir Clements Markham says that at the time of his visit to Peru in 1859, when he was on that famous mission that secured Chincona plants from eastern Peru for transportation to India, war was imminent between Peru and Bolivia and one casus belli was that the Bolivian government persisted in coining and deluging Peru with debased half dollars. These ill-omened chickens have certainly come back to roost, for one never sees them now in Peru and they are all too frequent here. Perhaps that is one reason why the local banks are so unusually well built.

There is also a pretentious "legislative palace," and at the time of my visit a large theatre was in the course of construction. It was hoped to have this completed in time for the celebration of the one hundredth anniversary of the beginning of the War of Independence.

The market-place is neither so interesting nor so picturesque as that of Potosí. A few of the men wore curious helmet-like hats with small visors turned up in front and back. It would be interesting to know whether this were the original hat of the vicinity or whether it had been copied from the head-gear of the armored Spaniard conquistadores of the sixteenth century. The corresponding women's hats were twice as large as the men's but the brim was turned up in the front and back in the same fashion.

Most of the women wore felt hats of native manufacture, picturesque coats of white cotton decorated with many little pieces of colored calico, and as many heavy woollen petticoats as they could afford. The majority wore rough rawhide sandals without socks but a few had elaborately patterned knitted stockings.

A considerable quantity of chocolate is manufactured here and, as in the mountains of Colombia, no meal is considered complete without it. They appreciate better than we do the advantage of having the drink as light and airy as possible, and consequently never serve any without beating it to a light froth by means of a wooden spindle that is inserted in the pot and rapidly revolved between the palms of the hands.

There are several Indian silversmiths here, as well as in Potosí, where filigree-work, spoons, and simple silver dishes are hammered out. The director of the mint in Potosí told me he was frequently offered pure silver family heirlooms that have come down from the extravagant days of the seventeenth century when in a well-to-do house every imaginable utensil was made of silver.

Another specialty of Sucre is the manufacture of tiny dolls out of pieces of fine wire, lace, and tinsel. They range in size from four inches down to half an inch. Sometimes an effort is made to copy a native costume, but more generally the dressing is entirely fantastic or suited only to high carnival. Similar dolls are made in south central Mexico.

CHAPTER XII
THE ROAD TO CHALLAPATA

WE were not sorry when the time came to leave Sucre. It not infrequently happens that interior provincial cities of considerable local political importance are not very lenient toward strangers, particularly if the latter are dressed in breeches that seem at all outlandish to the provincial mind. I understand that Chinese have found this to be true in the capitals of our Western States. The thing had happened to me before in Tunja, the capital of the province of Boyacá, Colombia. And it happened here in Sucre. Whenever we walked the streets examining the public buildings or visiting the market-place, we were considerably annoyed by loafers, both men and boys, who, recognizing us as strangers and foreigners, regarded us as the proper target for all manner of witticisms.

An hour after leaving the city, we turned to look back, and found the view from the west quite attractive. In the foreground, dry gulches, stony hillsides, and an occasional thatched mud hut. In the distance, hills sloping down so abruptly that one could not see the bottom of the gulch that lay between us and the city. Immediately beyond, the white walls of Sucre overshadowed by a mountain whose twin peaks rise beyond the eastern suburbs. There was just a suggestion of green, reminding us that this is the last fertile spot on the outskirts of the great arid plateau, towards which we now turned.

As the road between Sucre and the railway is one of the most important thoroughfares in Bolivia, it was to be expected that there would be postes every four or five leagues. The first one we came to was that of Punilla, four leagues from Sucre. All we needed was a guide, but the only postillon we could secure had a very sore foot, scarcely protected at all from the stony road by the primitive rawhide sandal that he wore. Yet he came along quite cheerfully.

The postes between Sucre and Challapata are larger than those in southern Bolivia. They are modelled on the Inca tambos that used to exist on all the more frequented trails in the highlands of Peru and Bolivia; a range of low, windowless buildings, either of stone or adobe, sometimes completely surrounding a courtyard, at other times only on three sides, containing a few rooms of which one is furnished with a rough and very shaky table and three or four adobe platforms intended for bunks; mud floors that have accumulated dirt and filth of every description ever since the building was constructed; poorly thatched roofs from which bits of straw and pieces of dirt occasionally dislodge themselves to fall on the table where we spread our canned repast, or to alight on our faces just as we were trying to get to sleep.

The trains of pack animals that we met on the road, whether llamas, burros, or mules, were all engaged in bringing freight from the railway. This consisted mostly of boxes of soap and canned goods, cases of wine and beer and condensed milk, and small packages of general merchandise.

The next poste, Pisculco, four leagues beyond Punilla over a good road that wound through semi-arid hills, was an extremely primitive affair. The master of the poste and all the postillons were "absent," but we secured the services of a small boy who bravely girded his belt, slung a horn over his shoulder, received his pay and started out as our guide and escort. He soon fell behind, however, and before we knew it, disappeared among the brown bushes. Both his scanty raiment and his skin were so nearly the color of the ground that it was a hopeless task to look for him, and we went on, trusting we should be able to follow such a well-travelled highway without the necessity of a guide. Unfortunately, the road forked, and in choosing the more travelled branch, we followed a short cut in the steps of llama pack trains. As they camp in the open at night, we missed the road for Moromoro, took the wrong turn, and after a perilous descent down a mile of treacherous, slippery rocks, found ourselves at the abandoned tambo of Challoma, whose only inhabitants were an old woman and her pigs. She was greatly alarmed at our arrival and told us in shrill tones that we were three leagues off the road. Nevertheless, as it was rapidly getting dark and we had had a hard ride of forty miles, we decided to take shelter under the leaky roof of the ancient poste.

Beyond Challoma the trail crossed a cañon and a shallow stream and finally came out on a series of flat lands where we saw a few burros and llamas

AN ABANDONED TAMBO

OUR FIRST VIEW OF THE GREAT TABLE-LAND OF BOLIVIA

grazing on the dry grass which had been left over from the last rainy season.

In the middle of one such plain stood the next poste, Caracara, built like a fortress in the desert. There are only three openings in the great square inclosure: a barred window high up in a gable end near one corner; a little door leading to a cantina where one could purchase a few drinks, matches, candles, and cigarettes; and a small arched entrance through which loaded animals and travellers pass to the courtyard. Although on one of the most important highways in Bolivia it did not afford any food for the animals or ourselves.

After leaving Caracara, we passed a few pink roses blooming under the shelter of some rocks. They looked strangely out of place in this Thibetan wilderness but they gave signs of the coming spring and the rainy season. In the afternoon we had several thunder-showers. The result of the showers of the past few days had been to stimulate also the growth of an occasional geranium, or modest little fern. In general there was little to relieve the monotonous brown wilderness.

For league after league we continued our march westward through a confused mountainous region. In southern Bolivia we had followed a long valley running in a north and south direction, but here our route lay across the valleys. Sometimes we followed the coach road for several leagues and then took a short cut down a steep hillside. At times we did not see a single hut in the twelve or fourteen miles separating the postes. While not quite so sandy and desolate as the region farther south, still it impresses one as being extremely inhospitable and unlikely ever to support a larger population.

In the evening of the second day we reached Ocurí, eighty miles from Sucre. Just outside the town we crossed a very swampy plain where cattle, horses, and pigs were feeding in treacherous bogs.

Ocurí is a brown little Indian town of perhaps two thousand inhabitants, with houses of sunburned brick and thatched roofs, lying high up on the side of a mountain whose peak shelters it somewhat from the easterly winds. It is higher than Potosí and has much the same cold, dismal climate. It likewise owes its existence to the presence of mines of silver and tin. There are several small smelters just outside the town. We could get nothing to eat in the poste, but a pleasant-faced mestiza woman who kept a sort of boarding-house near by, gave us a supper of beefsteak and fried eggs, a welcome change from the canned food which was our mainstay.

The principal street in the town was lined with small shops where a considerable variety of domestic and foreign merchandise was offered for sale. This does not mean that there were any attractive window displays but that when Mr. Smith felt brave enough to venture to step over the little Aymará brats and the fierce Bolivian dogs who were playing around the prostrate forms of drunken arrieros, he found hidden away in the dark recesses of dusty shops, quite a variety of articles. Cigarettes, onions, eggs, bread, canned salmon, sardines, home-made woollen ponchos, imported cotton cloth, candles, cheap domestic pottery, straw hats, shoes, belts, gloves, and condensed milk. It is a very poor place indeed in Bolivia where one cannot buy a small can of Swiss condensed milk, the one thing that is generally good.

At Ocurí, we entered the country of the Aymarás for whom this is a kind of outpost town. Our first evidence of their being here was the fact that the postillons in the tambo unloaded our mules very carelessly, allowing the bags to fall with a crash to the ground. They seemed to think it a great joke to treat us as ignominiously as possible. From here to Oruro, La Paz, and Lake Titicaca the Aymarás are in full sway. They seem to be inserted like a wedge between the Quichuas of Peru and those of southern Bolivia.

The Quichuas are a mild and inoffensive folk, but the Aymarás, heavier in build, coarser featured, and more vigorous in general appearance, are brutally insolent in their manner and unruly in their behavior. We were even regaled with stories of their cannibalism on certain occasions, but unfortunately had no opportunity of proving the truth of such statements. Neither Quichuas nor Aymarás are at all thrifty, and we were everywhere impressed with their great poverty. Their clothing is generally the merest rags and their food is as meagre as can possibly be imagined. Coca and chicha (i. e., cocaine and alcohol) seem to be beginning and end of life with them. We rarely ever saw one riding, although occasionally we met a postillon returning to his poste with a mule that had been placed in his charge.

A great majority of the population show little or no desire to vote or to have anything to do with politics. They are uneducated, but have very fixed ideas with regard to their absolute rights over land which they have occupied for any length of time. Their ideas of squatter sovereignty sometimes interfere with the desires of the government to develop the resources of the country.

It is unfortunate that no efforts are being made to establish a good system of public schools and enforce attendance. One of the greatest difficulties in the way of such an undertaking is the fact that the Indians not only have no interest in securing the education of their children, but also that they find it to their advantage to speak their own tongue rather than Spanish. Probably less than fifteen per cent of the population speak Spanish with fluency. They are lacking in ambition, seem to have no desire to raise produce, bear ill-will towards strangers, and prefer not to assist travellers to pass through their country. Even if a man has plenty of chickens and sheep, he will generally refuse to sell any although you offer him an excellent price. With coaxing and coca you may succeed. Sometimes he pretends not to understand Spanish and replies to all questions in guttural Quichua or Aymará.

So large a percentage of the population are Indians that nearly all the whites are actively interested in politics and would like to be office-holders. It is said that all elections are merely forms through which the party in power goes, in order to maintain its supremacy.

The majority of the inhabitants are in no sense fitted to be the citizens of a republic. However much the theoretical lover of liberty may bemoan the fact that Bolivia is in reality an oligarchy, one cannot help feeling that that is the only possible outcome of an attempt to simulate the forms of a republic in a country whose inhabitants are so deficient both mentally and morally. Mexico has given a splendid example of what can be accomplished in a region populated largely by Indians and descendants of Spanish monarchists. The benevolent despotism which President Diaz has exhibited now for more than a generation has done wonders. The great San Martin foresaw the advantages of oligarchy or monarchy and advocated something of the kind for the Spanish provinces of South America when they secured their independence. Unfortunately, his far-sighted statesmanship ran counter to the bombastic notions of "liberty" held by the uneducated creoles who had secured control of the reins of government and the result was the creation of republics. The extreme difficulty of communication throughout Bolivia has made the way of revolutions fairly easy. An entire province can rise against the government before sufficient troops can be sent to quell the disturbance.

Whenever we got an early start from a poste, we were pretty sure to come upon a llama camp before long; the drivers engaged in slowly rounding up their grazing beasts and inducing them to receive their loads for another day's work. In the absence of rain, the loads are merely piled up on the ground so as to form a shelter from the wind during the night. If showers threaten, ponchos and tarpaulins are thrown over the heap of merchandise.

Many of the llama drivers carried primitive musical instruments. The most common form was a bamboo flute or flageolet with six holes. On these the Indians succeed in playing weird, monotonous airs in which a fantastic reiteration of simple strains is varied with occasional bursts of high, screechy notes. Some of the drivers had little guitars of a very primitive construction on which they thrummed rather monotonously. Some had their wives and children with them. The women were nearly always engaged in spinning yarn with a wooden spindle which they handled with the dexterity of a professional juggler. Two or three men, and a boy or so, generally accompanied a caravan of sixty or seventy llamas. Each driver carried a knitted sling made of llama wool and found no lack of ammunition by the roadside with which to urge forward his flock or to head off a stray animal. We were always amused when we met a drove. The leaders would approach gingerly, stretching their long necks and looking very much like timid, near-sighted dowagers. They scarcely knew whether to advance or to retreat. A few flying rocks from the slings of the drivers, followed up by encouraging shouts, generally decided the leaders to proceed, but some were so palpably "frightened to death" by everything they saw, we were surprised they had managed to live so long. Occasionally a herd coming from Sucre laden with chocolate or sugar and bound eastward, would meet one coming from the railroad with foreign merchandise. This nearly always resulted in great confusion and much shouting. The llamas looked so stupid we wondered how they ever succeeded in extricating themselves and proceeding in the right direction. At one point where the road almost disappeared among a wilderness of huge, scattered boulders, we met a large drove that had lost all sense of direction. Every attempt of the drivers to get their animals headed the same way met with failure. The beasts seemed to be infused with some centrifugal force which sent every one of them in a different direction from his neighbor. Owing to the huge rocks, it was impossible for the poor creatures to see one another or the drivers. They may be there yet.

There is something extremely amusing in the soft tread, the awkward gait, the large innocent eyes, and the inquisitive ears of the llama. Many had the tips of their ears decorated with bits of colored worsted. I saw two that were decked out with very elaborate headdresses. They never seemed to be in a hurry, any more than their Indian drivers, and their disposition is much more gentle and inoffensive than I had been led to suppose.

About ten miles from Ocurí I saw several fat lizards each about six inches long. The altitude at the time was about fourteen thousand feet, the record height for lizards, so I am told.

Soon afterwards we got a glimpse to the northwards of the sharp peaks near Colquechaca, one of the highest towns in the world, which owes its existence, as do so many of the Bolivian towns, to the presence in its vicinity of rich silver mines.

We reached Macha at noon on the third day, after a hot ride of thirty miles from Ocurí.

Macha is another dusty-brown, Indian town lying on the slopes of a large valley. Near by we saw some evidences of cultivation. The fields were surrounded with walls of dried mud and had large adobe gates reminding me of the Sogamoso valley in Colombia. That region, however, was so much greener and more fertile than this that the resemblance ceased with the gates and fences. It should be remembered that the rainy season here had only just begun.

As we descended the east side of the valley, we met a six-mule coach on its way from Challapata to Sucre. The curtains were drawn down on all sides to protect the passengers from the dust and glare. Their outlook was rather limited. A quarter of a mile beyond we met a drove of relay coach mules, in charge of two mounted postillons.

There is a moderately good coach-road two hundred and ten miles long from Sucre to Challapata. The coach runs fortnightly, in pleasant weather, and takes five days for the journey. Personally, I should prefer almost anything rather than to be shut up in a Bolivian coach and yanked over these rough, dusty roads, but I suppose some people would relish even that better than jogging along forty miles a day on a mule, as we chose to do.

We left Macha after a light lunch but had not gone a mile before we were pelted by a violent thunder-shower accompanied by hail, some of the stones being as large as marbles. To add to our discomfort the mules had made rapid marches since leaving Sucre and were very tired. The road out of the valley was steep and slippery. When we reached the summit, the storm renewed its fury, and we all shivered with the cold, in contrast to the burning heat of the morning. At this height, whenever the sun shines, the glare is trying and the heat really uncomfortable. As soon as the sun passes behind a cloud, however, one experiences all the rigors of winter.

We arrived at the lonely isolated poste of Aconcawa just at sunset. The Aymará postillons were as disobliging as possible. Four or five Bolivian travellers had reached the poste ahead of us and taken possession of the only available sleeping room. The night was bitterly cold and wet. The altitude was something over thirteen thousand feet. After some difficulty, we succeeded in forcing our way into a room where the cebada or barley straw was stored. South of Potosí the fodder for the mules is generally alfa or alfalfa but hereabouts it is cebada. The Indians were so afraid of our damaging the straw by sleeping on it that they swept it up and piled it on one side of the room as high as possible, raising clouds of fine dust in the meantime. The dust did not settle for many hours and brought on asthma when we tried to sleep. Soon after leaving Aconcawa, Fermin's sharp eyes detected three vicuñas, feeding, a mile away to the south of us. I could barely make them out with powerful field-glasses and should never have seen them at all but for the keen-eyed gaucho. It seemed strange that these should be the only vicuñas which we saw in a wild state in our entire journey in southern Bolivia. Travellers fifty years ago speak of meeting them constantly in the more desolate parts of the mountains. Before the great demand arose for vicuña rugs, those highly-prized trophies of the casual visitor, these graceful and beautiful creatures, with their fawn-colored coats, were one of the most interesting features of travel in the lonely upland pastures of the Bolivian and Peruvian mountains.

On the little plain near the vicuñas were a few pools of water that seemed to be a feeding-ground for a few pigeons and some birds that looked like Titicaca gulls. An occasional earth-colored guineapig was practically the only other wild animal we could discover.

Soon after seeing the vicuñas we continued to climb by a zigzag road until we reached the highest point in this journey, the ridge of Livichuco, fifteen thousand feet above the sea. Neither mules or llamas seemed to mind this altitude but we found it very chilly and disagreeable and were glad enough to descend as quickly as possible without wasting much time in enjoying the extensive view over the rock-strewn hills about us. It may seem strange that we did not stop to rhapsodize on the fact that we were now leaving the basin of the Rio de la Plata, or on the extensive panorama. But the latter was so cold, desolate, and forbidding, the only effect was to make us urge forward the mules at as rapid a pace as possible.

The mountains were not snow-capped although, at times, we had had light storms of hail and snow. This was particularly true of the afternoons, the

A FRIENDLY LLAMA BABY

MY MULE ON THE LAST DAY'S RIDE

mornings being generally fine and clear. As we went west, the valleys grew broader. We occasionally passed over level plains four or five miles wide. We had now crossed the watershed and left the basin of the Rio de la Plata and its affluents for that of Lake Poopo and the Bolivian tableland.

Descending, we came to valleys that offered sufficient grass to support a large number of llamas, alpacas, and sheep. This region seems to be a favorite breeding-place for the llamas and we saw a number of baby llamas. One of the latter, almost entirely black as to its body and legs, with black ears, resembling the horns of a carnival devil, and a white face that looked like a mask, was so interested in my efforts to take his picture that he walked up to within eight feet of my mule, much to his mother's alarm.

A cold wind and a cloudy sky that kept the sun from offering any warmth made our arrival at the poste of Livichuco anything but pleasant. To add to our discomforts, Bolivian travellers had again arrived ahead of us and monopolized everything in sight, as the scanty accommodations of this wretched tambo were insufficient to meet the demands of both parties. A few eggs was all the postillons could offer for our entertainment, and as these turned out to be rotten their willingness to sell food was not appreciated.

The morning had been cloudy, cold, and disagreeable but the afternoon was worse. Clouds of dust and peals of thunder ushered in the usual storm. Our road, however, was not as rocky and precipitous as on the preceding days. We crossed several broad plains, joined the Potosí-Challapata trail and passed near Vilcapujio, another of the battlefields of the War of Independence. In 1813 the soldiers of Buenos Aires had again invaded Bolivia to assist the patriots of Upper Peru. They reached Potosí in safety and were on their way north to Oruro when they were met here at the fork in the road and defeated by the Spaniards. A few days later came the battle of Ayoma, near Macha. The result was temporarily fatal to the cause of Bolivian independence.

We had another unpleasant experience on our arrival at Ancacato, on the evening of the fourth day. Bolivian travellers had, as before, taken possession of all the available rooms and we had a hard time persuading the master of the poste to allow us to remain.

At a distance of two or three miles from the tambo is the old Indian town of Ancacato lying spread out on the level floor of the valley which was at present brown and desolate although it had signs of being cultivated in the rainy season. Like other Indian towns, the only conspicuous feature of Ancacato was the tower of its large church. The rest of the town consisted of brown huts as much as possible like the color of the hills.

The next morning we met an unusually large number of llamas on their way from Challapata to the interior carrying small boxes of European merchandise. The monotony of this morning's ride was varied by the spectacle of a mounted Indian trying, like "Mac," to drive a pack mule that was quite unaccustomed to such service and most unwilling to keep the road. There are no fences or walls to mark off the road from the surrounding country and an active pack animal can take to the hill as often as he pleases. Most of them are either too weary, too tame or too well acquainted with the punishment that follows, to attempt such amusements, but this one was new at the game and he led his driver a merry chase over frightful rocky slopes, up and down precipitous hillsides, and through the dry bed of a stream. "Anywhere and everywhere" seemed to be his motto.

A short hour's ride brought us through the pass over the Cordillera de los Frailes and out onto the great tableland where the horizon on every side, except behind us, seemed to be as level as the ocean. Far away to the southwest we could just make out the dark lines and specks that denoted the whereabouts of Challapata and the railway station.

Challapata is an old Indian town, but there has grown up at some distance from it, near the railway, a little modern settlement where white-washed warehouses, hotels, stores, and a telegraph office offer a marked contrast to the brown mud-huts of the more ancient city. The population is said to be more than two thousand souls. Of these by far the larger part are Aymarás who speak little or no Spanish. The streets of the new town are wide and sandy, hot and glary like some of our western towns. We thought the hotel was most comfortable and even luxurious, after our experience of the past few weeks, but I dare say that the traveller coming the other way would turn up his nose at its primitive accommodations.

CHAPTER XIII
ORURO TO ANTOFAGASTA AND VALPARAISO

Notwithstanding its comfortable beds, wash-stands, and billiard-table, we were glad enough to leave the hotel at Challapata and take the train for Oruro. Our only regret was that we had to say good-by to old Fermin whose faithfulness in his care not only of the mules but of ourselves, had made us grow very fond of him. We gave him a little gratuity which he almost immediately offered to Mr. Smith in exchange for a cheap silver watch the latter had purchased in Jujuy!

On our way northward to Oruro we got distant glimpses of the saline waters of Lake Poopo that receives the overflow from Lake Titicaca by means of the Desaguadero River but has no outlet of its own. On our right were the low summits of the Cordillera de los Frailes and on the intervening plain was an occasional town with brown huts and a conspicuous church. Once in a while we saw chulpas, so-called "Inca tombs," really Aymará, in which interesting remains are often found. The Ferrocarril Antofagasta-Bolivia, a very narrow-gauge road constructed and managed by Englishmen, was built to reach the important silver mines of Huanchaca which, in the early '90's, exported annually eight million ounces of silver. Once on the plateau, it was an easy matter to connect the railroad with Oruro whose output of silver at that time was about a million and a half ounces. Furthermore, Colquechaca, with an equal output, was only two days away and pack trains could bring the silver readily to the railway.

The road has proved to be a splendid investment, yet Great Britain has never favored Bolivia with much capital. Apart from this line and a small bit of railroad near La Paz, there are almost no British enterprises in the country. It is said that even Ecuador, backward as it is, has twenty times as much British capital as Bolivia, while Argentina has two hundred times as much.

The ride to Oruro was devoid of interest except for a conversation which I had with a distinguished Bolivian physician who had recently come from the eastern provinces where he assured me lay the real wealth of his country. He was most enthusiastic about the possibilities of the Gran Chaco as a region likely some day to be well populated. Although a native of this part of Bolivia, he told me that every time he came back to this altitude, he suffered from soroche or mountain sickness. I was told by several other Bolivianos that they too suffered from soroche whenever they came up from the lower elevation, notwithstanding the fact that the author of a recent book on South America says that the Bolivianos themselves never suffer from this infirmity.

We reached Oruro shortly after dark and were met by a pleasant-faced Austrian hotel proprietor who obligingly put us on board of a mule-drawn tram-car. A few minutes later we stopped in front of the Grand Hotel de Francia y Inglaterra and were back in the civilized world again.

There are two comfortable hotels in Oruro and an excellent Union Club where all nationalities come to enjoy themselves. Besides this, a German club has recently been started. Another feature of Oruro, which we might not have noticed had we approached it from the civilized instead of the uncivilized side of the world, was a rather palatial public billiard-hall or casino where a dozen or fifteen good tables, and an elaborate bar, attracted every evening a crowd of foreign engineers, clerks, and bookkeepers.

The climate of Oruro is cold and forbidding, the thermometer in the shade usually being 50° F. The rainy season commences in November and lasts until March; January and February being the rainiest months. During our summer the weather here is intensely cold and snow-storms are not infrequent. To the west and south of the city are barren hills and the general lack of foliage makes the place rather melancholy, muy triste.

The next morning we crossed the plaza to the fine large government building where the Prefect lives and has his offices. The present incumbent, Dr. Moises Ascarrunz, was most kind and attentive. He received us in state, opened champagne, drank our health and then drove us out in the state carriage to a rifle range where, as it was a holiday, the local sporting club was holding a match.

The Prefect has taken great interest in the club and it has thriven under his patronage. The facilities for rifle practice are excellent, and we saw some

THE PREFECTURA AND PLAZA OF ORURO

capital shooting. After a light lunch of beer and sandwiches at the pleasant little club house, the Prefect showed us the sights of the town.

In his annual report which was just off the press at the time of our visit, he calls special attention to the bad condition of the postes on the road from Sucre to Challapata! We were not inclined to dispute his criticism.

One day during our stay, a government proclamation was heralded about town in the usual fashion. The local regiment of infantry paraded through the principal streets, stopping at the important corners while the colonel read the proclamation in a loud voice. The colonel seemed so strong and healthy that I was greatly surprised to learn on my return to Oruro a few weeks later that he had been taken down with one of the sudden pulmonary fevers of this altitude and died in less than twenty-four hours.

A pleasant German-American, in charge of the local agency of a large New York commercial house, told us that it was not at all uncommon for a man to get a chill on his way home from an evening party and die the next day of galloping pneumonia. The explanation seems to be that at this altitude (13,000 feet) one needs all the lung capacity one has, as the air is so rare. A congestive chill is followed by such a dangerous loss in the capacity to receive oxygen, that the patient soon succumbs and dies.

The shops of Oruro, as might be expected of a mining city that has been for several years in communication by rail and steam with the outside world, contain a great variety of imported merchandise. One, owned by Spaniards, is devoted almost exclusively to the manufactured products of Spain. Another, owned by a German, contains an indefinite variety of goods "made in Germany." Two or three book shops contain several thousand volumes of Spanish and French literature, law and medicine. There is also a small public library and reading-room and the city hopes to have a large accession to the number of its books in the near future.

I called on one of the local physicians, not professionally, but because I had heard of a remarkable collection of Bolivian pamphlets and manuscripts that he possessed. One gets so accustomed to shiftlessness and uncleanliness in South America that I could scarcely believe my eyes when I found myself in an office whose spotless white furniture and aseptic glass cases of modern surgical instruments would not have been considered out of place on Madison Avenue. The surgeon had been educated at the Chilean Medical School in Santiago although he was a Bolivian by birth. His collection of manuscripts and prints was an extraordinary one, but I must confess that his up-to-date professional methods interested and surprised me more than his extensive bibliographical learning. After having witnessed unspeakable conditions in the leading hospital of Venezuela at Caracas where, as readers of my "Journal" will recollect, surgeons educated in Paris and New York worked in an operating theatre that had for its motto, "Those who spit are requested not to stand near the table during operations," I am afraid my views of South American surgery, outside of such cities as Buenos Aires and Santiago, had hitherto been decidedly uncomplimentary.

Oruro owes its importance to valuable silver and tin mines in its vicinity. There are several large smelters on the outskirts of the town, and the offices of a number of important mining companies are to be found here. Certain parts of Oruro are not pleasant places in which to take a walk. In fact, I never felt more uncomfortable in my life than I did on a solitary expedition in which I found myself among a lot of half-drunken miners of all nationalities who were hanging about the doors of a choice collection of grog-shops. The fearless, impudent stare of the Aymarás was no less unpleasant than the menacing looks of three or four burly Anglo-Saxon miners who had spent their last cent for drinks and were looking for more.

The silver mines have largely been abandoned and the principal industry is connected with the tin deposits. No mines were discovered here until some years after those of Potosí and they never produced as much silver, although, during the colonial epoch, they ranked easily second.

Oruro was founded about the time that the Dutch landed on Manhattan Island. In the latter part of the seventeenth century there was already a population of 76,000. In the eighteenth century, the city stood next to Potosí in wealth and importance.

Some of the churches still show the marks of that elegance with which they were ornamented during the period of Oruro's palmy days. There are, however, few remains of any fine edifices. Indeed, we are told by "El Lazarillo" in 1773 that "in this great city one will not encounter a single building that corresponds at all to the immense fortunes which have been spent here, during the past two hundred years, in an excess of parades, shows, games, and banquets."

When the price of tin went up, a few years ago, Oruro enjoyed a boom. Old buildings were torn down and pretentious new ones begun. Some of them were only partly completed when tin fell and the boom collapsed. The population now is about sixteen thousand, although during the boom it rose to over twenty thousand, of whom more than five thousand were foreigners. A good percentage were Chileans.

Apart from its importance as a mining centre, Oruro has for some time been distinguished as a railroad terminal. A line from here to Potosí is planned. A line from Oruro to Cochabamba, on whose fertile valleys Oruro depends for its food-supply, is in course of construction. The Bolivia Railway's line to La Paz has recently been completed. The road to Antofagasta has been running since 1892.

Oruro is nearly six hundred miles from Antofagasta and the journey used formerly to take three days, for trains were only run by daylight and at slow speed. We found, however, that the roadbed had been improved, although the track was not widened, and a vestibuled train with two compartment sleeping-cars and a restaurant-car can now make the journey from Oruro to Antofagasta in two nights and a day. Three times a week a Bolivia

A QUAINT OLD BALCONY IN ORURO

A CORNER IN ORURO

railway train leaves La Paz in the morning and arrives at Oruro late in the afternoon. Once a week, as soon after the arrival of this train as possible, the new vestibuled train starts for Antofagasta. There is no chance for a through service, for the Bolivia Railway has a meter gauge, while the Antofagasta line is only three-quarters of a meter wide. Furthermore owing to some unfortunate squabble between the railroad companies, the stations are located at some distance from one another, and the traveller must get across the town as best he may.

When the Antofagasta line was completed, Oruro increased in population by leaps and bounds, and the admiring Bolivians called their city the "Chicago of Bolivia." The only resemblance, however, that I was able to discover was this forced transfer across the city. The streets of Oruro which one has to cross in going from one terminal station to the other are not paved, and the traveller who happens to take the journey in the rainy reason, when the roads are two feet deep in mud, will wish this were Chicago!

The departure of the weekly train for Antofagasta is just as much of an event for Oruro as that of the weekly steamer is for a port in the Hawaiian Islands or the West Indies. Every one who can comes down to the station, and those who can afford it crowd into the restaurant car, order drinks and enjoy the iced luxuries just as the residents of the Caribbean ports do when a mail-steamer calls.

We had been advised by friends in New York not to attempt to use this railway as it was only intended to carry ore and no one cared how many passengers were killed. It did give one a creepy feeling to see a heavy sleeping-car balanced on rails that were only twenty-eight inches apart. It seemed like riding on a monorail and I could not help wondering whether, if the berths on one side of the sleeping-car should happen to be filled first, the car would not capsize. Evidently this thought had occurred to the builders of the car, for by an ingenious arrangement the berths are all in the centre of the car, directly over the rails!

We left Oruro at dusk and during the night passed through Challapata, the end of our mule trip, and Uyuni, where Don Santiago's stages start for Potosí, Tupiza, and La Quiaca via Cotagaita.

The scenery early next morning was not impressive. Before long, however, gigantic volcanic peaks twenty thousand feet high rose into view, one of them, the volcano of Ollawe, emitting a tiny cloud of sulphurous steam that gives a yellow stain to its snow-capped peak. We soon left behind the great sandy tableland of Bolivia, that veritable Thibetan Sahara, and began climbing out of the great plateau through the western Cordillera.

At one of the stations an Indian came aboard the train with a young vicuña that he had raised as a pet and which he was taking to be sold to a gentleman in Chile.

About noon we crossed the frontier. Our train was boarded by two officials. One of them was a Bolivian, seeing to it that departing passengers did not take any gold out of the country and violate the law which prevents any exportation of the yellow metal. The other was a polite Chilean customs officer. Their inspection of the luggage was very superficial. In the afternoon, at Ascotan, after crossing a pass thirteen thousand feet high, we commenced the descent and soon reached the banks of that wonderful white sea of borax, glistening like snow in the sun, which has made this region famous.

The mountains were grand and inspiring but we were so tired of seeing barren brown hillsides that we longed for something green, and yet the further we went, the more desolate became the country. We had entered the nitrate region which is part of that magnificent desert that extends for two thousand miles up and down the west coast of South America.

In the evening we stopped for a few minutes at Calamá, a small town but important as a nitrate centre. It has a moderately good water-supply which enables it to present an attractive greenness in contrast to the absolute aridity of the surrounding desert. In this region are several mines of silver, gold, and copper.

Calamá was the scene of some skirmishing during the revolution against Balmaceda in 1891, but its chief claim to fame rests on a battle that was fought here in the war between Chile, Bolivia, and Peru in 1879, when Bolivia lost her seaport and Chile made a large increase to her territory at the expense of her two northern neighbors. The first thing that Chile did after war was declared was to attack the unprotected Bolivian seaport of Antofagasta. The majority of the population of Antofa gasta were Chileans and the small garrison was quite unable to offer any adequate resistance to the Chilean invaders, so the Bolivian authorities retreated at once to Calamá. Thither the Chileans sent six hundred men to attack one hundred and forty. Although the Bolivian forces took up a strong position the Chileans had the advantage of superior numbers and won an overwhelming victory. The affair was insignificant except that it destroyed all the hold that Bolivia had on her seacoast.

During the night, we passed through a large number of little stations in the nitrate country. Early the next morning, as the last half hour of the railway journey, came an exciting ride down a steep grade in full view of the beautiful blue waters of the Pacific Ocean. After weeks of everlasting browns, it was a tremendous relief to our eyes to see such an expanse of blue. Of course no green was to be expected in this vicinity. But blue did just as well.

The railroad runs for some distance parallel to the shore back of the town until it enters the terminal station. We had left Oruro Thursday at 6:30 P.M., were in Calamá by nine o'clock Friday evening, and reached Antofagasta soon after seven o'clock Saturday morning.

Hardly were we established in a hotel when we learned that the steamer Mexico, of the Pacific Steam Navigation Company, was to sail that morning for Valparaiso. We had had no chance to explore the sandy streets and well-stocked shops of Antofagasta, but this was the first steamer to sail for six or seven days and it might be a week before there would be another. Furthermore, there was little to tempt us in this modern seaport with its ugly, galvanized-iron workshops and warehouses. So we decided to board the Mexico as fast as possible.

The harbor was crowded with boats and barges. A few steamers and sailing-vessels were lying at anchor waiting for cargoes of minerals of one sort or another, mostly nitrates and copper.

Antofagasta is a seaport of considerable importance, being the port of entry for a large part of Bolivia and northern Chile. Yet it shares with Mollendo the reputation of being the worst harbor on the west coast of South America. There is little protection against westerly and southerly winds. Even in calm weather there is a considerable swell at the boat-landing.

Once in the boat, however, we were charmed by the gambols of inquisitive sea-lions who thrust their snouts out of the water, a biscuit-toss away from the boat. As a counter attraction great flocks of birds flew in circles overhead looking for schools of fish that swim in this bay. As soon as a school was located, the entire flock of birds would pause an instant and then dive with the rapidity of lightning from the airy height straight into the billows, leaving only a splash of white water to show where they had gone. Another moment and they came to the surface, shook themselves, flapped their wings, and were away again to enjoy another magnificent dive a little later.

I had heard much of the terrors of steamship travel on the West Coast. Passengers who had recently experienced it assured me that it was simply horrible. We must have been very lucky, for we found the Mexico most comfortable and quite as good as one could expect in this part of the world. Of course she was neither so large nor so luxurious as the average trans-Atlantic liner. On the other hand she was not intended to carry luxury-loving travellers three thousand miles over a rough ocean and keep them amused, contented, and well-fed for a week. Her task consists in stopping every afternoon, anchoring in a badly-sheltered bay or an open roadstead, landing passengers, merchandise, and cattle into row-boats and barges, taking on cargoes of hides, coffee, or provisions; and meanwhile acting as a home for itinerant greengrocers whose business it is to provide this two thousand mile desert with fresh vegetables. Furthermore she was built to sail over the comparatively smooth waters of the tropical Pacific Ocean and provide for passengers who are travelling in a climate of perpetual spring and summer. All of this she does admirably.

The staterooms opened onto the promenade deck. There was a well-stocked library of fiction with books in four languages. The Chilean stewards were polite and obliging. Altogether we had little to find fault with. The food might have been a little better, but when one looked toward the land and saw that bleak desert coast continuing for hour after hour and day after day and realized that in the mountains behind it there were even greater desert solitudes, it did not seem surprising that the food was not up to our ideas of what it should be on board an ocean steamer.

Most of the passengers were natives of the West Coast. To them the diet seemed quite luxurious. To us who had come from the postes of southern Bolivia the table fairly groaned with abundance. I can readily believe that a traveller, who, while on his way south from Panama to Lima, has his first South American meals on board of one of these West Coast steamers would find the fare distressingly bad and the boats not very clean. Perhaps the discipline would seem lax and the service execrable. It all depends on one's point of view.

If one is going to travel in South America at all, it is necessary to make up one's mind to put up with a lot of this sort of thing. It need only be remembered that these boats are as safe and comfortable as those in other parts of the world, and that they have better accommodations than will be found anywhere in South America outside of half a dozen cities.

The first day after leaving Antofagasta brought us to Caldera. On the second day we reached Coquimbo which seems to be a flourishing seaport. Of course there are no wharves, but the bay is fairly well protected and steamers are able to anchor within three quarters of a mile of the landing-stage. New villas in course of construction on the heights at the south end of the bay testify to the prosperity of two of the leading business men of the place.

Devoted as Coquimbo has been to commercial pursuits, very little attention has been given to making the buildings attractive, and only recently has an effort been made to improve the appearance of the plaza. I visited two book shops in the hopes of getting some local prints and found a recently published anthology of the poets of Coquimbo! The books for the most part were those such as are found in the usual South American book store: French novels, French text-books, a few Spanish novels, and the local legal commentaries and law books.

It is a night's journey by steamer from Coquimbo to Valparaiso. The temperature was much cooler than we had expected, and grew more so as we neared Valparaiso. To be sure, Valparaiso is as far south of the equator as San Francisco is north and the same general climatic conditions prevail.

The beautiful bay and harbor of Valparaiso have been repeatedly described by enthusiastic visitors for many years. Since the terrible earthquake of 1906, the city has lost much of its beauty, although many of the buildings have been restored and business is going on quite briskly. In the harbor were fifteen or twenty ocean steamers lying at anchor, two or three Chilean men-of-war and two large floating dry docks capable of taking care of the West Coast merchant steamers.

The naval dry dock is at Talcahuano. Although Valparaiso is the principal seaport on the West Coast, there are no wharves. The business section is built on the old beach and on a terrace. The hills rise abruptly from this narrow shelf and the residential district is on the hills. Elevators and trolley-lines connect the upper and the lower city. The railroad station is very near the boat-landing.

The railway fares were very moderate and the offi cials of the road seemed to us quite courteous and obliging although, during our stay in Santiago, we read in one of the local newspapers a letter from a lady globe-trotter who declared the Chilean railway officials were the rudest and most disobliging that she had found anywhere in the world. Chilean railways have grown tremendously during the past fourteen years. At the time of the revolution against Balmaceda, in 1892, there were barely seven hundred miles; while, at the time of the Scientific Congress, the trackage had increased to three thousand miles of which half is owned and operated by the government. More lines are in course of construction.

Valparaiso is the commercial capital of Chile and her Stock Exchange determines the rate of exchange. The shops of Valparaiso are filled with things that appeal to Anglo-Saxons, for there is a large British colony here.

Perhaps it was natural that we welcomed most eagerly of all the presence of an attractive English book shop where we purchased files of English newspapers and all the recent pictorial weeklies and magazines that we could find. Partly for this reason and partly because we had grown tired of looking at scenery, the four hours' railroad journey between Valparaiso and Santiago passed without making much impression on us so far as our immediate surroundings were concerned, and almost before we knew it, we had entered the political and social capital of Chile.

CHAPTER XIV

SANTIAGO AND THE FIRST PAN-AMERICAN SCIENTIFIC CONGRESS

FROM the railway station to the centre of Santiago is a two-mile ride on a fine parkway, the Alameda de las Deliciosas. It has rows of trees, muddy little brooks, and a shady promenade. Statues to some of Chile's more famous heroes have been placed in the centre of the promenade, and stone benches, more artistic than comfortable, line its sides near the brook. This sounds rather romantic, but the waters of the stream, which is in reality a ditch two feet wide, are so dirty that it suggests an open sewer rather than a mountain brook.

During our stay some one became disgusted with either the brook or the stone benches and exploded a bomb under one of the latter. It happened late in the night and nothing was hurt, except the bench, which was quite demolished. Had the bomb gone off earlier in the evening there would have been a list of casualties, for all the world walks up and down here in the cool of the evening admiring the view of the Andes. The strictly fashionable world confines itself more often to the pavements of the principal plazas where it may be found about nine o'clock, on evenings when the band is playing, walking slowly round and round, enjoying a glimpse of itself. But the broad Alameda, as wide as three or four ordinary streets, is distinctly the more popular resort, and on festivals like Christmas or New Year's, it is thronged with merry-makers.

At the end of the Alameda, beyond the centre of the city, is the romantic rock of Santa Lucia. Santiago owes its situation to the fact that this precipitous hill of solid rock was left by nature in the centre of a rich, fertile plain. The rock formed a natural fortress and was fortified by the Spaniards when they first came to Chile. After having been the scene of numerous bloody battles during Chile's colonial days, Santa Lucia is now a wonderfully attractive park with fine driveways, well-made paths that command splendid panoramas of city, plain, and mountains, and a theatre and restaurant on its summit. The view is remarkably fine. The city spreads itself out on all sides although the principal plaza and the business district lie more to the west. The snow-capped Andes, the most characteristic feature of Santiago scenery, rise majestically to the east. Low foot-hills bound the western horizon. The fertile plain, which is none other than the great central valley of Chile, lies to the north and south. Magnificent vineyards yielding a larger crop of wine than those of California itself, are scattered over this valley. Chile repeatedly reminds one of California by its climate, its fruit, its mountain scenery, and its arid coast. California has one advantage, its width between the ocean and the Sierras, particularly in the fertile region, is so much greater than that of Chile.

The hotels of Santiago are not so luxurious and modern as those of Buenos Aires, yet we found the "Annexo B" of the Oddo to be perfectly comfortable. It is really a "bachelor apartment hotel." No meals, except early coffee, were served there, so we took advantage of the generous hospitality of the two leading clubs, the Club Santiago and the Union. Wearied as I was by the dismal brown desert of southern Bolivia, the gardens and fountains in the patio of the Club Santiago seemed like Paradise itself. To be able to sit at small tables, served by courteous waiters, and enjoy immaculate linen and the best of food and drink, was sufficiently novel to be charming, but only half as welcome as the restful green of the trees and the pleasant splash of the fountains.

We soon discovered that the coolest and easiest way to see Santiago was from the second story of an electric car, especially when the upper tier of seats was covered. The fare on the roof is intended for the pocket-books of second-class passengers and is only five centavos (a cent and a quarter!) which makes it cheaper to take a car than to walk. Unfortunately for the pleasures of life in Santiago, fashion frowns on any one who climbs the stairs when he can afford to ride below.

Our friends would not even allow us to ride below, however, and put us instead into a kind of "hack" that is known here as an "Americano."

It seems that several generations ago, an American resident introduced a carriage which he thought peculiarly adapted to Santiago. It might be described as a two-seated rockaway. This vehicle soon became a vogue and is now the established style for hackney carriages. There are victorias for hire on the principal plazas, but their rates are extortionately high while those of the "Americanos" are ridiculously low. It is well they are, for otherwise no one would patronize them. They seem to be without springs, cleanliness, or any ordinary comforts. They are not without fleas and other insects. As you go bumping and rattling over the cobblestones of Santiago in one of these antiquated vehicles you come to wonder whether the Chilean's proverbial dislike of Americans has not been intensified by the discomforts he has suffered in the "Americanos!"

The first Pan-American Scientific Congress was the fruit of an idea started some years ago in Buenos Aires where delegates from a few of the South American countries met for the first Latin-American Scientific Congress. That was followed by a second which met at Montevideo, and a third, at Rio, each showing an increase in numbers and importance. Plans for the fourth Congress were left entirely in the hands of a Chilean organization committee who decided that the time was ripe to include the United States in the list of invitations and make the Congress Pan-American instead of Latin-American. The visits of a number of distinguished North Americans, including Secretary Root and Professors Moses, Rowe, and Shepherd, had done much to pave the way for friendly feeling between the scientific men of Chile and those of the United States, and the proposal of the organization committee met with hearty approval. Owing to the efforts of Secretary Root and Professor Rowe, the United States Congress passed an appropriation to send an official delegation to the Congress. A number of our leading universities likewise appointed delegates.

The programme suggested for the Congress was replete with all manner of topics for discussion and covered almost the entire field of knowledge, from questions of sanitation to those of international law, and from the antiquity of primitive man in America to modern methods of primary instruction.

As was to be expected from such a comprehensive programme, the intention was not so much to bring out the results of the latest research as to furnish topics that would be sure to interest the delegates. Even the meetings of our learned societies in the States are largely social. To many of those who attend the chief attraction is the opportunity of meeting others who are interested in the same lines, and the programme is merely an excuse for the meeting. The Pan-American Scientific Congress was not far different. It offered an excellent opportunity for the scientists of Latin-America to renew old acquaintance, and it gave the favored delegates from the United States a chance to make new friends among men whose interests are chiefly intellectual.

Under the circumstances, it is not surprising that few of the papers presented new facts or the results of prolonged and scholarly research. Nor is it at all remarkable that the most animated discussions took place in the sessions devoted to international law and politics, education, and political science. These are topics on which every man has ideas which he is not afraid to express. And these discussions served as a means of introducing men that might not otherwise have met.

Politics were kept in the background, as far as possible, but national feelings occasionally found opportunity for expression.

Chile is the one country in South America that has never had and cannot have a boundary dispute with Brazil. The Portuguese-American Republic is not likely to meddle with West Coast matters, and Chile has nothing to gain from troubling the beautiful harbors of Rio and Bahia. Indeed, so lacking have been any causes of friction between the two Republics that they are fond of emphasizing the entente cordiale that exists between them. It was natural, consequently, that the third Latin-American Scientific Congress, meeting in Rio under Brazilian organization, should have chosen Santiago as the seat of the fourth congress, and it was a return of the courtesy when the organizing committee at Santiago, composed of Chileans, selected the local Brazilian Minister as President.

The Congress opened with formal ceremonies, fine music, and much oration. In answer to the roll-call of republics, the leading delegate from each country responded with befittingly felicitous remarks.

It is true that the learned Brazilian who replied, when the name of his country was called, with a speech in Portuguese lasting nearly an hour in length, stretched the friendly feelings toward the Brazil ian delegation almost to the breaking point. Few of the audience could understand enough of what he said to follow his wordy address. Almost everyone thought that its unnecessary length, added to the fact of its being the only address of the evening that was not in Spanish, the official language of the Congress, was at least a breach of good manners.

The state of mind of the Chilean audience was reflected in the daily papers the next morning when full space was given to verbatim reports of the speeches made by the representatives of all the other republics and not even a synopsis was accorded to the speech of the learned Brazilian. The Brazilian delegation took umbrage at this and also at the ovation that was given the Argentine representative whose speech was short, crisp, and filled with expressions of friendship. Like the Mexican delegate, he had appreciated the fact that there were of necessity seventeen other addresses, and that five minutes devoted to cordial greetings was better than fifty minutes of erudite information. A month afterwards when the Brazilian delegation was on its way home, I read in the newspaper reports from Buenos Aires that the Brazilians felt that the Chileans had gone out of their way to make friendly overtures to Argentina, Brazil's natural rival. But the only things of which they had any cause to complain were brought about by their own unfortunate mistakes and in no wise indicated any desire on Chile's part to weaken the ties of her long friendship with Brazil.

Another interesting thing in the formal opening

BATTLEFIELD OF MAIPO NEAR SANTIAGO

meeting was that although the Peruvian delegate received one of the most enthusiastic and heartiest ovations of any, he took it in stolid silence, making no motion and giving no sign that he heard or understood what was going on. As a matter of fact, he and his colleagues felt out of place. Peruvians hate and dread Chile and feel grievously wronged by her continued occupation of Peru's southernmost provinces, Tacna and Arica. Consequently, they accepted all the Chilean overtures with very bad grace, feeling that it would have been much more desirable to have had fewer fine words and more kind actions. It was apparent that the Chileans were doing everything in their power to try and patch up the quarrel and let bygones be bygones, but the Peruvians felt that the demonstration lacked the essential quality of sincerity which, of course, could only have been given by a sacrifice of the provinces of Tacna and Arica which Chile had no intention whatever of making. Throughout the meetings the Peruvian delegates held themselves somewhat aloof and took part in the exercises with a certain dignity which showed how little they enjoyed being the recipients of Chilean hospitality. The Chileans were undoubtedly annoyed at the cool reception of their friendly overtures. It is entirely possible that this contributed not a little to Chilean excitement over the incident of La Corona, of which I shall have occasion to speak later on.

The greater part of the time of the Congress, counted by hours, was given over to receptions and teas, breakfasts and dinners, visits to vineyards, public works, and exhibitions, military tournaments, picnics, and balls.

Hardly had we got settled in our hotel before invitations began to pour in, and we soon found that the hospitable Chilenos had made up their minds to overwhelm us with kindnesses from the moment of our arrival until our departure. Never did a city give itself over more heartily and more gracefully to entertaining an international gathering. For three weeks, hardly a day passed that was not marked by elaborate entertainments. Balls, distinguished by elegance and magnificence, were attended by the youth and beauty of the most aristocratic society in South America, clad in the height of fashion and behaving just as society does in other parts of the world. The Club Santiago was repeatedly the scene of banquets whose brilliance would have rather startled those good people in the United States who think of South America as being something like an African jungle.

Most of the outdoor festivals were held at the racetrack where a fine large grandstand, capable of seating ten thousand people, faces a beautiful field and the magnificent snow-capped Andes. Here, on a sunny afternoon, Santiago society met in a battle of flowers for the benefit of charity. The participants, either standing on the terrace in front of the grandstand or driving by in handsomely decorated equipages, were neither noisy nor boisterous and yet entered heartily into a very pretty event.

One evening was devoted to the volunteer firemen of Santiago. Following a parade was a distri bution of premiums for bravery and length of service. As there is no paid fire department, the city depends on these volunteers for fire protection, and it has always been fashionable to belong to one of the best companies.

For over three hundred years Santiago has been the home of Spanish families of distinction. Their income has never been so swollen as to tempt them to extravagant display or so small as to drive them to petty pursuits for the sake of gaining a livelihood.

In such matters as magnificent hotels, expensive restaurants, luxurious clubs, and showy automobiles, Santiago readily yields the palm to Buenos Aires. There has been no great boom in Chile at all comparable to that which Argentina has seen. Furthermore, earthquakes and fires have done their worst to impoverish a nation not too bountifully supplied with natural resources. To be sure, the enormous nitrate deposits of northern Chile have made the government able to distribute millions of dollars among its followers without overtaxing the population.

Money has come in so easily from the export duties on nitrate that no Finance Minister has been greatly troubled by his budget.

Although Santiago cannot boast of as many evidences of wealth as Buenos Aires, she has other qualifications which give her the right to hold her head higher than any city in South America. The chief of these is her literary preëminence.

She has produced during the past generation more writers of ability than any other South American city. Easily first among these is José Toribio Medina, whose untiring industry and genius for bibliography have made him famous all over the world. Aided by a devoted wife, he has produced more scholarly works than any other man now living in South America, and more volumes of first-class bibliography than any in the western hemisphere. A born collector, he spent years in various parts of the world purchasing rare books in out-of-the-way places and making notes of unpurchasable volumes in the great libraries, until he had built up a magnificent collection of early Americana that is almost unparalleled.

His modest house is replete with interest. Three large rooms are lined from floor to ceiling with his treasures. One room is devoted almost entirely to early Mexican imprints. To see gathered together in one place ten thousand pamphlets printed before Mexico secured her independence, leads one to modify somewhat those conceptions of Spanish intolerance for learning which we have inherited from some of our older writers. To be sure, the pamphlets are mostly of a religious character. However much one may disagree with the dogmas they contain one cannot but admit that the intention of their publishers was to raise the religious and moral tone of the community. In the back part of Sr. Medina's house are the rooms of the "Elzevir" Press. Here have been printed those sumptuous bibliographical quartos that are the envy of every librarian and the despair of the average scholar. As Sr. Medina was originally a printer, it is his recreation to assist in putting his volumes into type. It is not often in the modern world that one finds the whole process of making a book existing under one roof. Here are the sources; here lives the scholar who knows them; here he extracts their virtues; and from this same place he sends forth to the world the results of his investigations, printed and bound, ready for the use of the student.

Besides Sr. Medina, Santiago has produced a number of historians, men like Vicuña Mackenna and Diego Barros Arana who for careful statement and concise diction have not been surpassed in South America. Even the late Bartolome Mitre of Buenos Aires, one of Argentina's greatest statesmen and her greatest historian, never succeeded in getting away from the Spanish trick of efflorescence in language which greatly marred his work from the literary point of view.

Santiago's literary preëminence is further shown both by the fact that in no other city in South America are there so many people who are fond of books and reading—witness the large number of new and second-hand book stores—and the excellent list of works that are published here every year. While Buenos Aires, with a population three times as large, can boast of a few booksellers whose shops are devoted to showy imprints, and who cater to the needs of those who buy their libraries by the yard, there is little evidence in Argentina of a discriminating group of booklovers like those who patronize the score of old book stalls in one of Santiago's streets near the university.

On the outskirts of Santiago is an excellent man ual training school where several hundred boys are lodged, fed, and taught all manner of trades, from printing to forging, and carpentry to carving. Particular attention is paid to electricity, and a large number of the students become practical electricians. At the exhibition of the year's work we were particularly impressed with the fact that the school is able to sell nearly all the articles made by the students. Churns, derricks, chairs, and bells, well made and cheap, gave evidence that the school was run on sound business principles.

Not far off is the Quinta Normal, a fine large reservation where normal and agricultural schools rub shoulders with museums of fine arts and natural history. The result is a charming place for study and a delightful public park.

During our visit, the annual fine arts exhibition was in progress and included a number of extremely meritorious paintings by Sotomayor, a Spanish painter who has recently been engaged by the Chilean government to teach in the Art School. Chile is certainly to be congratulated on the class of teachers that she brings from abroad for her schools, and her latest acquisition is well up to the standard.

Chile's appreciation of art and her policy of securing able foreign talent to teach her youth are greatly in her favor. She is in fact a young and vigorous nation. Her people are bred in a splendid climate, well suited to the development of a strong race. In fact the Araucanian aborigines were superior to anything that the Spaniards found in either North or South America. The early Spanish immigrants were an unusually good lot. And there has been a striking admixture of Anglo-Saxon blood as is shown by the frequency of English family names in Santiago.

As is well known, in the south of Chile there are many Germans and it is commonly cited as one of the danger spots of German expansion in South America. Those who argue so fail to take into consideration the remarkably strong hold that Chile has on her children. In no other part of South America do foreigners become so fond of the soil as in Chile. Even those of English ancestry are prouder of the history of Chile than they are of that of England. I have heard them go so far in praise of their adopted land as to deride England and predict her downfall. In Buenos Aires, on the other hand, they continually revisit the homeland and pride themselves on their close connection with it. There one sees little of that devotion to the country of their adoption which is in evidence here.

Among the spectacles provided for the benefit of the delegates, the most interesting was a military tournament that was worth going a long way to see. The Chilean cavalryman is a remarkably daring horseman. His Spanish and Araucanian ancestry have given him qualities that appeal to the eye and to one's admiration of courage. Perhaps the most remarkable feat of the afternoon was the charge made by a squadron of cavalry over a burning hurdle. A brush fence, well soaked in kerosene, was erected in front of the grandstand and set on fire. Starting to windward, the squadron charged, vaulted over the flames and dashed away in the smoke, only to turn in the face of a strong wind which blew the smoke and flames into the very faces of the horses, dash back again, and in perfect order clear the fiery obstacle with as much ease and grace as though it had been a peaceful country fence. As an exhibition of training it was extremely significant.

President Montt,[1] who was extremely kind and courteous to us, and is one of the most able and honest officials that South America has ever seen, sent us an invitation one morning to attend the official inspection of the Military Academy. All the Chilean officers speak German and most of them have spent from two to three years studying in Germany. Like the army, the school is run on German models and is extremely well kept up. The neatness, discipline, cleanliness, and excellent sanitary arrangements were in marked contrast to most public buildings in South America. The cadets are a fine-looking lot of boys who are largely put on their honor. Few rules are made for their guidance but when any one is guilty of conduct unbecoming in an officer and a gentleman, he is permanently discharged from the academy. The instructors lay great stress on map-making. The exhibition of maps made by the students was remarkably interesting. The students are taught not only to make outline maps, but also to construct models of battlefields and even to draw sectional panoramas on a uniform scale. Three cadets are sent out to survey a position and to return in half an hour, each with a drawing which, fitted to that of his mates, will make a panorama that will enable the commanding officer to understand the situation and direct his forces intelligently. This is only one instance of the thoroughness with which the cadets are instructed. It is not remarkable that several other Latin-American countries have sent for Chilean officers to teach their cadets, and have even sent their own boys to study here.

The Congress closed on the evening of the 5th of January, 1909, with a grand banquet that was a blaze of glory. Eloquent speeches of mutual congratulation were delivered by the representatives of various parts of the two continents. Perhaps the most striking thing of the evening was the contrast between the speeches of that member of the American delegation who had been chosen to respond to the toast, "The United States," and the one that followed it delivered by a brilliant young orator from Uruguay. As might have been expected, the latter was fiery, flowery, and ecstatic, while the former was dignified and well within the bounds of reason even in his compliments. The unexpected and very striking difference was that the American spoke better Spanish, pure Castilian, melodious and graceful. The Uruguayan speech was in the offensive dialect of Montevideo, harsh to the ear, resembling Portuguese in its guttural quality.

The only other speech of the evening that equalled the North American's in beauty of diction was that of General Uribe Uribe, the delegate from Colombia. He ably upheld the reputation of his country for speaking the best Castilian in America. So far as one who is not a native may be permitted the priv ilege of judging by the effect on the ear, the inhabitants of Colombia and Peru speak the best, while the people of the countries of the River Plate speak the worst and most impure Spanish of any on the continent. The impurity is a natural result of their century-long dealings with the Portuguese in Southern Brazil; of the presence in their midst of a very large number of Italians whose speech is so like the Spanish that it

---

[1] His sudden death in August, 1910, is a very great loss to Chile.

easily corrupts it; and also of the fact that during the colonial epoch, Buenos Aires was not a centre of Spanish culture like Bogotá or Lima. On the contrary, as is well known, Buenos Aires was filled with a fairly rough lot of traders who made their fortune by smuggling and other illegitimate transactions. However much we may be inclined to justify such actions on their part by the injustice of the Spanish trade laws governing the commerce of the Indies, we cannot be oblivious to the fact that the kind of individual who would be willing to make his living by smuggling would probably not take pains to speak his native tongue with either elegance or careful attention to grammatical rules. In Lima and Bogotá, on the other hand, society was dominated by the official class, and however critically we may regard these proud Spaniards who were sent by their King to govern America, we must be willing to admit that they were likely to speak the beautiful language of Castile as perfectly as possible.

So much has been said of the inability of Americans to learn Spanish properly and to speak it gracefully (it is a common proverb in South America that English and Americans murder the soft Castilian) that it was a great pleasure to hear the official language of the Congress spoken better by a North American than by a South American. Furthermore, it was characteristic of their courtesy that the Spanish-American delegates at once complimented us on such an achievement.

CHAPTER XV
NORTHERN CHILE

Two days after the closing banquet, we rose early and hurried down to the station to take the morning express for Valparaiso. Notwithstanding the unseasonableness of the hour and the fatigue of recent entertainments, a large number of the hospitable folk of Santiago were on hand to bid us "Godspeed" on our journey. It is an extremely pleasant custom, this taking the trouble to welcome the coming and speed the parting guest by going out of your way to greet him at the railway station, or if in the country, to saddle your horse and ride out of town for a mile or two to accompany him. It takes time, to be sure, and time that, according to American standards, might be more profitably expended on attending to the business of adding up dollars and cents. Yet it does increase the store of friendly feelings in the world. The casual visitor to the United States too often has occasion to feel that we are so wrapped up in money-making that we have no time to be polite. As a recent British visitor said in comparing us with Mexico, "when one crosses the Rio Grande, the brisk and selfish American atmosphere is left behind."

After an uneventful journey of four hours in a parlor car, we reached the water-front of Valparaiso.

Before going on board the steamer we had a few hours to give to sight-seeing and the purchase of furs brought here from the Straits of Magellan and the Andean highlands. We had time also to feel something of the excitement caused by the rapid fluctuation in the value of the paper dollar on the floor of the Valparaiso Stock Exchange.

The national currency fluctuates considerably from day to day and is the most serious drawback to commercial prosperity in Chile. During my stay in Santiago it fluctuated so violently that some of the prominent business men were very evidently less interested in their legitimate business than in speculating in currency. The unit of value is the peso, worth, while we were there, about twenty-five cents. It has gone as low as fifteen cents, and as high as forty cents. All current accounts in the large importing houses are carried in pounds sterling.

British commercial houses have a very strong hold on Valparaiso. So important are the dealings with Great Britain that English is actually the language of commerce. This is the more noticeable because, although no educated South American would for a moment admit that he could not read and speak French, outside of the larger cities very few South Americans can even understand English. Nor do I remember to have met more than one or two, outside of Chile, who pretended to any knowledge of German. A knowledge of English is generally limited to those who have been in the United States or England and to those who have had large business dealings with British commercial houses. At the same time, English is taught in many of the schools in Chile and we repeatedly met young Chileans who were anxious to practice it on us.

Great Britain has always favored Chile ever since her merchantmen, headed by the gallant Admiral Thomas Cochran, Earl of Dundonald, created the Chilean navy which swept the West Coast clean of Spanish ships in the Wars of Independence. It was the Chilean navy that enabled San Martin's troops to reach Peru and strike at the last stronghold of Spain in South America. In those days, most of the vessels were commanded by English and Scottish officers. The tendencies of the navy are still British, and this extends even to the uniform of both officers and cadets. In a word, the navy is as English as the army is German. Furthermore, it has long maintained its preëminence among the navies of South America. When Brazil gets the dreadnoughts for which she has contracted, this supremacy will temporarily disappear.

When we boarded the Chilean steamer Limarí, we found among our fellow passengers quite a number of pleasant-faced little naval cadets bound for some point up the coast where they were to join their training-ship. They smoked too many cigarettes, and their manners on board were not particularly good, although they were probably no worse than a similar group of American schoolboys would have been under the circumstances. Certainly our fellow passengers were not as bad as those cadets whom Hugh de Bonelli encountered in his journey from Panama to Lima in 1850 and describes in his enter taining "Travels in Bolivia." In one corner of the saloon on his steamer "sat an elderly gentleman and a maiden lady, brother and sister, surrounded by parrots, a monkey, two cats, and three ugly little dogs, all of whom they alternately kissed and hugged. Two young cadets of sixteen, in uniform, who, without a figure of speech, may be said to have smoked themselves away—for they were scarcely perceptible behind the volumes of smoke they emitted,—got into disgrace with these worthy people. One of these young sparks threw down, on the sly, a lighted cigar upon the monkey, who had been watching him. The animal seized it, and put the lighted end of it into his mouth; then screamed, chattered, and cried—jumped upon the head of the old lady, who was so frightened that she fainted away; then upon that of the old man, from which he fell to the ground with the old gentleman's wig firmly held between his jaws!"

We found the Limarí well crowded with passengers, most of them Chileans bound for Coquimbo, Antofagasta, and Iquique. The absence of a railway makes the semi-weekly steamers the only means of communication on this desert coast. Yet it was not until we had experienced the decided inconveniences of overcrowding and felt the relief caused by the heavy disembarkation at the northern Chilean ports that we fully realized how dependent the Chileans are on the control of sea-power. They are now planning to construct a longitudinal railway that shall run parallel to the shore line, and make them less dependent on naval predominance.

The next day after leaving Valparaiso, we reached Coquimbo. The cable had been used to warn the authorities that there were distinguished passengers on board, and the leading citizens of the town came out to invite the delegados ashore and took us for a delightful drive along the beach from Coquimbo to the old Spanish settlement of La Serena. At the latter place we were entertained at the Club where an informal reception was held, with the aid of the usual cocktails and champagne.

At Caldera we were spared from official recognition and spent our time catching lizards on the sandy hills back of the town.

The third day brought us to Antofagasta where several of the delegation left to take the railroad to Bolivia over the route by which I had come out a month ago. The sea-lions and the diving birds were playing about the harbor in the same fascinating manner as when I first saw this port. But the effect, after living for several weeks amid the green parks of Santiago and enjoying several days of blue ocean, was far less striking than when we came from the bleak brown deserts of the Bolivian plateau.

The morning of the fourth day saw us at Iquique, once the centre of Peru's nitrate industry, now rivaling Valparaiso as the scene of Chilean commercial activity. Numbers of sailing-vessels were lying in the roadstead waiting for cargoes of the precious fertilizers. It was a pleasure to see several of the vessels actually flying the American flag! The West Coast depends largely on Oregon and Puget Sound for its lumber-supply and these three-masted American schooners find a profitable trade in bringing lumber and returning with nitrates. The Limarí's cargo consisted largely of merchandise which had come from Europe and America through the Straits of Magellan. While this was being discharged we had time to see the city, where a few months before an angry mob of strikers from the nitrate works, had been mown down by well-trained government troops.

We were entertained here by Mr. Rea Hanna, the enthusiastic American Consul, who has a difficult rôle to play in a town where Chileans are in control but where the Peruvian Club is the centre of aristocratic society. That he is universally liked speaks volumes.

At the southern end of the town there is good bathing; and in addition, pavilions and beer gardens to entice the weary clerk from the nitrate offices. The well-arranged grounds of the Jockey Club afford opportunity for social intercourse, polo, and tennis. But the most interesting place in Iquique is what is known as the Combination, the central office of the Nitrate Association, where the different companies, mostly English, unite to arrange scales of prices and quantity of output and maintain an efficient Bureau of Propaganda.

People frequently confuse Chilean nitrates with guano. One is a mineral, the other an animal product. Whether the nitrate fields were not originally guano deposits is a moot point, but I believe this idea has been abandoned. There is, however, considerable difference of opinion as to the actual origin of the great nitrate desert.

As there is a heavy export duty on the nitrates, Chile has been, and will continue to be, as long as the supply holds out, in the very enviable position of making foreigners pay the bulk of her taxes. How long this exceptional state of affairs will last is a problem for the geologists to settle. As there is undoubtedly enough material in sight to satisfy the demands of the present generation and the next, no one has any very stringent reason for husbanding the output or for investing the national income from the export duties in such a way as to provide for the exigencies of future tax-payers. The natural result of this easy method of securing a revenue is a tendency towards extravagance in the Chilean budget and an absence of careful supervision. Few people care whether the money is spent for the best interests of the country. Political scientists say that when the voter has a very light burden of taxes to bear, he does not mind seeing the government's money wasted or his favorite politicians grow wealthy. Doubtless in time such a condition of affairs will have a serious influence for evil on Chilean character. As yet the whole industry is too young to have produced any marked effect. Fortunately for the race, the nitrate fields will probably become exhausted before any lasting harm is done. Nevertheless Chile would do well to take warning from the experience of Peru, whose revenue for many years depended almost exclusively on the yield of guano from the Chincha Islands. The exhaustion of that valuable product left the country in a far worse state than she was before her easily acquired income had commenced to corrupt her politicians and financiers.

We left Iquique late that night and arrived early the next morning at Pisagua, the northern limit of the nitrate country. Like all the other ports at which we had touched since leaving Valparaiso, it is the terminus of a little railway that goes back a few miles into the interior and brings down minerals of one sort or another; sometimes copper ore, generally nitrate, more rarely tin and silver.

In the course of the afternoon we reached Arica. The southern side of the bay is guarded by a picturesque cliff, not unlike Gibraltar, which is celebrated in Peruvian history as the site of a memorable battle in the war with Chile. At its crisis the commandant of the Peruvian garrison, rather than fall into the hands of the victorious Chileans, spurred his horse over the summit and was dashed to pieces among the rocks and waves at the base of the cliff. To the Anglo-Saxon mind, he would have died more creditably had he killed as many Chileans as possible first, and fallen face to the front. But the more spectacular death that he chose appeals strongly to the Latin temperament.

Yet this trick of committing suicide instead of fighting to the last breath is not a characteristic of Spanish heroes generally. It is not easy to say whether the gallant soldier was influenced or not by any Quichua ancestor that he may have had. Readers of Prescott's "Conquest of Peru" will remember that in the attack on Cuzco, made by one of the Pizarros, a Quichua noble who had greatly distinguished him self in the Inca army, seeing that his cause was irretrievably lost, jumped over the precipice on the south side of the Sacsahuaman hill, and preferred to be dashed to pieces rather than to see how many Spaniards he could kill first. He in turn may have inherited the tendency from remote ancestors in the Pacific Ocean. On the Island of Kusaie there is a picturesque waterfall where, according to tradition, two young chiefs, defeated in battle, ended their lives by casting themselves from the precipice into the boiling pool below. The habit of jumping over a precipice in preference to being killed in battle by one's enemies is not uncommon in the history of the Pacific races, both in the Carolines and in the Hawaiian Islands.

Arica is particularly interesting to Americans because it was here that the U. S. S. Wateree was carried inland by the great tidal wave of 1868. Not only has the port been devastated by earthquakes and tidal waves but also by fire. At present it has a very squalid appearance. Before the completion in 1871 of the Southern Peruvian railway from Mollendo to Puno, Arica was an important port of entry for Bolivia. When the Chileans finish the railway which they are building to connect this port with La Paz by a line that shall cross the mountains back of Tacna, this importance will be restored.

At the close of the war between Chile and Peru the Treaty of Peace known as the Treaty of Ancon stipulated that the territory of the provinces of Tacna and Arica should remain in the possession of Chile for ten years from 1883 to 1893. The Treaty continues: "The term having expired, a plebiscite shall decide by popular vote if the territory of these provinces shall remain definitely under the dominion and sovereignty of Chile, or if they shall continue to form part of the territory of Peru. The Government of the country in whose favor the provinces of Tacna and Arica shall be annexed shall pay to the other ten millions of dollars Chilean silver money or Peruvian soles, of equal percentage of fine silver and of equal weight as the former. A special protocol, which shall be considered an integral part of the present treaty, shall establish the form in which the plebiscite shall take place, and the terms and conditions in which the ten millions of dollars shall be paid by the nation remaining in possession of Tacna and Arica."

As is well known, the special protocol, establishing the form in which the plebiscite is to take place, has never been agreed upon. The principal obstacle is that since 1883 a large number of Chileans have settled, voluntarily or otherwise, in the provinces, enough to decide the vote of the plebiscite in favor of Chile. The Chilean government says all present residents should vote. The Peruvians maintain that the voters in the plebiscite should consist only of those who were residents of the provinces at the termination of the war. Naturally, the Chileans will not agree to this as there is no doubt but that the majority of such persons are of inherent Peruvian preferences.

It is now seventeen years since the plebiscite was due to take place and the question is still an open one. The fact, however, that in a recent treaty with Bolivia, Chile promised to construct, at her expense, a railway from Arica to La Paz, and has since granted a contract to a reliable company to build that railway, would seem to indicate that Chile considers the question settled although no plebiscite has been held. No nation voluntarily commits itself to spend millions of dollars in building a railway in a province which it considers in the slightest degree likely to become the property of a neighbor. The Peruvians have not overlooked the calm way in which the Chileans take it for granted that Tacna and Arica are to be permanently Chilean territory, but they are in no position to dispute such a conclusion.

Their fighting strength is far below the Chilean standard and they know it.

The whole question was brought vividly to the fore just at the time of our visit by a little international episode known as the "Incident of La Corona." Peru had erected a magnificent memorial to her soldiers that fell in the conflict with Chile. As was customary and proper, the representatives of the various foreign powers resident in Lima, requested permission to deposit formal wreaths at the base of the monument as an expression of the friendship of their governments. The Chilean diplomat was not behind the others, and his request was granted, only to be denied later on when his funeral wreath had been made ready for the exercises. At this he took great umbrage, demanded his passports, and sailed for home. His arrival in Santiago was the occasion of a popular outburst. There was a strong demand on the part of a portion of the public that the government resent the Peruvian "insult" in a very practical way, viz., by holding elections in the provinces of Tacna and Arica and summoning representatives to the National Congress in the same manner as from the other Chilean provinces. This would be taking the last step in formal annexation of the disputed territory and final recognition of it as a definite part of the national domain.

I was travelling in the interior of Peru at the time of these demonstrations and it may be imagined that the press reports in the Peruvian newspapers did not underestimate the gravity of the situation. The fact that the Chilean government did not take any active steps toward formally annexing Tacna and Arica in response to the popular demand was attributed by many Peruvians and not a few Chileans to the fact that in the harbor of Lima there happened to be at this time a powerful squadron of American battleships. The long-standing friendship between the United States and Peru, and the active hostility between the United States and Chile at the time of the fall of Balmaceda and the "Baltimore" episode, were regarded by the Peruvians as sufficient guaranty of an intention on the part of the United States to interfere in case trouble arose over an attempt on the part of Chile to terminate the territorial dispute in a high-handed manner.

Whether or not the government at Washington indicated its wishes in any way or expressed any opinion whatever; whether or not the presence of our battleship fleet in the waters of the West Coast at this time was intentional or purely accidental, are matters about which I know nothing and which do not affect the actual results. As it stands, the Peruvians having avoided trouble with Chile feel grateful toward the United States, and the Chileans feel correspondingly irritated that their government was apparently kept from an overt act by the influence of the Yankis. An enthusiastic Chilean, a vigorous "anti-American," told me some time afterwards that he had endeavored, to the best of his ability, to find out from political friends in Valparaiso why nothing was done when it would have been so easy to settle the whole matter. The reply in every case was "fear of offending the United States."

After leaving Arica our next stop was to be at Ilo, the southernmost harbor of Peru, a fact that was emphasized by the very marked depletion of our passenger list. Few Chileans care to go to Peru. Because we came from the "polluted" ports of a hated rival, the Limarí was subjected to a thorough-going fumigation, a process rendered the more unnecessary and offensive because nearly all of the Peruvian ports actually had cases of bubonic plague and smallpox while the Chilean ports were free from the pest.

We reached Mollendo on the afternoon of January 14th, just seven days after leaving Valparaiso.

CHAPTER XVI
SOUTHERN PERU

Mollendo is one of those places where nature never intended man to live. The natural port, and the one that was used for centuries, is the bay of Islay, a few miles north. As a matter of fact, this was to have been the terminus of the Southern Railway of Peru, the outlet for the commerce of the Lake Titicaca region. But the owners of real estate at Islay were so convinced that there had arrived that "tide in the affairs of men which, taken at the flood, leads on to fortune," that they attempted to make the most of their opportunity and asked the railway prohibitive prices for land and water-front. The result was that Islay missed its high tide and the railway engineers carved out of the desert coast what is now the port of Mollendo.

It claims to be the worst harbor on the West Coast. In fact, the author of a recent book on South America was so impressed with the terrors of disembarking here that he described it fully in three separate chapters of his book! Although there was quite a little breeze blowing at the time of my landing, I confess to being very much disappointed at the tameness of the procedure. The reverend author had led me to expect "a surf-lashed landing-place—a tremendous tossing and bouncing on the moun tainous swell." Even in calm weather the boat was "tossed about like a cockle shell, now thrown up to heaven on the crest of a wave, now dropped down towards the nadir in its hollow. The swarthy Peruvian oarsmen strain at the oars, they avoid the jagged rocks between the boat and the pier by a hair's breadth!" etc. etc.

One gets very little idea from such language of a busy little basin and a dock where half a dozen steam cranes are at work loading and unloading large freight barges. As would be expected from the fact that this is the chief port in southern Peru, the docks were crowded with boxes and bales of every description. Occasionally as many as eight or ten freighters are anchored in the offing, and a large number of lighters are kept busy most of the time. A new breakwater is being built of enormous cubes of concrete, which it is hoped will resist the action of the waves better than the natural rock of the neighborhood which disintegrates rapidly.

A climb of fifty or sixty feet up the face of a steep cliff back of the landing stage brought us to the little platform and gate of the local custom house. Our arrival here was not expected by the officials, and we received the customary hard looks that are given every one coming from Chile. Mollendo has not forgotten the war.

Nevertheless it needed but the mystic word delegado to the collector of the port to cause all our luggage to be passed graciously through the custom house without even the formality of an examination.

Our next difficulty, after landing on Peruvian soil,

MOLLENDO

was in finding some one who would relieve us of our Chilean money and give us coin of the realm in exchange. At first the local bank flatly refused to oblige us, saying that so few people ever went from Peru to Chile that there was no demand for Chilean money, and that they could not realize anything on our Chilean currency without sending it by mail to Valparaiso or Antofagasta, an expensive and risky undertaking which they did not care to assume. In a word it was "against the rules." So it was necessary to say "delegado" again. As was to be expected, the obliging cashier was now only too glad to relieve us of all our Chilean money. How many bank cashiers in the States, after laying down a rule of the bank to a foreigner, would be willing to break it because the stranger was able to prove that he was an official delegate to a Scientific Congress? I fear we are behind our southern neighbors in realizing what is due to "science"!

The only thing we could find of interest in Mollendo, was a cock-fight in one of the side streets. An audience of fifty or sixty boatmen and their friends, relieved from their duties at the end of the day, were hazarding their silver soles on whichever bird they judged would last the longest in the tiresome and bloody battle that was being fought out on the cobble-stones. The excitement grew fast and furious as the fight neared its close, and one poor bleeding rooster, nearly totally blind, and almost dying, received a few final pecks from his victorious opponent, himself dripping with blood. I have occasionally watched these Spanish-American cock-fights in an effort to understand why the spectator with Spanish blood in his veins gets so excited over them. Apart from a realization that at present cock-fighting is the national sport of South America, and as such, takes the place that baseball does in the United States, and cricket does in England, I must admit that I have failed to work out any reason to account for the frenzied interest.

Probably the Peruvians would have been just as bored if they had been sandwiched into a crowd of "fans" at a baseball game.

We had not expected to stay over night in Mollendo, which has the usual reputation of West Coast ports for harboring persons afflicted with contagious diseases. But the daily train for Arequipa had gone and there would not be another until the following noon, so we were obliged to make ourselves as comfortable as possible in the Hotel Ferro Carril which was not at all bad. The worst feature of it was the partitions, which were extremely thin. The room next to ours was occupied by an English-speaking individual who received a call in the course of the evening from a fellow countryman, resident here, who tried to frighten him out of his senses by vivid details as to the number of cases of "yellow fever, bubonic plague, and smallpox" now raging in the town. "More deaths occurring every day than the undertakers could possibly attend to!" "Scarcely a house without its sick folk!!" "Not a family still intact!!!" etc., etc. What effect these remarks may have had on the person for whom they were intended, I am unable to say. I do know they caused no little uneasiness among those delegados who had landed here on their way to the interior. We did not stop to make personal investigations as to the truth of the rumors but were promptly on hand the next day to take the train for Arequipa.

As there was not nearly enough space for all the people who desired to leave Mollendo that morning, we were very much crowded for the first hour or so. This exodus from town was not due to any fear of the prevailing pest, but rather to the fact that January is the season for leaving town and enjoying a short stay in the country. The train followed the coast for eight miles to the south until it reached the bay and beach of Mejia, a summer resort where many of the families of Mollendo have built little villas. From here the road turns inland, east and then north, climbing slowly and affording one a view of the pleasant green valley of the Tambo River with its little country houses and its plantations of sugarcane. Still climbing, the train continued almost due north across the sandy plain known as the Pampa de Islay, or the desert of Arequipa. For miles on either side of the track as far as the eye could reach, there was not a green thing to be seen. Although there was no animal or vegetable life, it is not exactly correct to say there was not a living thing, for this is the home of the medanos, those extraordinary crescent-shaped sand-dunes that travel across the hard ground of the desert floor, driven by the prevailing southwesterly winds. Each hill is a perfect crescent exquisitely drawn, the delicate horns tapering off toward the north, away from the wind. They cause the railroad no end of trouble, for when a medano approaches the track, it must get across some way or other. It is of no use to shovel back the horns of the crescent as they encroach on the rails, for the main body of the mound, twenty feet high and sixty feet or more wide, will advance just the same and must be helped along.

Although we had started from Mollendo immediately after lunch and the journey is only one hundred miles in length, it took us seven hours to ascend the 7500 feet, and it was dark when we left the train at Arequipa. We found on the other side of the station a long line of mule-trams, one of which was reserved for intending guests of the Gran Hotel Marone. After some delay incident to transferring a train-load of passengers and their hand luggage to this caravan of tram-cars, we started off and jingled our way through poorly-lit streets of one-story houses where attractively carved stone doorways, dimly visible in the semi-darkness, told of well-built mansions of former Spanish grandees, whose walls had withstood Arequipa's earthquakes.

To a person who has experienced a great earthquake, the mere mention of the word is terrifying, and yet we were told by one of the astronomers at the local Harvard Observatory that their seismograph recorded three earthquakes during the four days of our stay here. In fact, scarcely a week goes by without one or more disturbances. Fortunately for us, and for Arequipa, these daily earthquakes that are so faithfully recorded by the delicate instruments of the observatory are not usually perceptible

THE CATHEDRAL OF AREQUIPA AND
MOUNT CHACHANI

AN OLD DOORWAY
IN AREQUIPA

CHACHANI AND MISTI

to human beings. However, like San Francisco, Valparaiso, and many another city of the west coast of America, Arequipa does have a serious shake once or twice in a century and people do not build two-story houses unless they can afford to use very strong construction.

We were most agreeably surprised and delighted with our accommodations at the Hotel Marone. None of us had expected to find anything nearly so comfortable outside of a South American capital. With this excellent hotel and with the promised improvement of steamship service on the West Coast, Arequipa is bound to become a Mecca for travellers. Charmingly situated, with a delightful climate, picturesque streets, and remarkable churches and monasteries, it offers the additional inducement of being a base from which many pleasant excursions can be made. Mountain climbers and those fond of mountain scenery will be attracted by the active volcano El Misti, 19,000 feet high, and the snow-capped peaks of Chachani that look down upon the city from their lofty altitude of over 20,000 feet above the sea. Arequipa is the distributing centre for southern Peru and contains a number of banks and the warehouses of several large importing houses. To the explorer intending to penetrate the continent, it is an excellent place in which to purchase part of his outfit. It was the base of the DeMilhau-Peabody Museum Expedition to the Upper Amazon. I was astonished to find at the time of my visit, that in one of the English warehouses it was not only possible to get a complete supply of excellent canned goods, but even such luxuries as folding-cots and Caracas chocolate. Professor Bandelier, that most distinguished student of Spanish-American lands and peoples, says in his recently published "Islands of Titicaca and Koati" that Mt. Koropuna, lying about one hundred miles northwest of Arequipa, is probably the highest mountain in America. Aconcagua is 6940 metres, while, according to Raimondi's map of the Department of Arequipa, Koropuna is 6949 metres. Here is a chance for a well-equipped exploring expedition.

For the less ambitious tourist there are shops where one may buy all manner of foreign and domestic supplies, and excellent photographs, the best of which I regret to say were stolen from a scientific expedition many years ago by a native photographer. The lover of curious costumes and quaint shops will be abundantly repaid by long strolls through the Indian quarters.

As soon as the Prefect of Arequipa, Sr. Don Lino Velarde, heard of our arrival, he made haste to call and place himself "entirely at our disposal." Sometimes this gracious Spanish extension of hospitality means very little, but in this case it was genuine, and the Prefect did everything in his power to make our stay both pleasant and profitable. Horses and a military escort were provided for an excursion to the Harvard Observatory, and the Prefect's secretary was detailed to act as our cicerone and see to it that we were shown the treasures of the local monasteries.

We found the old Jesuit church the most interesting of all the sights that the city afforded. It had once been superbly adorned and embellished with elaborate gilded carvings and magnificent altars. The last earthquake had overturned and destroyed three of the altars, but the four remaining are well worth a visit, and there are many beautiful paintings still on the walls. The west front of the church is a marvellous example of stone-cutting and like the towers of the Jesuit church in Potosí shows what excellent manual training the Jesuits taught their followers. Their expulsion from South America was one of the most serious in the long list of mistakes that Spain made in the government of her American colonies.

The atmosphere of the Franciscan monastery took one back to the middle ages. Everything was scrupulously clean and in good order. In the sacristy we found a beautiful Madonna by some artist of the sixteenth century. The monks treasure it highly and with good reason for the face is as beautiful as any I have ever seen. A pleasant-faced, communicative monk, who seemed glad enough to be permitted to break through the monotony of his quiet life in the cloisters, took us to his favorite spot in the gardens where, under the grapevines, a rude seat had been made from a great millstone that dated back to Spanish days. From here he led us to different trees in the orchard and begged us to sample the pears, peaches, and plums that it was his delight to cultivate. We were permitted also to visit the library and found it well stocked with rare and beautifully printed old books. Naturally most of them were devoted to theology and religious philosophy, but there was one section into which old-fashioned works on natural history had crept, including a fine set of Buffon. On the door of the library was posted a notice telling the monks that on Mondays and Thursdays they could consult books on piety; Tuesdays and Fridays, works on theology; Wednesdays and Saturdays, other classes of religious books, etc., etc. We looked in vain for any day on which it was permitted to use the books on natural history. Much has been written of the degenerate conditions prevailing in the South American religious houses. The Franciscan monasteries we visited here and in Santiago, where an electric dynamo runs a modern printing press for the dissemination of religious information, cannot be included in that category.

As we wandered about Arequipa enjoying the picturesque Indian shops and the bright colors of the native costumes, the Indians themselves were courteous and polite and gave little evidence of any justification for their reputation for turbulence.

The only evidence which we witnessed of any eagerness to join an uprising was on the arrival of Dr. Durand, a notorious revolutionist, who had fled from the country on the failure of a revolution which he had instigated not two years ago, and was now being allowed to return, thanks to the clemency of the Government. He had taken refuge in Bolivia and in going to his home at Lima, had to pass through Arequipa. We happened to be calling on the Prefect when the chairman of the local committee of the Liberal party came to request the privilege of giving Dr. Durand a popular reception. The Prefect had evidently received orders from the Government to allow any kind of a demonstration short of rioting, and after warning the Liberal chairman that there must be no disturbance of the peace, gave him permission to carry out the plans for the reception. We were somewhat surprised at the daring, one might almost say the bravado, of the Government in extending clemency to a notorious agitator who had done his best to upset the administration by violence.

Our feelings were confirmed the next day on the arrival of the train from Puno. The exile was received by a mob of three or four thousand noisy Liberals who, inspired by the sight of their hero, went to the limit in their manifestations of joy. It goes without saying that the horses were taken from the exile's carriage and that he was dragged through the streets in triumph by his loyal supporters. The flat roofs of the houses were crowded with interested spectators who did not care to ally themselves with the Liberal party by joining the procession in the streets. A few of the bolder Liberals, encouraged by cognac or chicha, ventured to cry "Down with the Government!" "Down with the President!" "Viva Durand!" "Long live the Liberal party!"

It may seem ungracious to criticise the policy of a country where one has received as much hospitality and kindness as I have in Peru. At the same time I cannot help expressing the conviction that if Peru wishes to give the world evidence that she belongs to the same category of nations as does Mexico, for instance, where capitalists may safely invest and de velop the resources of the country; if she seriously proposes to do away with revolutions and make them matters of ancient history rather than of present politics, she cannot afford to allow the instigators of revolutions to enjoy public triumphs such as are usually accorded to the true heroes of a nation.

There is too much of a tendency among South Americans to regard revolutions as a popular game. One of the rules is that after the conflict is over, your enemies must be treated with all the honors of war, and that it will not do to be too severe on the conquered revolutionist for fear that he may take revenge on you when the next revolution succeeds. If these politico-military agitators were put to death after being convicted of treason by a properly constituted tribunal, Peru would enjoy an era of peace and prosperity such as she scarcely dreams of at present—and the Peruvians are good dreamers. But just as long as she enthusiastically welcomes home, after a brief exile, men like Dr. Durand, she offers an extra inducement to any hot-headed young firebrand to start another revolution. If he succeeds, all honor and glory will be his, besides the emoluments of office and the satisfaction of enjoying political power. If he fails and makes good his exit from the country, it can mean at the worst but a brief exile and then a triumphal return, crowned by an ovation. In either case, unless he is so extremely unlucky as to get shot in the scrimmage, he is sure of plenty of honor and glory and those plaudits so dear to the Latin heart. Such a state of affairs insures more revolutions.

In talking the matter over among ourselves the evening after we had witnessed this extraordinary reception to a man whom we could not help regarding as an enemy of his country, we ventured to predict that before the end of the year Peru would see another revolution. It was an easy prophecy and we were not surprised at its speedy fulfillment. In fact, in less than six months a revolution broke out in Lima that for a time seemed as though it would succeed in overthrowing the Government whose mistaken clemency we had witnessed. The President and the Minister of Foreign Affairs were captured and dragged through the streets, and narrowly escaped death in the resulting collision between the revolutionists and the government troops. Fortunately, like so many of its predecessors, the revolution was a failure. But coming as it did just at a time when the city of Lima was endeavoring to sell its bonds on the New York market, it acted as a very effective warning to capitalists who were attracted by an eight per cent municipal bond.

CHAPTER XVII

LA PAZ, THE DE FACTO CAPITAL OF BOLIVIA

IT is a twelve hours' run from Arequipa to the wharf at Puno where one takes the steamer across Lake Titicaca. The distance is only two hundred and eighteen miles, but there are fifteen or twenty stops, and there is no hurry.

Our train was mixed passenger and freight and one first-class coach was amply sufficient to accommodate everybody.

Shortly after ten o'clock, we stopped for breakfast at a primitive little railway inn, where, although we had good appetites and were accustomed to native fare, the food seemed exceptionally bad, and some of it was quite inedible. Whether it was the result of this or not, several of the passengers soon began to show signs of mountain sickness. Arequipa is 7500 feet above the sea, but Crucero Alto, a water tank station, which we reached about half past two, is 14,666 feet, so there was good excuse for any one who is at all affected by rarefied atmosphere.

The eastern edge of the plateau brought us to the two mountain lakes of Saracocha and Cachipascana. Although there was no green in the landscape, the snow-capped mountains that surround the lakes lent an atmosphere of romance and charm to the otherwise desolate view. Continuing eastward, the train went rapidly down grade for two thousand feet, stopping occasionally at little Indian villages until it reached the important railway junction of Juliaca. Here the passengers for Cuzco left us, and in the dusk we turned south and hurried over the remaining thirty miles of level road. On reaching the wharf at Puno, we found to our dismay that the steamer scheduled to cross Titicaca this evening was the Yavarí, the smallest and oldest on the lake, and the first steam vessel to be propelled at an altitude of 12,500 feet above sea-level. She had already received her full complement of freight, and her deck was covered with railway-ties brought from Oregon for the new Bolivia Railway System. It took but a few moments to get passengers and their luggage transferred from the train to the steamer, and before we realized it, we were plowing through the troubled waters of the highest large body of water in the world. The sky was beautifully clear and the stars shone with wonderful brightness, attracting us to spend the evening on deck, to the amazement of the natives who preferred to sit in the stuffy little dining saloon. It did not take us long to agree with them that it was too cold and damp to make the starlight very enjoyable.

Our slumbers were disturbed by a terrific thunder-storm that made the little Yavarí toss about like a cork. The rain descended in torrents and obliged us to close our porthole. Of course, it was not the first squall nor the worst that the stout little vessel had weathered, but out of consideration for her age, we had unpleasant dreams of swimming in the water of a lake which is so cold that none of the Indians who live on its banks and navigate their crazy balsas over its surface have ever learned how to swim.

We were up at daylight just in time to see the islands of Titicaca and Koati and the promontory of Copacavana, the old centre of civilization on the plateau. It is still the scene of many quaint Indian festivals. The ancient terraces are still used in slow rotation for raising crops. We passed quite close to the peninsula of Taraco which abuts from the eastern shore and is thickly populated. In fact, so far as we could see, all the valuable lands on the shores of the lake were cultivated to the limit.

Mr. Bandelier says there are probably more Indians here now than there were in the days before the Conquest, all the sentimentalists to the contrary notwithstanding.

The atmosphere was wonderfully clear, and with the aid of glasses, we could see people miles away going in and out of picturesque little churches, driving their cattle to pasture, tending crops, and working on the primitive threshing-floors where donkeys and oxen were treading out the barley. Occasionally the effect was heightened by a mirage that raised the shores up from the lake and enabled us to see new towns and villages. Far in the distance snow-covered mountains added to the charm of the scene.

On the marshy shores the fisherfolk began to embark in their balsas, those curious canoes, made of bundles of reeds tied together, quite comfortable when new but most disagreeable when water-logged. At one time we were able to count forty of them dot ting the waters of the lake. Not less interesting was a species of wild duck or diver that amused us by swimming directly in the path of the steamer, then becoming suddenly frightened, and with the aid of its wings, running over the surface of the water with incredible swiftness.

Numerous as have been the travellers that have crossed the lake, and easy as it is of access, still Mr. Bandelier is able to write: "Lake Titicaca in most of its features is as unknown as the least visited of the inner African lakes. The shores are so indented and their topography is so complicated, that a coasting voyage of a year at least would be needed to achieve a complete investigation."

There is only a narrow channel between the peninsula of Copacavana on the west and that of San Pedro on the east so that after one passes through the narrow straits of Tiquina, one loses sight of the great expanse of Titicaca and is in reality in a small lake at its southern end. It took us several hours to cross this, however, and it was noon before we entered the little artificial harbor of Guaqui. The only lake traffic that pays is freight and the boats run frequently, but irregularly, starting as soon as their loading of cargo is completed. One reads in the guide-books that they have a regular schedule. The natives say that you can never tell when the steamers will sail. As a matter of fact, it is usually possible to find out a day or two ahead from the railroad officials the hour and date of sailing.

Soon after our arrival the daily train started. The first stop was at the famous town of Tiahuanaco. We could see enough of the wonderful ruins from the train to arouse the greatest curiosity, which a few boys increased by trying to sell us trinkets which had possibly been dug up in the vicinity.

Beyond Tiahuanaco the country, part of the great tableland of Bolivia, is covered with loose stone and an occasional low shrub. Not a single tree breaks the monotony. Trees are rarely seen anywhere on this plateau. A three hours' run over the level plains brought us to Alto de La Paz.

My impressions of the approach to La Paz were so much like those of our old friend Edmund Temple who came here from Potosí in 1828, that I shall quote in full his quaint and vivid description. "After travelling twelve, thirteen, and, as I imagined, every mile of the distance from Ventilla to La Paz, my astonishment was excited by not perceiving on so level a plain any object indicating the existence of a town. Sundry groups of Indians, droves of mules, llamas, and asses, some unladen, some with burdens, were indeed to be seen passing and repassing, as in the bustle of business, but no buildings or habitation whatever; no turret, dome, or steeple of church or convent appeared in view, although the tolling of their bells occasionally struck faintly on the ear. Huge, barren, weather-beaten rocks, and snow-covered mountains, apparently close at hand, rose directly before me, and presented an impassable barrier.

"I could not perceive where I was to find a town; and, as I rode onwards in strange perplexity, endeavoring to solve the enigma, I arrived suddenly at the verge of an abrupt and prodigious precipice, at the

MONOLITHIC IMAGE AT TIAHUANACO

bottom of which I beheld, in diminutive perspective, the large and populous city of La Paz.... Through this fairy town may be faintly seen, winding with occasional interruptions, a silver thread marked with specks of frothy white, which, upon approaching, proves to be a mountain-torrent, leaping from rock to rock, and sweeping through the valley. In casting a glance farther round, you perceive squares and patches of every shade of green and yellow, which, to a European, is perhaps the most striking part of the interesting scene. Corn, and fruit, and vegetables, and crops of every kind, may be seen in all their stages, from the act of sowing to that of gathering them in; here, a field of barley luxuriantly green; there, another in full maturity, which the Indians are busily reaping; next to it, a crop just appearing above the ground. Farther on, another arrived at half its growth; beyond it, a man guiding a pair of oxen yoked to a shapeless stick, the point of which scratches the earth sufficiently for the reception of the seed which another man is scattering in the furrows; trees bearing fruit and at the same time putting forth buds and blossoms complete the scene of luxuriance.... Yet it requires only to raise the eyes from the lap of this fruitful Eden to behold the widest contrast in the realms of Nature. Naked and arid rocks rise in mural precipices around; high above these, mountains beaten by furious tempests, frown in all the bleakness of sterility; higher still, the tops of others, reposing in the region of eternal snow, glisten uninfluenced in the presence of a tropical sun.

"I stopped for some minutes on the verge of the precipice to look upon a scene so wonderfully strange; indeed, my horse, of his own accord, made the first pause, and with outstretched neck, ears advanced, and frequent snorting, showed that he was not unaware of the abyss beneath, and seemed to inquire how it was to be descended, for the road, in a sudden turn, winding round the face of the precipice, is at first completely concealed from view; and, although it appeared as if I could have 'thrown a biscuit' into the town from the heights where I first discovered it, a short league is the calculated distance, and full three quarters of an hour were occupied in descending, before I entered the suburbs. Here, again, I was surprised to find that the town, which, from the height I had just left, appeared to be on a flat, was in reality built upon hills, and that some of the streets were extremely steep, which circumstance alone must convey a tolerable idea of the depth of the valley in which the city of La Paz is situated."

The only change since the days of Temple, whose graphic pencil has so ably described the scene, is that a well-built electric railroad winds down the face of the western cliff into the town. At the time of his visit he was obliged to go from tambo to tambo in search of a lodging but found them all so full that there was no place for him. It gave him the opportunity of putting to test those often proffered services and complimentary generosities of the South American. Addressing the first decent-looking person he passed, he made inquiry who was the owner of a large and respectable mansion near by. On learning that it belonged to a worthy and excellent man, he determined to present himself and ask for lodgings. At first he was rather brusquely received by the lady of the house, who "stood for some time like a pillar of salt to my politely-studied address"; but he explained his predicament and was soon given a kind and affable reception.

Fortunately, we were not obliged to experiment upon the proverbial Bolivian hospitality, but were met at the station by kind friends, representatives of W. R. Grace & Co., who did everything in their power to add to the debt of gratitude which I had owed their house ever since I started on my journey. Comfortable quarters were found for us in the Sucursal, a huge, modern, three-story building intended for a convent, but now used as the annex of the leading hotel. It was not long before we were exploring the streets and enjoying the sights of the most picturesque Indian city in Spanish-America.

There are, to be sure, the usual earmarks of a Latin-American capital: well-stocked warehouses owned by English, German, and American firms; native politicians, unmistakable, in frock coats and silk hats, who spend their time chatting around the benches of the principal plaza near the Government House; a telephone company with four hundred subscribers; fine residences on a shady alameda, owned and occupied by people of European descent; etc., etc. Nevertheless the general impression that one gets of La Paz is that it is an Indian city, quite distinct from any city seen anywhere else. Its In dians are not like the Quichuas of Cuzco and Potosí, or the Chibchas of Bogotá. They are Aymarás.

It is said that La Paz, with a population of sixty thousand people, has thirty thousand Aymarás who neither speak nor understand a word of Spanish. Judging by my experiences in the streets and in the market-place, the proportion of people who do not understand Spanish is considerably larger. I found very few, even of those who were most anxious to sell their goods, who could so much as count in Spanish.

The result of having such a large part of the population untouched by Spanish language or custom is to make the streets much more picturesque. The brilliant colors completely threw into the shade my impression of Potosí. Never have I seen such gay ponchos and such kaleidoscopic effects as in the La Paz market-place and the streets and squares near it.

The reason is not far to seek. In no other city of the Andes are the aborigines so powerful as here. La Paz owes its political supremacy, and its present possession of the President and Congress, to the fighting qualities of the Aymarás. They are a barbarous folk whose cupidity, low cunning, and savage cruelty is quite unlike their mild cousins the Quichuas. Pampered and befriended by the Government, made to feel their power and importance, they stalk unabashed through the streets of the city and take pleasure in carrying their savage tastes to an extreme. The natural result is to give the city an

THE MARKET-PLACE OF LA PAZ

A REMARKABLE STAIRWAY AT TIAHUANACO

atmosphere of barbaric glitter which is lacking elsewhere. In cities like Bogotá, Cuzco, and Potosí, although the Indians far outnumber the whites, the latter are so absolutely dominant, and the Indians so peaceable and humble, that there is an opportunity for ridicule to mitigate against the more picturesque features of Indian costume. But in La Paz few of the Spanish-speaking boys would dare to jeer at a stalwart Aymará carrier, no matter what garb he chose to wear.

In fact, the Aymará attitude is a striking example of the truth of Mr. Bryce's dictum that "serfs, when they have attained a measure of independence, resent the inferiority, be it legal or social, to which they find themselves condemned. Discontent appears and social friction is intensified, not only because occasions for it grow more frequent, but because the temper of each race is more angry and suspicious." We had noticed their insolent demeanor when we first met them in the village of Ocurí on the road from Sucre to Challapata. Poor Mr. Bandelier had many unpleasant experiences with them.

The streets of La Paz, picturesque at all times, are particularly so on Sunday, especially on Children's Sunday. In 1909, that event came on January 24th, when we had been in La Paz nearly a week.

The fair held on that day was unusually interesting. From early morning until the middle of the afternoon, the plazas and streets were thronged with thousands of gaudily dressed Aymarás, bent on enjoying themselves, and purchasing toys and other trinkets of the hundreds of peddlers who displayed their wares in every inch of available space on the three principal plazas and the streets connecting them. While the characteristic feature of this fair is the number of toys that are offered for sale, and the miniature models of everything the Indians use and wear, the chance to sell all kinds of articles that appeal to Aymará taste is not lost sight of. Spread out on ponchos on the edge of the sidewalk and in the middle of the streets was pottery, large and small, useful and ornamental; tinware, woodenware, and crockery; dresses for women, girls, and dolls; ponchos of every grade and description, from the expensive vicuña, worth forty dollars, to the cheapest kind of llama, worth only two or three; musical instruments: little guitars with bodies made of the hard shell armor of the Bolivian armadillo,[2] Aymará flutes and flageolets of bamboo, drums and horns made in Germany; and dolls made in France; in fact, everything that one can think of that would appeal to the Indian and at the same time be within the possibilities of his pocket-book.

The proper thing to do, and the one that seemed to appeal most to the half-tipsy Aymará porter that had saved up a few pesos from the rewards of his labor, was to purchase a fat little doll eight or ten inches high, made in the form of a humpbacked clown, buy gaudy clothes for it, and then load it down with tiny models of brandy bottles, coca wallets, and chicha jugs, in short everything it might be supposed to desire. The result was not unlike a heavily laden Santa Claus, although the face of the manikin, instead of being like our genial old saint, was that of a hideous, debauched vagabond.

The most interesting things that were offered for sale were little plaster models of Aymará types; a carrier or porter with a red knitted cap and a bit of rope in his hand, on the run to get his load; a woman seated on the ground before a miniature loom on which she had begun to make a bright-colored poncho; a chola with her white straw hat, yellow fringed shawl, jewelled neck, close-fitting bodice, gaudy petticoats, and high-heeled French boots. Besides there were rudely made little rag and wooden dolls, clad in characteristic native costumes; clay models of llamas, cows, birds, and mythical animals; little balsas fifteen inches long but resembling in every particular the craft of Lake Titicaca; small packages of coca leaves done up in burlap exactly like the bundles that the burros bring across the Andes from the warm valleys to the eastward; little copper kettles from Coracora; tiny clay models of cooking utensils, water-jugs, and little rawhide sandals scarcely more than an inch in length, faithful imitations of the clumsy Aymará footwear.

One of the smaller plazas was given over almost entirely to games of chance. The favorite variety consisted of a form of dice. Instead of being marked with the usual aces and deuces, the dice were cov ered with grotesque figures. Each outfit had a different set, but nearly always one face bore the representation of a drunken man, another that of a devil with forked tail and horns, and a third the effigy of the sun. The others frequently carried pictures of wild animals such as lions, tigers, or jaguars. As three dice were cast at a time, it was possible to win three for one, provided all came up the same way, and you had staked your money on the lucky figure. The gambling booths were well thronged. Most of the betting was done with reals, a nickel coin worth about four cents. On the pavement in the middle of this plaza a number of games of lotto were going on, a game which I used to play in my childhood when anything connected with gambling was strictly forbidden. The La Paz game was played as usual with discs and cards. Instead of numbers as

[2] Mr. Thomas Barbour, of the Museum of Comparative Zoölogy, Harvard University, tells me these are generally Dasypus vellurosus. Colored plates of many of the interesting Aymará toys and textiles can be found in Stubel's Kultur und Industrie Süd Amerikanischer Völker.

in our game, each disc had a gaudily painted picture on it, and each card several pictures and lines. The discs were drawn from a greasy calico bag by an Indian boy, who called out the name of the figure in a droning voice, and the corresponding grotesque picture on the cards was then covered. The player who first covered all the pictures on his card won the pool, less the bank's percentage. I should have liked to join the game, but as it was conducted entirely in Aymará, I found it a little too difficult to learn the names of the different men and animals that figured on the cards.

Another game of chance that attracted a dense crowd consisted in selling ten numbers at a real apiece. If your number was drawn, you won five reals and the bank got the other five. The only novel feature of the game was the way in which the drawing was made. At the top of a little pole, five feet high, were ten wooden arms radiating from it like the spokes of a wheel. From the end of each hung a little clay figure of an animal, lions, llamas, dogs, and cows. These had numbers pasted to them. By means of a spring, a wooden monkey was made to climb the pole, carrying a stick in his hand with a hook on the end of it. In the meantime, the wheel of numbered animals was rapidly revolved until the monkey manikin made a jab with his hook and pulled off one of the clay animals. This decided the winning number. To see how it worked, I bought two numbers for two reals. The other numbers were soon sold in the crowd; the monkey clambered painfully up his stick, and owing to some defect of the mechanism, pulled off two clay figures instead of one. It happened that both of them bore the numbers which I held in my hand, but as I was a foreigner, and as the monkey had not played the game squarely, the figures were re-arranged, the spring again set, and my luck changed, much to the delight of the Aymarás.

The home of Bolivia's millionaires, and the centre of Bolivian capital, is in Sucre, nevertheless there are nine banks of issue in La Paz, including several small ones that have no agencies in southern Bolivia and whose bills have only local circulation. While we were here, the banks put into operation a new rule to the effect that bills torn in two, after the favorite custom in Bolivia for making change, would be no longer accepted at the bank at their face value. It seemed natural and proper enough to us, but greatly disturbed the small tradesmen, and seemed likely to cause considerable inconvenience owing to the scarcity of subsidiary coinage.

During my entire visit I was treated most courteously by the government officials and I regret to feel any necessity of offering serious criticism of anything in La Paz. Nevertheless I cannot pass by the barbarous state of affairs which we found in the city prison, an institution which is entirely inadequate for a city of this size and a disgrace to any modern capital. The prisoners are herded together without regard as to whether they are detained on suspicion of misdemeanor or convicted of murder.

Not all of the prisoners are treated so humanely. For our satisfaction, the jailer unlocked the door of one cell, six feet high, three feet wide, and eighteen inches deep. As the door opened, the occupant of the cell tumbled out onto the floor. He was a police officer in full uniform who for some delinquency had been imprisoned for twenty-four hours in this torture chamber where he could neither stand up nor lie down. I shall offer no further criticism because I am conscious of the fact that travellers in nearly every country are prone to find fault with the methods of punishment employed there. Coming from a different atmosphere, things seem dreadful to the stranger that attract no attention from local observers, and which are really not as hard on native prisoners as they would be on foreigners. Furthermore, the distinguished Bolivian statesman who had politely but regretfully yielded to our request to see the prison, told us he was very sorry we had seen it and that it "would be improved before long."

The traveller in search of new itineraries or out-of-the-way routes will have plenty of suggestions made to him by the hospitable English and American colony in La Paz, and if he is at all uncertain in his mind as to just what he wants to do, he is likely to become bewildered by the number of attractive trips which he can make from La Paz as a base. La Paz contains the principal offices of a number of mining and exploration companies. The general manager of one of those that is engaged in gold-mining in the valley of the Beni, very nearly persuaded me to abandon my proposed trip overland from La Paz to Lima, and go across the mountains to the Beni, thence to the Amazon, and so home. Had it not required more time than I had at my disposal, and been a somewhat uncertain venture at this time of the year, I should have accepted his invitation. For the benefit of any who would like to plan a journey across South America by one of the new trade-routes which few travellers have yet seen, I give the itinerary as it was given me. It makes no allowances for missing connections:—

La Paz to Sorata by coach or mule-back, 2 days.

Sorata to Guanay, a hard trip on mule-back, 7 days.

Guanay to Rurrenabaque, on the river Beni, by raft, 4 days.

(In the rainy season, that is from January to April, there are very few rafts to be had. The route then would be from Sorata direct to Rurrenabaque, an interesting but rather difficult trip that would take fourteen days on mule-back.)

Rurrenabaque to river Alto at the junction of the Beni and the Madre de Dios by steam launch, 4 days; or by boat, 18 days.

From river Alto to Port San Antonio by boat, 6 days.

From Port San Antonio to Manaos on the Amazon, by steamer, 5 days.

Total: La Paz to Manaos, not counting time lost in making connection, 28 to 45 days.

BALSAS NEAR GUAQUI ON LAKE TITICACA

AN OLD CHURCH NEAR THE BOLIVIA RAILWAY

CHAPTER XVIII
THE BOLIVIA RAILWAY AND TIAHUANACO

In order to attend the Scientific Congress, I had been obliged to interrupt my journey from Buenos Aires to Lima and had left my saddles and impedimenta at Oruro. It was now necessary to return thither and pick up the overland trail.

Leaving La Paz early one morning by the electric train for the Alto, we took the Guaqui train as far as Viacha, the northern terminus of the Bolivia Railway.

This railway was built to order for the Bolivian Government by an American syndicate, and we found it equipped with American-made locomotives and cars, and operated by American railroad men. Most of them had had some experience in Mexico and were familiar with the difficulties of handling Indian laborers, and also with the use (and abuse) of the Spanish language. None of them seemed to be particularly enthusiastic over the prospects of the country, and all were looking forward with pleasure to the time of their vacation when, according to the terms of their contract, they would be sent back to the States.

The construction of this road over the plateau offered no great engineering difficulties such as are met with by the roads that cross the Cordillera. The heaviest grade is not over ten per cent, and there are no tunnels. To offset this advantage, however, rock ballast is difficult to procure, and the earth that has been dug up on each side of the track to form the roadbed seems to lack cohesion. The gauge is one metre. The ties are of California redwood and Oregon pine. Owing to the high cost of rails and ties and the distance which they had to be brought, the railroad has been an expensive one to build. There is only a difference of eight hundred and sixteen feet between the highest and lowest portion of the line, yet the hundred and twenty-five miles have cost two million dollars and a quarter, or eighteen thousand dollars per mile.

The Bolivia Railway is remarkable for the promptness with which it was constructed after the signing of the contract. The National City Bank of New York and Speyer & Co. agreed, on the 22nd of May, 1906, to build the line from Viachi to Oruro. Work was commenced seven months later, and the line was opened for traffic in less than two years. Everything considered, the prompt completion of the work is a great credit to the American engineers who had the line in charge.

There is another side to the story, however. Owing to the fact that the opening of the road had to be rushed in order to please President Montes of Bolivia, trains began to run before the road was really finished, and it has been necessary to continue the service in order to avoid criticism. The South American is not as patient as the North American and is ever ready to enter vehement and furious protests against anything short of perfection in railway management. Not content with actual progress, and not having had any practical experience in the difficulties of railroad construction and maintenance, he imagines that all accidents and all shortcomings on the railway are due to gross carelessness on the part of the chief officials. Every time a train is late, he blames the management and accuses it of bad faith, although he knows many of his friends and neighbors would miss any train that started on time. The necessity of catering to the desires of the politicians has made it extremely difficult to get the roadbed into good shape. At the time of my visit six hundred Indian laborers, conscripts, were still employed in getting the track properly ballasted. Their wages average a trifle over fifty cents a day.

I had heard that accidents occurred "every trip," but thought it only one of those extravagant criticisms that are so common, until I asked the conductor. He admitted that some of the wheels generally left the rails at least once a day. For an hour or so nothing happened, and in my interest in the landscape, dotted here and there with mud-colored villages and ancient tombs, I was beginning to forget the delightful sense of approaching danger, when suddenly, with a rattle and a bang, we came to a sharp stop. One of the forward cars had left the rails and plowed its way across the ties for some distance. The train crew, well experienced in such matters, soon had the refractory car back on the rails again and, nothing the worse for our accident, we proceeded merrily southward for another half hour until brought up with a sudden jerk by a repetition of the rattle and bang. This time it proved to be the tender whose wheels had found a weak spot in the roadbed. Upon further examination, it looked as though we were going to be delayed for at least four or five hours. The tender had lost its balance and was lying over partly on one side, kept from a complete upset by the weight of the engine and the strength of the couplings. In ten or fifteen minutes, however, the crew, well trained by daily practice, had the port wheels back on the track, but the starboard wheels continued to remain in the air five or six inches above the rails. As the water tank had recently been filled, the centre of gravity was too high to allow the tender to assume its normal position, and the added weight of several men failed to bring it down. The engineer suggested that a bend in the track less than a quarter of a mile away would "do the business," and so he was allowed to pull down to the curve. It looked like an extraordinarily clever acrobatic performance to see this refractory tender going merrily along on a single rail. True to the engineer's expectations, as soon as the wheels felt the changed angle of the track, down came the tender with a lurch that almost capsized it on the other side. In less than twenty minutes we were again on our way, thankful that we had experienced wreckers instead of the ordinary train crew of the eastern United States, whom I have seen take several hours to perform what these men did in a few minutes.

Notwithstanding our two accidents we arrived at Oruro about five o'clock in the evening, after a journey of nine hours, on time!

We found the Government House surrounded by throngs of people. Presently a company of infantry marched through the streets from their barracks and took up a position in the courtyard. The occasion was the death of the major who, six weeks before, had read the proclamation in the streets and now had just died after an illness of twenty-four hours.

The scene at the railroad station the next morning at eight o'clock, when I left Oruro to return to La Paz, was characteristic. The local regiment was drawn up in front of the train after having escorted the remains of their major from the Prefecture. Several hundred citizens thronged the platform and tried to crowd into the cars. Friends of the deceased major and his family, men and women, were weeping loudly, and some of the women uttered piercing shrieks and wild cries. Altogether, it was rather trying.

The plain over which we passed for a good part of the journey was very flat, treeless, and covered only with small, scrubby growth. At one station we were met by thirty or forty Indians who had brought bundles of fagots, dry brush from the neighboring mountains. These they piled onto a flat car and carried down the line to one of the new settlements which have sprung up near the tracks, and which depend on the trains for both fuel and fresh water. The latter is carried in tank cars, like oil.

At the principal stations, a dozen or more Aymará women, seated in a long line on the ground, offered for sale chicha, cakes, buns, and little pears, brought from the fruitful valleys far to the eastward.

The only part of the road that offered any attractive scenery was that near the river Viscachani, an affluent of the Desaguadero. Near Ayoayo, there are a number of ancient tombs east of the track. Some of them have been opened by the railroad people and artificially flattened skulls found. The railroad men told us that when they were building the line they saw many vicuñas and biscachas, but these have now almost entirely disappeared.

We stopped for lunch at a little station whose new adobe buildings and corrugated iron roofs told of railroad enterprise. The restaurant was kept by a pleasant American, who did his best to please all of his patrons, but chiefly the railroad "boys" on whom he depends for most of his income. On my way down to Oruro, I had had the good fortune to sit at the same table with part of the train crew, but this time the two seats nearest me were occupied by Bolivian army officers who were as rude and ill-mannered as possible. If I had introduced myself as a delegado they would have been the pink of politeness. Any one connected with the Government would be sure to receive their kind attention. But, so far as they could see, I was simply an American traveller. Accordingly they proceeded to act as though they owned the restaurant and everything in it, presuming that I would be glad enough to get whatever they chose to leave. There is, however, a certain relief in avoiding the excessive attentions which such men as these bestow on any one with a government "pull," and it was instructive to see how they behave toward foreigners who were apparently travelling without official recognition. It enabled me the better to appreciate the different attitude that is taken toward South Americans by distinguished foreign visitors who are in the hands of attentive friends during their entire stay, and by casual travellers who have failed to fortify themselves with official letters of introduction. I do not mean to imply that one who merely wishes to visit the chief centres of interest will fail to be comfortable unless he supplies himself with important looking documents tied with red tape and sealed with a great seal, but I do know from personal experience that such a preparation can give one, in at least eleven Latin-American republics, a very different impression of the country and of the courtesy of its inhabitants.

There does not seem to be much likelihood of any large amount of traffic being developed along this desolate plateau. The railroad must depend for its freight on foreign merchandise coming to La Paz via Oruro and the port of Antofagasta. As it has a longer haul than that of its competitor, the Peruvian Southern from Mollendo to Puno, it will have some difficulty in getting much of this. Furthermore, there is the new Chilean government railroad now under construction, a direct line to La Paz from the port of Arica. When that is finished, it is difficult to say how the line from Oruro to La Paz can secure enough freight to pay expenses. There will always be a certain amount of passenger traffic, but at present one train, three times a week, is amply sufficient.

A branch of the Bolivia Railway is now in course of construction from Oruro to Cochabamba, which will bring to La Paz the food and coca cultivated in the warm valleys northeast of Sucre where frost is unknown and there is an abundance of rain. There is an imperative demand for coca all over the plateau where it cannot possibly grow. Furthermore it does not keep well, loses its flavor after four or five months, and fresh supplies have to be brought continually from the eastern valleys. This makes it an important article of commerce to be reckoned as one of the surest sources of revenue for the Bolivia Railway.

Shortly before reaching Viacha we passed a truncated hill, the Pan de Sucre, that has been a favorite camping-ground in revolutionary wars. It is easily defended and its summit is spacious enough to furnish refuge for quite a number of troops. On the hills west of it, romantically perched on an almost inaccessible peak, is a little church where services are held once a year. To the eastward we could begin to see the magnificent snow-range of the Bolivian Andes. Words fail to describe adequately the grandeur of the Cordillera Real with its two hundred and fifty miles of snow-capped mountains, scarcely one of which lies at a lesser elevation than twenty thousand feet. It must be seen to be appreciated. Still, one can get a very vivid impression of it in the pages of Sir Martin Conway's fascinating "Climbing and Exploration in the Bolivian Andes."

The next day after my return from Oruro, through the courtesy of Mr. Rankin Johnson, I enjoyed the privilege of visiting the village and ruins of Tiahuanaco on the plains several miles south of Lake Titicaca.

Leaving La Paz at eight o'clock in the morning, we had six hours in and around the village and returned in time for dinner the same evening. It was necessary to take our lunch with us, for there is no inn and the little village shops afford scarcely anything that is fit to eat. The Tiahuanaco station is within a mile of the most interesting ruins. The railroad track passes within a few feet of three of the monolithic images and one of the monolithic doorways.

At the station we secured the services of a picturesquely dressed old Aymará who the station master assured us was a competent guide. He took us across the dusty plain towards a large mound which had once been surrounded by terraces and stone walls. It is popularly known as the "fortress." Originally a truncated pyramid about six hundred feet long, four hundred feet wide, and fifty feet high, treasure-seekers have dug great holes in its sides and excavated part of its summit in an effort to find the "buried riches of the Incas." Besides the fortress there seems to be evidence of a great "temple" and also of a "palace." The "temple," roughly outlined by rude stone blocks, occupies an area of nearly four acres. For the most part the blocks are from six to ten feet in height and three feet in thickness. Within there is still evidence of a terrace, and from this on the eastern side there leads a remarkable stairway. Scattered about over the mound and all over the plain are many rectangular stones whose purpose has been entirely lost, thanks to the activity of treasure-seekers who have ruthlessly moved them from their original position and left them lying in indescribable confusion. There seems to be evidence that many of the blocks were held in place by strong metal pins, for there are round holes drilled into the stones and insertions made to receive "T" clamps.

The principal ruins are in a broad level part of the plain where the soil is firm and dry. They consist of rows of erect, roughly-shaped monoliths, sections of foundations, portions of giant stairways, monolithic doorways, some bearing carvings in low relief, monolithic statues, and innumerable small cut stones strewn about on all sides.

Great stone platforms, weighing many tons, aroused our keenest curiosity. One looks around the plain in vain for a near-by quarry from which they could have come. The most natural supposition is that they must have been quarried on the spot from ledges outcropping here, for it would seem scarcely possible that blocks twenty feet long, ten feet wide, and four feet thick could have been transported any distance by the primitive methods at the disposal of those prehistoric people.

The ruins were much more complete in 1875 at

"GREAT PLATFORMS OF STONE WEIGHING MANY TONS"

PART OF THE GREAT MONOLITHIC DOORWAY

the time of the visit of the American archæologist, E. G. Squier, who spent some time here, and whose account of the ruins in his book on Peru is one of the most complete and satisfactory that we possess. Unfortunately, his drawings give an erroneous impression of the size of many of the monuments which are not so large as he has represented them.

Squier saw no subterranean vaults or passages, but we were more fortunate, for only a short time previous to our visit, thanks to the activity of Mr. John Pierce Hope of La Paz, who has taken a great interest in the work of exploration, a small vault was discovered and we were able to enter and examine it. It is about six feet square and the same in depth and is made of beautifully cut stones, accurately fitted together. Nothing of value was found in the vault and it is probably one of those to which Von Tschudi, who was here before Squier's visit, refers. The winds that blow over these sandy plains will soon fill the vault and cover it up again and leave it to be rediscovered by some future traveller.

The largest monolithic doorway, now broken, is covered with figures not unlike some of the Central American monuments. It is very different from anything else here or in Cuzco. The story goes, that when the Spaniards first arrived, it was lying on its side, and there appears to be no record to show who raised it nor when the crack developed which led finally to the door breaking into two parts. The southern and larger half has lost its balance and will soon be lying on the ground. By a curious coincidence, Mr. Barbour, who made a careful photograph of the carvings on this doorway, afterwards secured from a grave near Pachacamac in the vicinity of Lima, a textile that was decorated with a similar pattern.

After examining the ruins, we spent an hour or more in the village itself where we were struck by the great number of finely cut stones inserted into the walls of the huts and used as paving in the streets. The church on the plaza is built entirely of blocks brought from the ruins. It has a fence or wall in front composed of a row of arches that reminded me of Potosí and Bartolo. The exterior of the church gives no evidence of the extraordinary magnificence within, which is quite in keeping with the ancient importance of this little village. Here we found religious paintings, some of them very good, elaborate gilded carvings, and an altar built of pure silver, beautifully worked.

La Paz has two or three remarkable collections of antiquities which consist largely of material brought from Tiahuanaco. Perhaps the best is in the National Museum, which owes its existence to the enlightened patriotism of Sr. Don Manuel Vicente Ballivian, a descendant of one of the most distinguished Bolivian families, and the leading antiquarian in the republic.

Of the ancient Tiahuanaco, there is comparatively little left now. Not only did the Spaniards use cartloads of it in building the churches of La Paz and Guaqui, but the modern Guaqui-to-La Paz railroad has taken away within the past ten years more than five hundred trainloads of stone for building its bridges and warehouses. From the point of view of the railroad manager, whose business it is to secure lasting results with the greatest possible economy, it must have seemed a most fortunate circumstance that within a few rods of his tracks there should be such a quantity of nicely cut stone, and "a lot of old stone walls," all ready to use! O tempora! O mores!

CHAPTER XIX
CUZCO

WE left La Paz on January 26, 1909, at 8.30 A.M. When we reached Guaqui we found that our steamer was to be the old Yavarí that we had before. She was late in arriving from Puno; the afternoon was spent in unloading her cargo; and we did not sail until eight o'clock that evening.

The night was wet and chilly. Thunder-storms and squalls made the lake quite rough and we had the usual discomforts. The storm and the late start kept us from reaching Puno before 11 A.M. The regular train had gone, but a special was made up for the convenience of the Arequipa passengers and we reached Juliaca at one o'clock. Here I bade the last of the delegados farewell and asked for the train for Cuzco. "It had left several hours before and the next train was due to leave day after to-morrow!"

Thanks to the courtesy of the railway officials, however, a special train, consisting of half a dozen freight cars and a small passenger coach, was made up to take me as far as Checcacupe.

The coach which had been put at my disposal was old and very small, about the size of an ancient bob-tailed horse-car. Moreover, it was already occupied by a dozen native passengers who, like myself, had missed the regular train. As usual, they had no end of bags, bundles, and boxes. There was hardly room to squeeze inside the door. Undoubtedly they had better right on the train than I did, for they had paid their fares while I was riding on a pass. So I relinquished any claim to the coach and took the fireman's seat in the locomotive, which afforded me a better opportunity of seeing the country.

We pulled out of Juliaca shortly after two o'clock and rattled along over the plains north of Titicaca. Here I saw for the first time llamas tied to stakes. Of all the thousands of llamas seen in Bolivia, I do not remember one that was tied. But I soon found that the practice is customary in and around Cuzco.

The inquisitive Indians who gathered at the stations to stare at our train while the engine was getting a drink of water were mild-mannered Quichuas. Puno is the northern limit of the Aymarás. The Quichua women here wore broad-brimmed black hats covered with velvet and ornamented with tinsel.

We did not reach Ayavari until six o'clock and it was dark before we approached the upper part of the valley of the Pucará River and began to climb up over the Vilcanota mountains. The night air was exceedingly cold, but fortunately, by this time, most of the native passengers had left the train and I was able to get a seat in the coach.

The highest station on the road, La Raya, is 14,150 feet above sea level. From here, there is a rapid descent of 2500 feet to Sicuani which was for many years the northern terminal of the railroad. Here, in search of supper, I stumbled through the dark streets with the train-crew to a filthy little Indian chicheria where a half-drunken brigand and his besotted spouse were persuaded to give us hot tea, beer, and stale bread. The conductor of the train said I would have to spend the night at Sicuani as he did not propose to go any further in the dark. Unfortunately for him, orders came directing him to proceed at once twenty-five miles further to Checcacupe in order that I might catch the north-bound morning train. The engineer declared that it was a dreadfully risky run from Sicuani to Checcacupe and that we would probably never reach our destination at all. But I was too tired and sleepy to care very much, and as soon as I got back into my little bobtailed car, pulled out my sleeping bag, and promptly forgot all about the train and the danger of falling into the Vilcanota River. The next thing I knew the Checcacupe station agent was flashing his lantern in my face and telling me to lie still as this was much the best place for me at this time of night (1 A.M.), and I should not be disturbed until morning. I thanked him and dropped off to sleep again, dimly conscious that some kind of an animal was scratching about on the floor of the little car among my dunnage bags. When I woke up, aroused by the shouts of the train-men who were making up the train for Cuzco, I found that my visitor was a little seven-year-old Quichua street-Arab who could speak no Spanish, but who said as plainly as possible that he would be my slave for ever after and desired to travel in my company. I gave him part of my breakfast and thought little more about it, especially as Mr. Clarence Hay, who had kindly agreed to accompany me overland from Cuzco to Lima, met me here. Mr. Smith had gone back to New Haven to pursue his studies.

Mr. Hay and I were soon installed on the train for Cuzco. We were already well on our way when the polite Peruvian conductor smilingly informed us that there was a boy in the second-class car who insisted he belonged to me. It was too late to put the little fellow off, so I decided to be responsible for him; but he was a foxy little rascal, slipped out of the train at some station before we reached Cuzco, and disappeared. Children mature early in the Andes.

At the time of our visit, the Cuzco railroad had only just been completed. The track runs along the steep side of a valley which has an embarrassing habit of sending down landslides quite unexpectedly, so the journey was a bit slow and uncertain. The natives are fond of exaggerating its irregularities, and said it would take several days, but we were to reach Cuzco on time, notwithstanding all their dismal forebodings.

The scenery was very pretty. The Vilcanota valley rapidly narrows as it descends, and the river becomes a roaring torrent. The climate is delightful and has been likened to that of Italy. The soil is extremely fertile and produces a remarkable variety of crops.

The road follows the west bank of the Vilcanota until it is met by the Huatanay River. Here it turns abruptly to the left and enters the lovely region that was once the very heart of the Inca Empire. The valley of the Huatanay is still densely populated, as it always has been. In quick succession the train passed the large Indian cities of Oropeza, San Geronimo, and San Sebastian. Suddenly we stopped in the fields and took on a group of laughing Peruvian sports who had waved a piece of red flannel to save themselves the trouble of going to the nearest railway station. One of the joys of this railroad is that everybody that is anybody flags the train whenever he pleases. The habit interferes somewhat with the time-tables, but no one cares (except the railroad people), and it gives an individual a great sense of his own importance to make a train stop while he climbs on board. A few minutes later we reached the temporary Cuzco station, a group of small, corrugated-iron buildings which stand in a plain a quarter of a mile south of the city.

The most agreeable approach is by way of the Alameda, an ill-kept avenue with a double row of alder trees, on the west bank of the Rio Huatanay. From it we had a fine view of the convent of Santo Domingo, the ancient Temple of the Sun, across the ravine to the east. On the west of the Alameda is the new rifle range of the local shooting club. The avenue itself leads into one of the principal streets of the best residence quarter, where Spanish houses have almost completely obliterated all traces of Inca occupation. As soon as we reached the centre of the city, long walls of beautifully cut stone, laid without cement, and fitted together with the

LLAMAS OF CUZCO

CUZCO FROM SACSAHUAMAN

patience of expert stone-cutters, assured us that this was verily the Cuzco of Pizarro, Garcilasso de la Vega, and the Spanish chroniclers. The one distinctive feature that separates Cuzco from all other cities in America is the prevalence of these long, dark, sombre walls. When you look at a building from a distance, it seems to be an ordinary two-story Spanish house with a red-tiled roof, wooden balconies, and white-washed adobe walls. As you come a little closer, it strikes you that the whitewash has been worn off the lower part of the walls, but when you come closer still, you find that this portion consists of unpainted Inca stone-work, still fresh and attractive.

The most striking wall in Cuzco is that of the palace said to have belonged to the Inca Rocca, which is composed of very large irregular boulders. They are of all sizes and shapes, some with as many as a dozen angles, but all fitting perfectly. The stones used in most of the ancient palaces and temples are more nearly rect-angular. The corner-stones of buildings are frequently rounded off, but there are almost no circular walls in Cuzco. The principal exception to this is in the Domini-can Monastery, once the temple of the Sun, where the end of one of the buildings is rounded like the chancel of a church. This is, perhaps, the finest bit of stone-cutting in Cuzco, and is shown off by the Dominican Fathers with great zest. E. G. Squier, who lived for some time in the convent and made a minute examination of these walls, found that the sides of contact of each stone are true radii of a double circle, and that the line of general inclination of the wall is perfect in every block.

In some of the walls, the outer surfaces of the stones are perfectly flat, but in general, they are slightly convex. The blocks vary in length from a few inches to several feet, although it is very rare to find any more than five feet long. All are laid with remarkable precision and at first sight appear to be absolutely rectangular. On closer examination, you find that there is scarcely an absolute right angle in the whole wall. Each block is slightly irregular, but this irregularity matches so exactly with that of the next that there is no space for a needle to enter. The result of such careful workmanship, combined with the use of dark-colored stone, is to produce a dignity and solidity that is very impressive.

The characteristics of Inca architecture are in part the same as those of the older Egyptian ruins: individual blocks of great size; doors narrower at the top than at the bottom, and walls with a base markedly wider than the apex so that the sloping front is a distinct feature. Probably the same methods which the Egyptians evolved in order to put in position large monoliths too heavy to be lifted by hand, were employed by the Incas. They seem to have thought nothing of fitting carefully into place, on top of a wall fifteen feet high, boulders weighing several tons.

The followers of Pizarro who divided Cuzco among themselves, built their homes on the massive walls of the Inca palaces. Sometimes they left the Inca wall standing to a height of six or seven feet. In other instances it still rises to fifteen or twenty feet.

It is unfortunate that the Incas did not use cement. In that case the Spaniards would have found it much more difficult to have destroyed the ancient palaces, and more would have been left for the delectation of students and travellers today. Under the circumstances, it was a simple matter for the faithful disciples of the church to raise temples and towers of great beauty by the simple process of tearing down Inca palaces and using the material according to the ideas of ecclesiastical architecture which they had brought with them from Spain.

Many travellers have studied Cuzco but none with so great care as Mr. Squier, in whose "Peru" may be found many drawings and plans of the rooms.

Thirty years ago, when he was here, there was no inn, and he was obliged to depend on the kindness of the local officials and the hospitality of the monasteries. But there is now a commodious Hotel Comercio where reasonably good meals and decent bedrooms enabled us to be very comfortable. Of course, the "plumbing" was conspicuous by its absence, and there was by no means so much luxury as at the Hotel Marone in Arequipa. However, even the Incas were not remarkably cleanly and it is as well not to have too many of the conveniences of the twentieth century when living in a metropolis of the fifteenth.

Cuzco has long been notorious as one of the dirtiest cities in America; and it justifies its reputation. The stone paving of the streets is extremely rough and unspeakably filthy. To add to the slime, the sewers are open conduits running through the middle of the narrow streets. In the wet season, they are kept flushed by heavy downpours. In the dry season, they are unspeakable.

One has to be very careful where one steps while investigating the ancient structures, for the present inhabitants are no more cleanly or sanitary in their habits than their predecessors. It is pathetic to see the filth and squalor that surround the walls of the magnificent old edifices.

Although we rarely forgot to pick our way carefully through the streets, the practice soon became a habit and did not interfere with the enjoyment of the brilliant colors affected by the Quichuas. Their home-made ponchos and shawls, fastened with one pin instead of two as in Potosí, are woven of native wool and cotton. Yet though the material may be as rare and uncommon as real alpaca, vicuña, or llama wool, the brilliant hues are unmistakably aniline. In fact, in the market-place of almost every city in the Andes, one is pretty sure to find a native peddler whose specialty is the sale of German dyes.

The most striking part of the Cuzco Quichua costume is the pancake hat. It is reversible, being made of a straw disc with a cloth-covered hole in the centre. On one side, for rainy weather, the disc is lined with coarse red flannel or some other worsted stuff, but the dry weather side is elaborately covered with tinsel on black velvet. Likewise, the loose, baggy cloth that covers the opening in the centre is lined with velveteen on the fair-weather side and coarse woolen stuff for rain. The men's hats are slightly larger than the women's, but otherwise the fashion seems to be alike for both sexes.

Opposite our hotel was the church and convent of La Merced. Its cloisters are noted for their fine old paintings, their elaborately carved stone columns and arches. Its gardens are filled with rare flowers and shrubs. In the crypt beneath the altar, Pizarro's partner, Almagro, and his son are supposed to have been buried. The obliging Brother who showed us the monastery had never heard of any such tradition. "Quien sabe?" and a shrug of the shoulders was all he would reply.

Not far from La Merced is the warehouse of Sr. Lomellini, Cuzco's leading merchant, an Italian gentleman who, while building up an extensive business, has devoted himself to a study of the Inca civilization. He has brought himself in as close touch with it as possible; the very entrance to his warehouse is a fine old Inca doorway, while his home, half way up the side of Sacsahuaman, was once the site of the palace of Manco Capac, the first famous Inca. He showed me with a sad smile a few elaborately carved bronze figures or idols that looked very much as though they had been buried for centuries in the mould of a royal mausoleum, but instead were "made in Germany." Later I found similar specimens in Lima, where one "anti quarian" had the effrontery to have three of identically the same pattern, differing only in color, exposed for sale in the same showcase.

West of Sr. Lomellini's warehouse is the monastery and plaza of San Francisco. The plaza is chiefly interesting for the Beggars Fair which is held here every Saturday evening. There are practically no pawn shops in Cuzco, but this fair takes their place. We were told it was an excellent opportunity to obtain bargains. It may be so for the natives, but as we were branded at once as "foreigners who had plenty of money," the prices of everything were put up to the highest possible notch and kept there. I was surprised at the amount of old rubbish, rusty nails, bits of broken pottery, and worn-out second-hand clothing, hundreds of things that one rarely sees exposed for sale in a pawn shop, and many on which no one but a junk dealer would advance a penny. As a picturesque spectacle, however, the Fair was most attractive. The plaza was lit up by smoking torches and crowded with a swarm of bargain hunters who jostled each other noisily up and down the long lines of traders seated on the ground behind their wares.

Nearly all the fairs in the Andes are held on Sunday mornings. The market-places are usually entirely deserted in the evening. I suppose in this fair it would not do to expose cast-off household treasures to the full light of day. Not only is the chance of making a sale much greater when the article can only be seen by torch-light, but the newly-poor individual, who is forced to bring hither his household goods, may more easily avoid the scrutiny of his newly-rich neighbors.

Looming up in the darkness, above the torches, the tall tower of the Franciscan church added a touch of solemnity to the scene. One afternoon we had an opportunity to visit the monastery and examine the beautiful wood-carvings in the choir. Like all the Franciscan establishments that we visited, the rule of the order is strictly enforced, the gardens are well kept, and although one can easily see that the Order has seen better days, there is little to criticise.

The Great Plaza of Cuzco, once much larger than it is now, and the scene of many Inca carnivals, is still very attractive. On its east side stands the massive cathedral and its chapels, said to have been built entirely of stones taken from Inca palaces near by.

On the south are the beautifully carved stone towers of what was formerly the Church of the Jesuits. Flanking these are picturesque two-story buildings with red-tiled roofs and overhanging wooden balconies supported by a row of columns and arches. In the arcades numerous small tradesmen display their wares. On the west and north of the plaza are more two-story houses with arcades filled with interesting little booths. Here, and on the stones of the Plaza, are cloth merchants who have gathered their wares from England and the Continent, North and South America; venders of pottery and Quichua toys, made in the neighborhood; market gardeners with corn and potatoes; and peddlers of every variety of article imaginable; some protected from the rain by cloth shelters that look as though they had been taken from the top of a prairie schooner in the "days of '49"; others squatting on the rough pavement, their wares spread out on the skins of sheep or llamas, exposed to wind and weather.

The Plaza has had a varied history. Perhaps its most tragic day was when it witnessed the death of Tupac Amaru. It was on the morning of the 18th of May, 1781, that the Inca was brought forth to his execution from the old Jesuit church. In order to prevent a repetition of Indian uprisings, such as he had started, the Spanish authorities felt it necessary to practice the most diabolical cruelties on both him and his wife. She was placed on a lofty scaffold, her tongue was cut out, and an attempt was made to garrote her with an iron screw. When it was found that her neck was so small that she could not be strangled in this manner, the executioners placed a lasso around her neck and pulled and hauled until she was dead. After witnessing the death of his wife, the Inca was taken into the centre of the square, his tongue was cut out, and his body was drawn and quartered by four horses.

The immediate effect of his revolution was to cause laws to be promulgated prohibiting the use of the native language, ordering the Indians to give up their national customs and to destroy all their musical instruments. Fortunately, these laws were not carried out. In fact, the Quichua tongue is

SACSAHUAMAN

THE CATHEDRAL—THE JESUIT CHURCH—THE PLAZA-CUZCO

still used to a large extent. It was supposed by Sir Clements Markham and other travellers fifty years ago that owing to the constantly increasing corruption of the ancient dialect and the introduction of Spanish modes of expression, the language of the Incas would soon be a thing of the past. We found, on the contrary, that nine out of ten Indians, even those who occupied stalls in the market-place of the largest cities, either could not or would not converse in Spanish. There was usually an Indian in the crowd who was willing to act as an interpreter, but the great majority of the people seem to have no acquaintance with Spanish. Furthermore, we found that the Spanish-speaking residents all recognize the necessity of learning Quichua.

The Prefect of Cuzco put his orderly at our disposal for the entire time of our stay. He proved to be most useful and agreeable. A word from him opened to us the doors of monasteries and churches, and his knowledge of prices enabled us to get examples of Quichua handiwork without being obliged to pay much more than the regular price. In our shopping excursions whenever we began to accumulate more Indian toys and trinkets than we could easily carry in our pockets, the orderly would summon the next police officer and tell him to act as our porter. It was rather hard to keep from laughing. Imagine a Broadway policeman toddling up Murray Hill carrying bundles for a foreign delegate to a Scientific Congress!

After my experience in the La Paz jail, I was curious to see what that of Cuzco might be like. Our obliging cicerone willingly consented to show all there was to be seen. The jail consists of an old-fashioned Spanish dwelling built around a large courtyard. Into this inclosure all classes of prisoners are put without any regard as to whether they are awaiting trial or condemned to life imprisonment. There did not seem to be any cells, and the forty or fifty prisoners were enjoying themselves after the fashion of the inmates of English prisons of the eighteenth century. The Government's provision for food does not include any luxuries, but it is possible for the prisoners to earn money and purchase what they need. So far as we could see, there was no forced labor, and the men were thrown entirely on their own resources. Several were busily working at hand-looms making ponchos which they were glad enough to sell. Others had cups carved out of horns. One unfortunate, who happened to be asleep at the time of our visit, sent to the hotel a gaudily painted trinket with a note saying that he hoped we would purchase it for a good price, as he was much in need of funds. On the whole, although the building was old, dilapidated, and quite inadequate, according to our ideas, the prisoners seemed to be having a good time, and there was no evidence of cruelty. The Quichuas are such a mild, inoffensive folk that the jailers do not have the same incentive to punish them severely as do those in La Paz who have to deal with the cantankerous Aymarás.

On the south side of the historic plaza, next door to the Jesuit Church, is the University of Cuzco, rather squalid by comparison with the church, but containing some fine stone cloisters. It was founded in 1598, thirty-eight years before Harvard College. I had a very pleasant call on its distinguished Rector, a well-read lawyer. The principal work of the University at present consists of training men for the law. According to the annual report of the Rector, during the year 1907 the University conferred the degree of Bachelor of Philosophy and Letters on four candidates, that of Bachelor of Jurisprudence on two, Bachelor of Political Science on two, and Doctor of Jurisprudence on four. There are eighteen instructors. They receive salaries of $35 a month, and give, on the average, one hundred and thirty-five lectures a year. The Faculty of Letters has a three-year course and thirty-three students. The Faculty of Jurisprudence, a five-year course and forty-six students. The Faculty of Political Science, a three-year course and twenty-four students. The Section of Natural Science, a three-year course and nine students. The total income for the year is in the neighborhood of $10,000. Of this the Government gives $5500, and the rest is made up largely of students' fees. One source of revenue for 1907 was $40 in fines levied on the members of the Faculty, "for failing to attend their classes and for other acts"!

The question of the education of South American youth is an interesting one. The opinion of the majority of British residents has been well expressed by an English mining engineer who has recently published a book on Peru. He says: "The Spanish-American youth educated in the United States, is not a happy product. London is the real home for the cosmopolitan refinement suited to their character"!

South American institutions of learning are built on such different lines from those in the United States that it seems to me extremely unlikely that a large number of students from South America will ever come to American universities. Ought we to do anything to encourage more to come? Spanish-Americans now studying in the States are devoting their attention chiefly to engineering and dentistry. Very few South Americans are likely to care for our academic or collegiate course or anything corresponding to it. It does not fit in at all with their customary scheme of education. To the average South American, a "college" means a kind of high school from which a student graduates to enter at once upon his professional studies. At first glance it looks like the familiar German idea of a gymnasium course followed immediately by professional studies in the university. But it would be unfair both to the gymnasium and the colegio to place their curriculum in parallel columns.

A large number of physicians in South America claim to have studied in Paris. The dentists usually advertise the fact that they were educated in Philadelphia or New York. Lawyers rarely ever receive any special training outside of the local university. On the other hand, while a large percentage of the native civil engineers are trained in the local engineering schools, a very considerable number have studied abroad. It is a generally recognized fact in South America, outside of Argentina and Chile, that the best engineers are Americans.

On the whole I am not disposed to agree with those who disparage American training for Latin-American youth. I am inclined to believe that it increases their efficiency more than the "cosmopolitan refinement" of London.

CHAPTER XX

SACSAHUAMAN

To defend Cuzco from attack by enemies coming from the north, the Incas built a great fortress on a hill overlooking the city. To reach it, the easiest way is to take a mule and ride through Cuzco's narrow streets, up the ravine to the ancient gateway in the east side of the hill. At first sight it might seem ridiculous not to walk, as the fortress in only 600 feet above the city. But Cuzco has an elevation of 11,500 feet, and hill-climbing at this altitude is best done on mule-back.

The Prefect kindly supplied us mules and an escort. On our way we passed the church of Los Nazarenes whose superstructure is laid on ancient walls that are noteworthy because of the many serpents that are carved in relief on the stones. Among the crude pottery dishes that I bought in the streets of La Paz was one decorated with these same little wriggling serpents.

Beyond Los Nazarenes the street narrowed until presently it became simply a path in a rocky gorge. As we entered the gorge there was at first little to be seen. Then in its narrowest and most easily defended part we came suddenly upon a pile of massive rocks, roughly hewn. Huge blocks of stone, five or six feet high, slightly rounded off and accu rately fitted together, are here built into a gateway twelve feet high that opens into a passage defended by a wall of large boulders. This leads to the hilltop. On the side toward the city, the slope is nearly precipitous, but the approach was made even more difficult near the summit by a series of three terraces each twelve or fourteen feet high. There is nothing remarkable about the summit except the beautiful view of Cuzco which one gets from here.

The immediate front of the hill just below the upper terraces is extremely steep. About half-way down to the city the spur broadens and flattens out. It was there the first Inca built his palace. On the lower continuation of this spur, between two rivulets, the palaces and temples of the later Incas were built.

It is the north side of Sacsahuaman, the side away from Cuzco, that is the chief object of interest. Here the slope is very gentle and it was necessary to fortify the place artificially. Furthermore, it was on this side that attacks might be expected, not only from the savages of the Amazonian wilds, but also from the hostile tribes of the Andean plateau, including the Caras of Ecuador. Accordingly, here the Incas exerted their utmost skill in the construction of a powerful line of defence.

The fortifications extend for a third of a mile entirely across the back of the hill, and are flanked by steep valleys at each end. They consist of three lines of zigzag terraces, one above another, each faced with walls of colossal boulders, some of them twelve feet in diameter. The lower terrace has an average height of about twenty-five feet; the middle and upper ones are some six feet less. There are few sights in the world more impressive than these Cyclopean walls.

The Incas were accustomed to build great terraces and I have seen them in many places in Peru. In every other case, however, the terrace walls are straight, or nearly so. Here, although the walls are parallel, they are also zigzag and consist for the entire length of salients and reëntrant angles. The apex of each salient in the lower wall is usually formed by a conspicuously large block, twenty-five feet high and ten or twelve feet thick.

The size and strength of the walls and the employment of salients which enabled the defenders to cover the entire face of the fortification with a flanking fire, a device unknown even to the European Crusaders, made the Inca fortress practically impregnable. It was certainly quite secure from the assaults of any Indian assailants, armed only with such primitive weapons as bows and arrows, slings and spears.

Next to the colossal size of the stones which the builders used for the lower wall, the most impressive thing is the care they took to fit the stones together without cement, so that they should stand for ages.

It is said that most of the smaller stones have been carried off for building purposes in the city. Be this as it may, what remains is the most impressive spectacle of man's handiwork that I have ever seen in America. Photographs absolutely fail to

A SECTION OF THE LOWER TERRACE, SACSAHUAMAN

do it justice, for at best they show only a few boulders, a small part of one of the walls. If taken far enough away to show the whole fort, the eye loses all sense of the great size of the stone units owing to the fact that they are so much larger than any stones to which it is accustomed.

The Inca author, Garcilasso de la Vega, wrote, in the sixteenth century, as follows of Sacsahuaman: "This was the greatest and most superb of the edifices that the Incas raised to demonstrate their majesty and power. Its greatness is incredible to those who have not seen it.... It passes the power of imagination to conceive how so many and so great stones could be so accurately fitted together as scarcely to admit the insertion of the point of a knife between them. And all of this is the more wonderful as they had no squares or levels to place on the stones and ascertain if they would fit together. How often must they have taken up and put down the stones to ascertain if the joints were perfect! Nor had they cranes, or pulleys, or other machinery whatever.... But what is most marvellous of the edifice is the incredible size of the stones, and the astonishing labor of bringing them together and placing them." Compare this with what a recent writer on the Caroline Islands says, in describing the colossal stone ruins on the Island of Lele near Kusaie: "Looking at their solid outlines, seamed and furrowed with the rain and sun of untold generations, one cannot help marvelling at the ingenuity and skill of these primitive engineers, in moving, lifting, and poising such huge and unwieldy masses of rock into their present position, where these mighty structures, shadowed by great forest trees, stand defying Time's changing seasons and the fury of tropic elements."

Also this from Captain Cook's "Voyages": "The platforms are faced with hewn stones of a very large size. They used no sort of cement, yet the joints are exceedingly close and the stones mortised and tenoned one into another in a very artful manner and the side walls were not perpendicular but sloping a little inwards." This is an accurate description of Sacsahuaman. Yet Captain Cook never came to the highlands of Peru and probably never even saw a picture of these walls. In this paragraph he is describing the stone ruins on Easter Island.[3]

The resemblances between the ruins of upper Peru and those of Easter Island and the Caroline Islands offer a remarkably interesting field for ethnological speculation. Unfortunately as yet they have told us but little of the builders of Sacsahuaman.

It is generally conceded that the fortress was commenced in the reign of the Inca Viracocha, two hundred years before the Spanish Conquest. Whether this tradition is well founded, it is difficult to say. It may be due to the fact that the name "Viracocha," as Sir Clements Markham points out, was simply the term applied to a powerful character, a term of admiration, equivalent to the word "gentleman" in English.

Whoever built it, the task was certainly heroic. Many of the stones were un-

[3] In Paymaster Thompson's report of his visit to Easter Island, he gives drawings and photographs of walls that bear a striking resemblance to Sacsahuaman. There is the same peculiar close fitting of one stone to another, the same striking size of the stones and lack of cement in the joints. See also Cook's Voyage Around the World in 1772-1775, London, 1777.

doubtedly quarried near by. As for methods of transportation, we know that the Incas understood the manufacture of strong cables, for they built suspension bridges across many of the chasms of central Peru. By the aid of these cables and of wooden rollers, it would have been entirely possible to have dragged very large stones for a considerable distance, up inclined planes. Although they had no draft animals, llamas being only accustomed to carrying, they had thousands of patient Quichuas at their disposal, whose combined efforts, extended over long lines of cables, would have been amply sufficient to move even the largest of these great blocks. Nevertheless, when one considers the difficulty of fitting together two irregular boulders, both of them weighing eight or ten tons, one's admiration for the skill of these old builders knows no bounds.

The modern Peruvians are very fond of speculating as to the method which the Incas employed to make their stones fit so perfectly. One of the favorite stories is that the Incas knew of a plant whose juices rendered the surface of a block so soft that the marvellous fitting was accomplished by rubbing the stones together for a few moments with this magical plant juice!

Discussion and speculation will undoubtedly continue indefinitely, yet one can come to at least two conclusions: the Incas had an unlimited amount of labor at their disposal, and time was no object.

Furthermore, they were apparently very fond of playing the game of stone-cutting. From the fortress we rode across the little grassy plain that separates the terraces from the rocks of Rodadero hill. On its summit, terraces have been hewn out of the solid rock, and it is said that the Incas were fond of sitting here to watch their patient workmen engaged in putting together the magnificent walls of Sacsahuaman. On the north side of the hill, the rock has been worn into grooves by the water and polished by the ponchos of generations of pleasure-seekers who have used this curious formation as a "toboggan slide." Our guides assured us that the habit of coasting down this hill on ponchos was started by the Incas. At all events, it is still a favorite Sunday amusement.

In the rolling country north of the Rodadero are numbers of rocks and ledges that have been carved into fantastic seats, nooks, and crannies by a people who seem to have taken a keen delight in stone-carving for its own sake. It is difficult to explain in any other way the maze of niches and shelves, seats and pedestals that are scattered about on every hand. Writers are accustomed to label as "Inca thrones" every stone seat they find in the mountains of Peru. But here the ledges are carved so irregularly as almost to bewilder the imagination.

A mile away to the northeast we discovered the dim outlines of a large amphitheatre where the Incas may have gathered on the grassy slopes to

AN INCA VASE FROM CUZCO

ARTICLES OF DRESS AND A DECORATED MULE HALTER FROM CUZCO

watch games and religious festivals. It offers an attractive field for digging, as it seems to have been entirely overlooked hitherto.

On our way back to the city we were invited to rest at Sr. Lomellini's country house which is built in the gardens of Manco Capac, the first Inca. The entrance is through a gate in the wall of the ancient outer terrace. Near the house stands a section of the palace wall, thirty feet long and ten feet high, containing a recessed door and window. In the outer terrace the stones are of irregular shapes while in this wall they are practically rectangular. In his house, Sr. Lomellini has collected a number of extremely interesting specimens of the ceramic art of the Incas. The most striking are two very large vases resembling in shape and marking the small one figured here. This is only six inches high; those are nearly three feet. There are quite a number of imperfect specimens in the American Museum of Natural History.

After the gardener had given us a handful of roses, we left the precincts of the ancient Inca and clattered down the hill over the rough cobblestones to the picturesque sights—and distressing smells—of modern Cuzco.

CHAPTER XXI
THE INCA ROAD TO ABANCAY

There are several ways of going from Cuzco to Lima. The easiest and most frequented now is by rail to Mollendo and then by steamer to Callao, the seaport of Lima. Before the days of railroads the common route was by mule via Ayacucho, Pisco, and the Coast. Since the building of the Oroya railroad and more particularly since the extension of the line south to Huancayo, instead of going west to the coast from Ayacucho the overland traveller continues north to the Jauja valley until he meets the railway. It was this road that we proposed to take.

For centuries the overland trail from Cuzco to Huancayo and the north was the most celebrated highway in Peru. The Incas used it in their conquests and improved it. When Atahualpa fell into the clutches of Pizarro, the largest part of his golden ransom was brought over this road. After the death of the Inca, Pizarro in his march on Cuzco found this road most convenient for his little cavalcade. During the civil wars that followed the conquest this highway was repeatedly the scene of action. For three hundred years it was replete with historic incident. Finally, the road that had seen the beginnings of Spain's conquest, was destined to see the

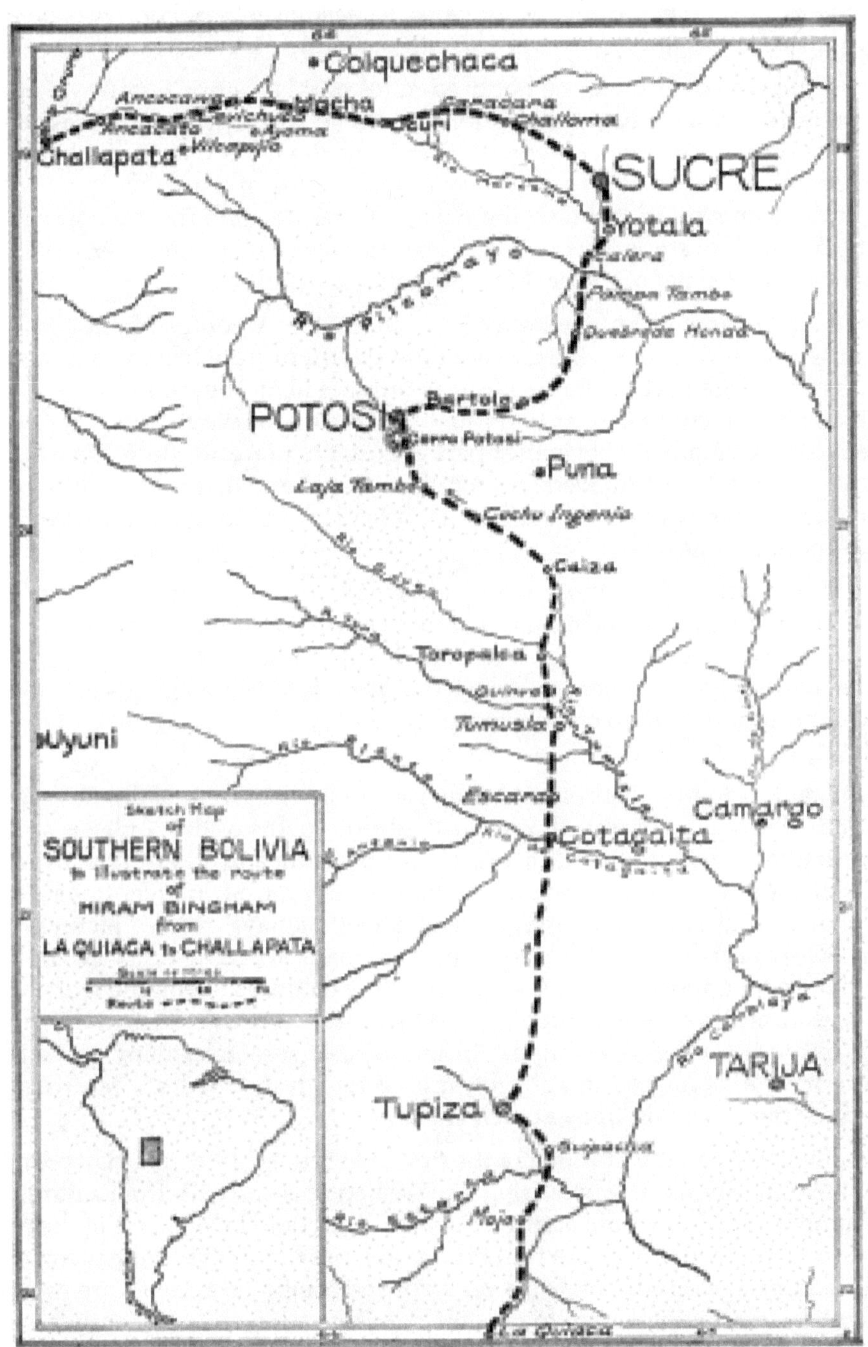

SOUTHERN BOLIVIA

bitter end. For, in 1824, it witnessed the last campaign, the final act in the drama of Spain's Colonial Empire, when La Serna, last viceroy of Peru, was defeated by the patriot forces under General Sucre in the battle of Ayacucho.

In journeying over the three hundred miles of this historic highway, I should have preferred to have hired mules for the whole trip, but nobody was willing to undertake the contract. We were told that "in the good old times" before the railway came to Cuzco, it was very easy to hire mules; and arrieros were willing enough to go anywhere, but now there was so little demand for this sort of thing that the supply had stopped. The best we could do was to get an arriero to take us to Abancay, the capital of the next Department.

Two American civil engineers whom I had met in Arequipa had told me that the journey from Cuzco to Huancayo would be full of trouble and countless difficulties, as a large part of the region was uninhabited! They said that if it were possible to buy a tent in Cuzco, to do so, by all means, as we should otherwise be obliged to spend many nights in the open, exposed to rain and snow. They had not been over the road but had lived for months in Cuzco and had "heard all about it." I mention this merely as an instance of the difficulty of finding out the truth about South America by hearsay.

We now learned from those who had actually been over the road that while there were no inns to be encountered anywhere except in Ayacucho, it would be only owing to extremely bad luck if we failed to reach the shelter of a village every night. Accordingly we contented ourselves with a few canned goods and kitchen utensils and found them to be all that was necessary.

In the Peruvian highlands the rains commence in November and continue until the end of March. February is supposed to be the worst of all. During that month the discomfort of travelling over the bridle-paths of the Andes is so great that the natives never undertake a journey for pleasure and stay at home as much as possible. Yet it was February that we had chosen for our march. It was "Hobson's choice," but I was not sorry. Several travellers have given a picture of the region as it appears in the dry season when the roads are comparatively good. We were to have an opportunity of seeing what they could be like in the worst of the rainy season, and we were further favored by the fact that this particular February turned out to be "the rainiest month of the rainiest season that any one remembered to have experienced in Peru for at least twenty-five years." In a word, we were to see the mountain trails at their worst.

We left Cuzco on the morning of the first of February, 1909. The day promised ill. Rain fell in torrents. The preceding day we had received calls from a number of local dignitaries, all of whom assured us that they would be on hand in the morning to escort us out of town. But the continuous downpour overcame their conscientious scruples. Even the Prefect's polite orderly, who had been unremitting in his attention, was glad enough to take our hint that we were sufficiently honored by his accompanying us for three blocks from the hotel.

The Prefect had been very solicitous about our welfare and, although we assured him that we preferred to travel without a military escort, he insisted that a sergeant and at least one soldier should accompany us as long as we were in his

Department. I never discovered why he was so insistent. There was no danger, and highway robbery is unheard of in Peru. Possibly he was afraid that the delegados might otherwise go hungry at villages where inhospitable, half-starved Quichuas would say that there was no food to be had; or he may have thought it undignified for us to travel without an escort. Whatever his reasons, he meant well and it was not a case of graft, for the soldiers were ordered to accompany us at the expense of the government.

We started off in a northwesterly direction, leaving Sacsahuaman on the right. After climbing out of the Cuzco valley we descended gradually to the great plain of Anta, famous as the scene of numerous battles in the wars of the Incas. We crossed it by the ancient Inca road, a stony pathway five or six feet wide, with ditches and swamps on either side. The Peruvians have allowed it to fall into decay, and for a good part of the distance it has disappeared. At noon we reached Puquiura, a village with a plaza very like that of Tiahuanaco. At half past three, after making a long detour in order to avoid the swamps and ponds that in the wet season cover the direct road, we crossed a little stone bridge and rode into the dismal plaza of the old Indian town of Huarocondo. This is only a few miles from Urubamba, and the remarkably interesting ruins of Ollantaytambo, which have been so graphically described by Squier.

Unfortunately we had no time to visit them and took instead the road to the southwest. Skirting the hills north of the plain of Anta, we passed several great terraces a third of a mile long and fourteen or fifteen feet high, and towards evening entered Zurita, a small Indian town. Here we were directed to the house of a hospitable Gobernador where we found that two Peruvian travellers had preceded us.

As in other houses of the better class in this vicinity, the entrance was through a large gate into a courtyard. Opposite the gate was a two-story building with a balcony running the length of the second floor. On another side of the court were smaller structures one of which had a wide stone verandah where the arrieros and the soldiers piled up the saddles and bags and spread their blankets for the night. Two unfortunate parrots, cold, sickly, and bedraggled, had their perches attached to the posts of the verandah.

An hour after our arrival, four Indian alcaldes and tenientes carrying silver-tipped canes as symbols of office, presented themselves in the courtyard in answer to the summons of the Gobernador. When that official appeared on the balcony, they humbly removed their hats and stood in silence while he told them how many bundles of fresh barley straw to bring for our mules. An hour later they returned with other Indians who, acting under their orders, brought the cebada. The conversation was carried on in Quichua, which we were unable to follow, but the Gobernador said that for the fodder the alcaldes wanted one sol, a Peruvian silver dollar worth forty-eight cents. This we cheerfully gave him, whereupon, in a most unabashed manner, he put the sol in his pocket, took out a few small coins worth about half a sol and threw them down into the courtyard where they were gratefully picked up by the alcaldes.

We left Zurita the next morning, accompanied by the Gobernador and our fellow lodgers. They were all well-mounted on excellent horses. The horsemen of this vicinity affect a bit of harness that seems to be a relic of the trappings of Spanish war horses. The crupper is covered with a V-shaped piece of solid leather elaborately stamped and marked. From it hang hip straps supporting very loose breeching that dangles almost to the points of the hocks and actually rests on the ham strings. Although it is of no use whatever, and in fact, actually impedes the horse's action, the effect is rather picturesque.

Leaving the arriero and his pack mules to follow in charge of our military escort, we pushed on at a good pace with our friends and found ourselves at noon at Challabamba on the divide that separates the waters of the river Urubamba from those of the Apurimac. In marked distinction to the grassy, treeless plain of Anta from which we had just ascended, we saw before us deep green, wooded valleys.

The trail, a rocky stairway not unlike the bed of a mountain torrent, led us rapidly into a warm tropical region whose dense foliage and tangled vines were grateful enough after the bleak mountain plateau. Beautiful yellow broom flowers were abundant. The air was filled with the fragrance of heliotrope. Parti-colored lantanas ran riot through a maze of agaves and hanging creepers. We had entered a new world.

A steep descent brought us to the town of Limatambo where there are interesting terraces and other evidences of an Inca fortress. The valley of the Limatambo River is here extremely narrow and the fortifications were well placed to defend an enemy coming against Cuzco from the west and north.

Rain had been falling most of the day and the river Limatambo had risen considerably. The ford was quite impassable, and we were obliged to use a frail improvised bridge over which our mules crept very cautiously sniffing doubtfully as it bent under their weight. Soon afterwards we crossed the river Blanco and left the old trail, which goes through the Indian village of Mollepata, described by Squier as "a collection of wretched huts on a high shelf of the mountain with a tumbled-down church, a drunken Governor who was also keeper of a hovel which was called the post-house, and a priest as dissolute as the Governor ... a place unsurpassed in evil repute by any in Peru." Fortunately for us, since the days of Squier's visit, an enterprising Peruvian has carved a sugar plantation out of the luxuriant growth on the mountain side, at La Estrella. Here we were given an extremely cordial welcome although Sr. Montes, the owner,—the fame of whose hospitality had reached even to Cuzco,—was not at home. Our military escort did not arrive until nearly three hours later, with a sad story of wretched animals and narrow escapes.

We were considerably surprised to find here at La Estrella an excellent piano in fairly good tune. It had been brought from Cuzco on the shoulders of Quichua bearers. This seems extraordinary enough, but before the days of the railroad, pianos were formerly carried by Indians all the way from the Pacific Coast to Cuzco. The next time I saw five stalwart Irish truckmen groaning and shaking under the weight of an upright piano which they had to carry fifty feet from the truck into a house in New Haven, I wondered what they would think of half-starved Indians who could carry it from sea-level over mountains fourteen thousand feet high.

The presence of the piano at La Estrella meant that here as everywhere else we were to be favored with the strains of the "Tonquinoise" and "Quand L'Amour Meurt." This is the kind of music that most appeals to the South Americans. Wherever there was a piano in the heart of Peru or Bolivia, it mattered not whether the place was Potosí or Arequipa, these tunes were everlastingly drummed into our ears.

The next morning we descended from the canefields of La Estrella by an extremely precipitous winding trail. In places it seemed as though our heavily-laden mules must surely loose their footing and roll down the fifteen hundred feet to the raging Apurimac River below. At length, however, we came to an excellent modern bridge which we were actually able to cross without dismounting, something that rarely happens with the bridges of Peru.

In the old days a wonderfully lofty suspension bridge made by the Indians in the Peruvian fashion, was the only means of crossing this river. Vivid pictures of it, no two alike, are given in Squier's "Peru," Markham's "Cuzco and Lima," and Lt. Gibbon's "Exploration of the Valley of the Amazon." Although they all differ as to its height above the water and its length, all were greatly impressed by the remarkable cañon that it crossed. Gibbon says "the bridge was ... 150 feet above the dark green waters"; Sir Clements Markham, who crossed the bridge two years later says, "the bridge spanned the chasm in a graceful curve at a height of full 300 feet above the river." As he crossed it in the middle of March just at the end of the rainy season when it may be supposed the waters were high, while Lt. Gibbon crossed it in August, the middle of the dry season, when the river is very low, the contrast between their estimates of the height of the bridge above the river is all the more striking. Unfortunately it has disappeared and travellers can no longer dispute over its dimensions.

The scenery to-day was superb; the great green mountains piling up on one another, their precipitous sides streaked with many lovely waterfalls. Green parrots overhead and yellow iris underfoot lent additional color to the scene. To add to our joy

THE GOBERNADOR OF CURAHUASI AND HIS FAMILY

the sun shone all day long. A comparatively easy journey over steep but well-travelled mountain-trails brought us to the town of Curahuasi where we were met by Lt. Caceres, who had been directed to act as our escort, and who proved to be a most genial and exceptionally spirited young Peruvian, a member of an old and distinguished family.

Immediately on our arrival at Curahuasi we were taken to the local telegraph office where Caceres sent off an important message announcing the approach of the "distinguished visitors"! To recompense us for waiting while he wrote the messages, bottles of stout were opened and toasts solemnly proposed. We expected to spend the night in the town, but found that the Gobernador, who desired us to be his guests, lived a couple of miles up the valley at Trancapata on the road to Abancay.

Although his establishment was a primitive one, it was charmingly situated on the edge of a deep ravine. The dining-room was an old verandah overlooking the gorge, and we enjoyed the view and the generous hospitality quite as much as though the villa had had all modern conveniences. In fact, neither of us had ever before experienced such a cordial welcome from a total stranger. We were to learn, however, before we left the Department, that such friendliness was characteristic of nearly every village and town that enjoyed the over-lordship of the genial Prefect of Apurimac.

The next morning when we finally managed to bid our cordial host good-by, it was not until he had accompanied us for a long distance up the deep valley. As we climbed the ascent under a bright sun, a wonderful panorama spread itself out behind us, the snowy peaks of Mt. Sargantay gleaming in the distance. We soon left the region of luxurious vegetation, lantanas, cacti, and tropical plants, and ran into a chilly drizzle at an elevation of thirteen thousand feet. Then we descended, came out of the rain, and had a delightful ride over a trail lined with masses of blue salvia and pink begonias.

At last we caught glimpses of the fields of sugarcane that have made Abancay famous throughout Peru. To one who has seen the broad canefields of Hawaii or the great plantations of Cuba and Porto Rico, the fame of this rather small district would be surprising. But after passing over the bleak highlands of Peru and experiencing the chill of the mountain climate, one feels more ready to appreciate that a warm, rich valley, eight thousand feet above the sea, where sugar can be easily raised, is a matter for profound congratulation.

A long descent down a very bad road brought us into a charming region. A mile from Abancay itself we were met by the sub-Prefect and a dozen sugar planters and caballeros who had taken the trouble to saddle their horses and come out to give us a fitting welcome. After an interchange of felicitations, we clattered gayly into town and were taken at once to the Prefecture. Here Hon. J. J. Nuñes, the genial Prefect, gave us a cordial reception and apologized for the fact that he had quite a large family and could not give us suitable sleeping quarters in the Prefecture. As it was, he placed the local club entirely at our disposal. We were only too glad to accept, for the club's two pleasant rooms overlooked the little plaza and commanded a very pretty view of the ancient church and steep hills beyond.

Hardly had we had time to turn around in our new quarters before the Prefect came to make a formal call. He at once broached the subject of the ruins of Choqquequirau and begged us to visit them.

It seems that in Quichua, the language of the Incas, still spoken by a majority of the mountaineers of Peru, Choqquequirau means a "Cradle of Gold." Attracted by this romantic name and by the lack of all positive knowledge concerning its last defenders, several attempts had been made during the past century to explore its ruins and to discover the treasure which it is supposed the Incas hid here instead of allowing it to fall into the hands of Pizarro with the ransom of Atahualpa. Owing to the very great difficulty of reaching the site of the ruins a tradition had grown up that the Incas built a great city that once contained over fifteen thousand inhabitants, high up on the mountain-side, six thousand feet above the river Apurimac. That the tradition had a basis of fact had been demonstrated occasionally by bold mountain-climbers who succeeded in reaching a part of the ruins.

We were told that the first man to reach there went and came alone. All he saw was a stone wall which he reached late in the afternoon, exhausted and without food. He slept in its shelter, left his gun as proof that he had been there, and came away early the next morning, anxious only to get home. A generation later a small party of adventurers succeeded in reaching the ruins with enough food to last them for two days. They excavated two or three holes in a vain effort to find buried treasure and returned with a tale of sufferings that kept any one from following their example for twenty years. They brought back reports of rocky "palaces, paved squares, temples, prisons, and baths," all crumbling away beneath luxuriant tropical vegetation. Then a local magistrate, dreaming of untold riches, so ran the tale, endeavored to construct a path by which it might be possible to reach Choqquequirau and to maintain a transportation service of Indian carriers who could provide workmen with food while they were engaged in making a systematic effort to unearth the "Cradle of Gold." This man had at his disposal the services of a company of soldiers and a large number of Indians, and it is said that he expended a large amount of time and money in his quest. He succeeded in reaching the top of the ridge 12,000 feet above the river and 6000 feet above Choqquequirau, but was unable to scale the precipices that surround the ruins, and all his labor came to nought. Others tried to utilize the path that he had made, but without success, until the present Prefect of the department of Apurimac, Honorable J. J. Nuñes, assumed office and became interested in the local traditions. Under his patronage, a company of treasure-seekers was formed and several thousand dollars subscribed.

The first difficulty that they encountered was the construction of a bridge over the frightful rapids of the Apurimac. All efforts failed. Not a Peruvian could be found willing to venture his life in the whirlpool rapids. Finally "Don Mariano," an aged Chinese peddler, who had braved the terrors of the Peruvian mountains for thirty years, dared to swim the river with a string tied to his waist. Then after much patient effort he succeeded in securing six strands of telegraph wire from which he hung short lengths of fibre rope and wove a mat of reeds two feet wide to serve as a foot path for a frail suspension bridge. Once on the other side, the company was able to use a part of the trail made twenty years ago, but even with that aid it took three months of hard work to surmount the difficulties that lay between the river and Choqquequirau. Cheered on by the enthusiastic Prefect and his aide, Lieut. Caceres, an exceptionally bold officer, the task which had defied all comers for four hundred years was accomplished. A trail that could be used by Indian bearers was constructed through twelve miles of mountain forest, over torrents and precipices, and across ravines from the river to the ruins.

With these and similar stories we were regaled by one and another of the local antiquarians, including the president of the treasure company and our friend the Prefect.

We felt at first as though we could not possibly spare the week which would be necessary for a visit that would be worth while. Furthermore we were not on the lookout for new Inca ruins and had never heard of Choqquequirau. But the enthusiasm of the Prefect and his friends was too much for us. The Prefect held it out as an extra inducement that no foreigners had ever visited Choqquequirau, a statement that I later found to be incorrect. Finally he said that President Leguia of Peru, knowing that we were to pass this way, had requested the company to suspend operations until we had had a chance to see the ruins in their original condition. In short so urgent were the Prefect's arguments, and so ready was he to make it easy for us, that we finally consented to go and see what his energy had uncovered.

That night he gave us an elaborate banquet to which he had invited fifteen of the local notables. After dinner we were shown the objects of interest that had been found at Choqquequirau, including several ancient shawl-pins and a few nondescript metallic articles. The most interesting was a heavy club fifteen inches long and rather more than two inches in diameter, square, with round corners, much like the wooden clubs with which the Hawaiians beat tapa. It has a yellowish tinge that gave rise to a story that it was pure gold. Unfortunately we had no means of analyzing it, but I presume it was made, like the ancient Inca axes, of copper hardened with tin.

The next afternoon, amidst a heterogeneous mess of canned provisions, saddles, rugs, and clothes, we packed, and received distinguished guests. Almost everyone who called told us that he was going to accompany us on the morrow, and we had visions of a general hegira from Abancay.

In the evening we were most hospitably entertained at one of the sugar estates. To this dinner a genial gathering came from far and near. The planters of Abancay are a fine class of caballeros, hospitable, courteous, and intelligent, kind to their working people, interested both in one another's affairs and in the news of the outside world. Many of them spend part of each year or two in Lima, and a few have travelled abroad.

One of our hosts had recently made an excursion to Choqquequirau, which "nearly killed him." He lost one mule: it slid down a precipice. He lamed another badly. On the whole, although urged to do so by his friends, he decided not to offer to go with us on the morrow. At least one man proposed to stay in Abancay!

CHAPTER XXII
THE CLIMB TO CHOQQUEQUIRAU

THE next morning, accompanied by a large cavalcade, we started for Cho-qquequirau. Most of our escort contented themselves with a mile or so, and then wishing us good luck, returned to Abancay. We did not blame them. Owing to unusually heavy rains, the trail was in a frightful state. Well-nigh impassable bogs, swollen torrents, avalanches of boulders and trees, besides the usual concomitants of a Peruvian bridle-path, cheered us on our way.

Soon after leaving our friends we had to ford a particularly dangerous torrent where the mules had all they could possibly do to keep their footing in the foamy waters. After the crossing we rested to watch Castillo, one of the soldiers who had been assigned to accompany us, cross the stream on foot. His mule, tired out by the dreadful trail, was being rested. It had forded the stream with the others and was standing by us watching the soldier take perilous leaps from boulder to boulder, where a misstep would have meant certain death. Hardly had Castillo gained our side of the stream when the mule decided to return to Abancay and plunged back across the dangerous ford. With a shout of rage, the soldier repeated his performance, gained the other side of the torrent, and started after the mule, now quite rested, and trotting off briskly for home. A chase of a mile and a half put Castillo into no very pleasant frame of mind, and the mule had little respite for the remainder of the day. At noon we stopped a few moments in the village of Cachora where the Prefect had instructed the Gobernador to prepare us a "suitable luncheon." This intoxicated worthy offered us instead many apologies, and we had to get along as best we could with three or four boiled eggs, all the village could provide.

All day long through rain and heavy mist that broke away occasionally to give us glimpses of wonderfully deep green valleys and hillsides covered with rare flowers, we rode along a slippery path that grew every hour more treacherous and difficult. In order to reach the little camp on the bank of the Apurimac that night, we hurried forward as fast as possible although frequently tempted to linger by the sight of acres of magnificent pink begonias and square miles of blue lupins. By five o'clock, we began to hear the roar of the great river seven thousand feet below us in the cañon. The Apurimac, which flows through the Ucayali to the Amazon, rises in a little lake near Arequipa, so far from the mouth of the Amazon that it may be said to be the parent stream of that mighty river. By the time it reaches this region, it is a raging torrent two hundred and fifty feet wide, and at this time of the year, over eighty feet deep. Its roaring voice can be heard so many miles away that it is called by the Quichuas, the Apurimac, or the "Great Speaker."

Our guide, the enthusiastic Caceres, declared that we had now gone far enough. As it was beginning to rain and the road from there on was "worse than anything we had as yet experienced," he said it would be better to camp for the night in an abandoned hut near by. His opinion was eagerly welcomed by two of the party, young men from Abancay, who were having their first real adventure, but the two Yankis decided that it was best to reach the river if possible. Caceres finally consented, and aided by the dare-devil Castillo, we commenced a descent that for tortuous turns and narrow escapes beat anything we had yet seen. Just as darkness came on, we encountered a large tree that had so fallen across our path as completely to block all progress. It seemed as though we must return to the hut. Half an hour's work enabled us to pass this obstacle only to reach a part of the hill-side where an avalanche had recently occurred. Here even the mules and horses trembled with fright as we led them across a mass of loose earth and stones which threatened to give way at any moment. Only two weeks previously, two mules had been lost here. Their crossing had started a renewal of the avalanche which had taken the poor animals along with it.

An hour after dark we came out on a terrace. The roar of the river was so great that we could scarcely hear Caceres shouting out that our troubles were now over and "all the rest was level ground." This turned out to be only his little joke. We were still a thousand feet above the river and a path cut in

A CHASM DOWN WHICH PLUNGED A SMALL CATARACT

THE WONDERFUL CAÑON OF THE APURIMAC

the face of a precipice had yet to be negotiated. In broad daylight we should never had dared to ride down the tortuous trail that led from the terrace to the bank of the river. But as it was quite dark and we were quite innocent of any danger we readily followed the cheery voice of our guide. The path is what is known as a corkscrew and descended the wall of the cañon by means of short turns each twenty feet long. At one end of each turn was the precipice, while at the other was a chasm down which plunged a small cataract which had a clear fall of seven hundred feet. Half way down the path my mule stopped, trembling, and I dismounted to find that in the darkness he had walked off the trail and had slid down the cliff to a ledge. How to get him back was a problem. It is not easy to back an animal up a steep hill, and there was no room in which to turn him around. It was such a narrow escape that when I got safely back onto the trail, I decided to walk the rest of the way and let the mule go first, preferring to have him fall over the precipice alone if that were necessary.

Two thirds of the way down the descent came the crux of the whole matter, for here the path crossed the narrow chasm close to and directly in front of the cataract, and in the midst of its spray. There was no bridge. To be sure, the waterfall was only three feet wide, but it was pitch dark. As I could not see the other side of the chasm, I did not dare to jump alone, but remounted my mule, held my breath, and gave him both spurs at once. His jump was successful.

Ten minutes later we saw the welcome light of the master of the camp who came out to guide us through a thicket of mimosa trees that grew on the lower terrace just above the river.

The camp consisted of two huts, six by seven, built of reeds. Here we passed a most uncomfortable night. Mr. Hay has described the next few hours so vividly in his diary that, with his permission, I am going to quote his account of it.

"Our luggage, including the folding cots, did not arrive that night till very late, so we slept on benches made of bamboo poles, in our boots, under an open thatch-roofed shelter. During the night the Prefect's secretary, el periodista, either in exuberance over reaching the bottom of the mountain in safety, or being unstrung on account of his recent experience, or simply because he was a bounder, fired his revolver off at three different times, the ball fortunately passing through the roof each time. I must admit that I was so sound asleep as to hear only one of the shots, though I was so near the "young idea" that I could have touched him with my hand. Even he, though, wearied of that form of amusement after a time, and quiet was restored until 3 A.M. At that hour a rooster, who had quietly been resting with his women-folk on a pole over our heads, decided that dawn was coming on, or if it wasn't, ought to be, and showed us conclusively what a healthy pair of feathered lungs, in a rarified atmosphere, was capable of. He was within reach, but I bided my time. Not half enough notice had been taken of the alarm to suit him, and I saw the chest of Sr. Chanticlerio expand for a supreme effort. He raised himself to his full height and let loose. With ever increasing volume the notes poured out, until just as it seemed he would burst, in the concluding notes of the anthem, I arose, and with the side of my hand, caught him in the place that needed it most. He summoned up the courage to give one defiant little crow three hours later. But his spirit was broken, and his style was cramped by the periodista, who, awake by this time, was firing at him with his revolver. There were no casualties."

While breakfast was being prepared we went out to take pictures and measurements of the bridge. This was 273 feet long by 32 inches wide, and the river 250 feet wide. "Don Mariano," the builder of the bridge, told us that when construction commenced, the water was nearly eighty feet below the bridge although at present the river had risen so that it was only twenty-five feet below it, an increase in depth of over fifty feet. An almost incredible bulk of water was roaring between its steep banks. It was estimated at 100 feet deep, and yet the water piled up on itself in such a way as to give the appearance of running against huge boulders in midstream.

We sent the Indian bearers ahead with our luggage. Pack animals could not possibly use the trail on the other side of the river and the bridge was not constructed to carry their weight. The surprising thing was that the Indians were very much afraid of the frail little bridge which Chinese courage and ingenuity had built, and crept gingerly across it on their hands and knees while they carried our luggage and supplies to the other side of the river. They had been accustomed for centuries to using frail suspension bridges much less strong in reality than this little structure. But they are not acquainted with the tenacity of wire, and it seemed the height of frivolity to them that we should be willing to trust our lives to such a small "rope." Yet the much larger fibre ropes of which their suspension bridges were constructed would not begin to stand the strain as well as these six telegraph wires.

After a breakfast of thin soup and boiled sweet potatoes, we girded ourselves for the ascent. The river at this point is about 5000 feet above sea-level. We had had little practice in mountain climbing, except on mule-back, for many months, and it seemed like a pretty serious undertaking to attempt to climb six thousand feet more to an elevation of 11,000 feet. This will sound tame enough to the experienced mountain climber although it was anything but easy for us. Our patient, long-suffering Quichua bearers, coming of a race that, at high altitudes, is in the habit of marching distances which appear incredibly long to those students of military history that have confined their attention to the movements of European troops, bore their burdens most cheerfully. At the same time they gave frequent evidence of great fatigue which was not at all to be wondered at under the circumstances.

Of one incident of the ascent Mr. Hay wrote: "Most of the party started long before the two 'Yanquis,' but in half an hour we caught up with

SUNRISE AT CHOQQUEQUIRAU

THE FRAIL LITTLE BRIDGE OVER THE APURIMAC

them. They had waylaid an Indian bearer and were having beer and other refreshments under a tree. Here we noticed an example of the height of generosity towards an Indian in Peru. This is to let him carry all day, among other things, the refreshments. Then take the beer, drink it, and return him the bottle. The bottle, be it noted, should be received with many expressions of thanks on the part of the Indian. We passed the revellers and plodded on up together. Unfortunately for history but fortunately for our nerves, at least, the periodista gave out soon after this and was forced to turn back. So the chronicle of the events at Choqquequirau must come only from the pen of an alien? Not for a minute! El periodista was ever with us in spirit, and the report for the Lima Journal fared far better at the hands of Imagination than it ever could have through plain Experience."

The enthusiastic Caceres kept shouting "valor" at the top of his lungs as evidence of his good spirits and in an effort to encourage the others. The two Yankis had a hard time of it and were obliged to stop and rest nearly every fifty feet.

At times the trail was so steep that it was easier to go on all fours than to attempt to maintain an erect attitude. Occasionally we crossed streams in front of waterfalls on slippery logs or treacherous little foot-bridges. At other times we clung to the face of rocky precipices or ascended by roughly constructed ladders from one elevation to another. Although the hillside was too precipitous to allow much forest growth, no small part of the labor of making the path had been the work of cutting through dense underbrush.

As we mounted, the view of the valley became more and more magnificent. Nowhere have I ever witnessed such beauty and grandeur as was here displayed. A white torrent raged through the cañon six thousand feet below us. Where its sides were not too precipitous to admit of vegetation, the steep slopes were covered with green foliage and luxuriant flowers. From the hilltops near us other slopes rose six thousand feet beyond and above to the glaciers and snow-capped summits of Mts. Sargantay and Soray. In the distance, as far as we could see, a maze of hills, valleys, tropical jungle, and snow-capped peaks held the imagination as though by a spell. Such were our rewards as we lay panting by the side of the little path when we had reached its highest point.

After getting our wind, we followed the trail westward, skirting more precipices and crossing other torrents, until, about two o'clock, we rounded a promontory and caught our first glimpse of the ruins of Choqquequirau on the slopes of a bold mountain headland 6000 feet above the river. Between the outer hilltop and the ridge connecting it with the snow-capped mountains, a depression or saddle had been terraced and levelled so as to leave a space for the more important buildings of the Inca stronghold.

At three o'clock we reached a glorious waterfall whose icy waters, coming probably from the glaciers on Soray, cooled our heads and quenched our thirst. We had now left our companions far behind, and were pushing slowly along through the jungle, when shortly before four o'clock we saw terraces in the near distance. Just as we began to enjoy the prospect of reaching Choqquequirau alone, Caceres and Castillo caught up with us. They had stayed behind in a futile attempt to encourage the Indian bearers, and the other adventurers to have more "valor." The others did not arrive until the next morning; not even the Quichua carriers on whom we depended for food and blankets.

Soon after our arrival, we clambered up to a little bit of flat ground, where evidently the Incas once cultivated their crops, to enjoy the view. Here we were discovered by a huge condor who proceeded to investigate the invaders of his domain. Apparently without moving a muscle, he sailed gracefully down in ever narrowing circles until we could see clearly not only his cruel beak and great talons, but even the whites of his eyes. We had no guns and not even a club with which to resist his attack. It was an awe-inspiring moment, for he measured at least twelve feet from tip to tip of wing. When within forty feet of us he decided not to disturb us, and seemingly without changing the position of a feather, soared off into space. We were told afterwards by Caceres and Castillo that they had been greatly alarmed by condors when they first commenced operations here.

Owing to the non-appearance of the carriers we passed an uncomfortable night in the smallest of the little thatched huts which the workmen had erected for their own use. It was scarcely three feet high and about six feet long by four feet wide. The day had been warm, and in our efforts to make climbing as easy as possible, we had divested ourselves of all our warm clothes. Notwithstanding the fact that a shelter tent was pulled down and wrapped around us for warmth, and stacks of dry grass piled about us, we were scarcely able to close our eyes for the cold and chilling dampness all night long.

The humidity was one hundred or nearly so during the four days which we spent on the mountain. Consequently we passed the majority of the time in thick mist or rain.

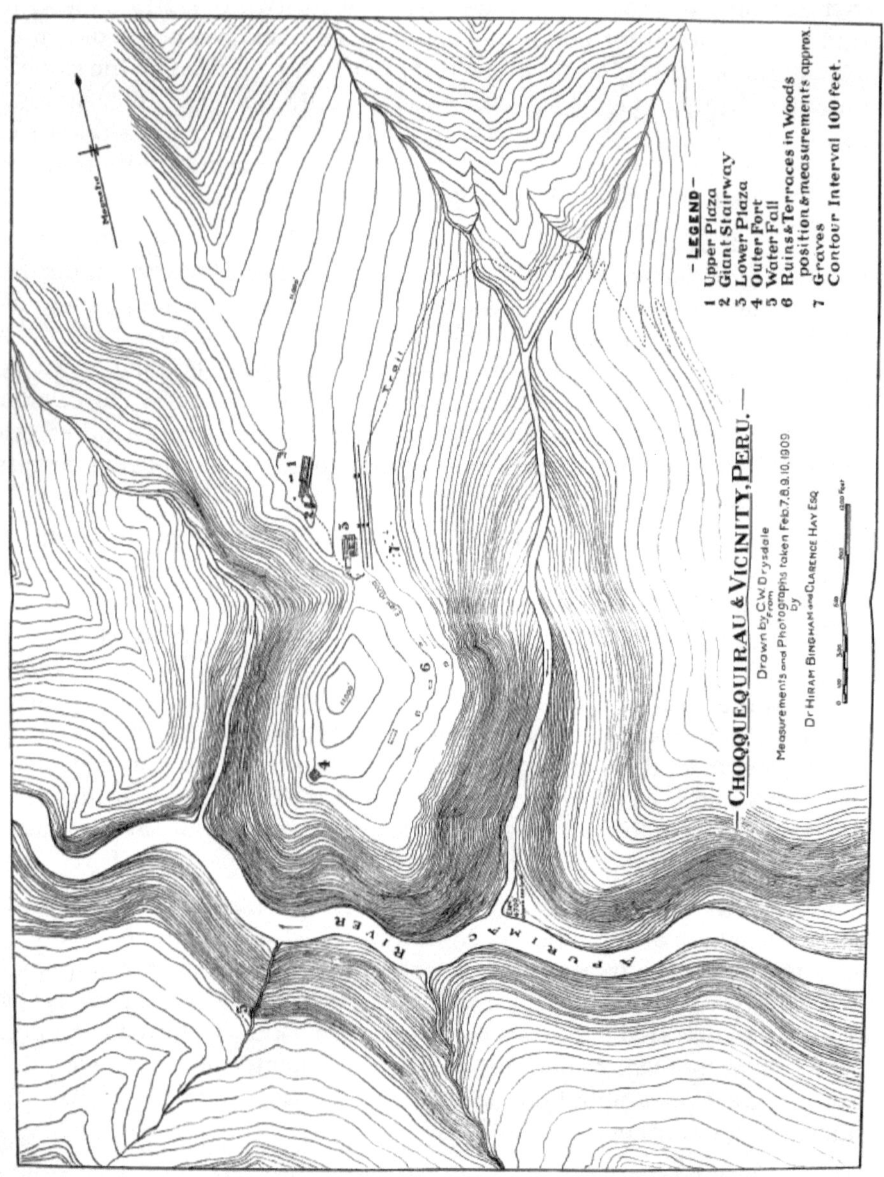

CHOQQUEQUIRAU AND VICINITY

CHAPTER XXIII
CHOQQUEQUIRAU

The next morning we began at once to take measurements and get what pictures we could. We found that the ruins were clustered in several groups both on terraces and natural shelves, reached by winding paths or stairways. Some buildings were long and narrow and of one story; others of a story and a half with tall gables. The buildings were placed close together, probably in order to economize all the available space. It is likely that every square yard that could be given to agriculture was cultivated.

Magnificent precipices guard the ruins on every side and render Choqquequirau virtually inaccessible to an enemy. Every avenue of ascent, except such as the engineers determined to leave open, was closed, and every strategic spot was elaborately fortified. Wherever it might have been possible for a bold mountaineer to gain a foothold, the Incas had built well-faced walls of stone so as to leave an adventurous assailant no support. The terraces thus made served the double purpose of military defence and of keeping the soil from sliding away from the gardens down the steep hillside.

As may be seen from the map, the ruins consist of three distinct groups of buildings.

All had been more or less completely hidden by trees and vines during the centuries of solitude. Fortunately for us the treasure-seeking company had done excellent work in clearing away from the more important buildings the tangled mass of vegetation that had formerly covered them. Dynamite had also been used in various likely spots where treasure might have been buried. But the workmen had found no gold and only a few objects of interest including, besides those we saw at Abancay, a few clay pots and two or three grinding stones of a pattern still in use in this part of the Andes and as far north as Panama.

At the top of the southern and outer precipice, five thousand eight hundred feet immediately above the river, stands a parapet and the walls of two buildings without windows. The view from here, both up and down the valley of the Apurimac, surpasses the possibilities of language for adequate description. The photograph gives but the faintest idea of its beauty and grandeur. Far down the gigantic cañon one catches little glimpses of the Apurimac, a white stream shut in between guardian mountains, so narrowed by the distance that it seems like a mere brooklet. Here and there through the valley are marvellous cataracts, one of which, two thousand feet high, has a clear fall of over one thousand feet. The panorama in every direction is wonderful in variety, contrast, beauty, and grandeur.

North of this outer group of buildings is an artificially truncated hill. It is probable that on this flattened hilltop, which commands a magnificent

BUILT OF STONES LAID IN CLAY

THE PARTY WALL RISES TO THE PEAK

view up and down the valley, signal fires could be built to telegraph to the heights overlooking Cuzco, intelligence of the approach of an enemy from the

Amazonian wilds.

We noticed on this hilltop that small stones had been set into the ground, in straight lines crossing and recrossing at right angles as though to make a pattern. So much of it was covered by grass, however, that we did not have a chance to sketch it in the time at our disposal.

North of the lookout and on the saddle between it and the main ridge is located the main group of ruins: a rude fortification fifteen feet high, running across the little ridge from one precipitous slope to the other; a long one-story building of uncertain use in which curious carved stone rings are set into the walls in such a manner as to serve possibly for the detention of prisoners; a long one-story building that might have been a grand hall or place of meeting, whose walls are surrounded with numerous niches; and a block of story-and-a-half houses whose gabled ends are still standing. The use of gables was almost universal in the central and southern part of the land of the Incas.

These double buildings stand transversely to the general line of the edifices and have a middle or party-wall exactly dividing the gable. It rises to the peak of the structure and once doubtless supported the upper ends of the rafters. These houses bear a striking resemblance to one of the Inca buildings at Ollantaytambo described by Squier[4] in the following words: "It is a story and a half high, built of rough stones laid in clay, and originally stuccoed, with a central wall reaching to the apex of the gables, dividing it into two apartments of equal size.... There seems to have been no access to the upper story from the interior, but there are two entrances to it through one of the gables, where four flat projecting stones seem to have supported a kind of balcony or platform, reached probably by ladders." This description fits these structures almost exactly. There are other resemblances between Choqquequirau and the Inca fortresses visited and described by Mr. Squier. In fact, one might use many a sentence from his accounts of Pisac and Ollantaytambo that would adequately describe Choqquequirau and its surroundings. Like the buildings of Ollantaytambo, these are nearly perfect, lacking only the roof.

The two-story houses had an exterior measurement of 42 by 38 feet. Similar ones measured by Squier near the temple of Viracocha north of Lake Titicaca, were also divided into two equal apartments and measured 46 by 38 feet. The fronts of each building have two entrances and the interior of every apartment is ornamented with irregular niches within which some of the stucco still remains. The walls are irregular but usually about three feet thick, and are composed of unhewn fragments of lava cemented together with a stiff clay.

In general, all the walls appear to have been built entirely of stone and clay. The construction, compared with that of the Inca palaces in Cuzco, is

---

[4] E. G. Squier, Peru, p. 503.

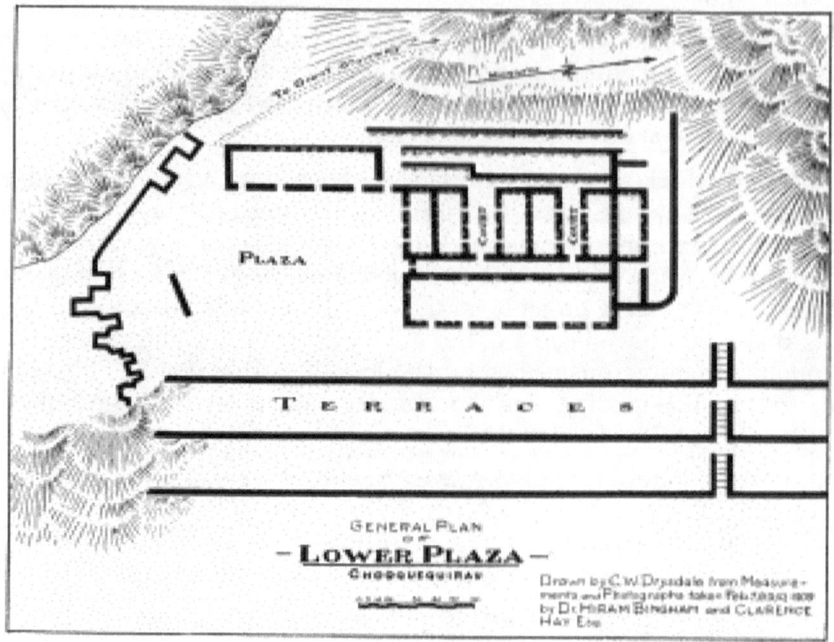

LOWER PLAZA CHOQQUEQUIRAU

extremely rude and rough and no two niches or doors are exactly alike. Occasionally the lintels of the doors were made of timber, the builders not having taken the trouble to provide stones wide enough for the purpose. One such lintel was still standing, the wood being of a remarkably hard texture.

Probably the ruins to-day present a more striking appearance than they did when they were covered with thatched roofs.

Ornamental niches which constitute a characteristic and constant feature in Inca architecture appear on the interior of all the Choqquequirau buildings and on the exterior of a few. Some of those on the outside are of the re-entering variety. Those on the inside are of two kinds. The larger ones about five feet high reach to the floors of the apartments and are mere closets, as it were, without doors, being slightly wider at the bottom, about thirty-four inches, than at the top, about twenty-eight inches, and of varying depth, thirteen to sixteen inches. A second line, smaller and not reaching to the ground, is also found in several of the structures. There is good evidence that some of the walls were faced with stucco and possibly painted in colors. In the case of one wall that had been partly pushed out of the perpendicular by the action of time, several of the niches retained almost entirely their coating of stucco, and so did some of the more protected portions of the wall.

Almost the only ornamentation which the houses contained besides the ever-present niches, were cylindrical blocks of stone about three inches in diameter projecting twelve or fourteen inches from the wall seven feet above the ground between each niche.

In one of the niches I found a small stone whirlbob of a spindle-wheel, in size and shape like those made from wood and used to-day all over the Andes by Indian women. This simple spinning apparatus consists of a stick about as large as the little finger and from ten to twelve inches long. Its lower end is fitted with a whirlbob of wood to give it proper momentum when it is set in motion by a twirl of the forefinger and thumb grasping the upper end of the spindle. It is in universal use by Indian women from the Andes of Colombia to those of Chile, and one rarely sees a woman tending sheep or walking along the high road who is not busily engaged in using this old-fashioned spindle. In the tombs of Pachacamac near Lima have been found spindles still fitted with similar whirlbobs of stone.

The third group of buildings is higher up on the spur, a hundred feet or more above the second group. Near the path from the lower to the upper plaza are the remains of a little azequia or watercourse, now dry, lined with flat stones. The southeast corner of the third group is marked by a huge projecting rock twenty feet high and twelve or fifteen feet in diameter. Beside it, facing the eastern slope, is a giant stairway. It consists of fourteen great steps roughly made and of varying dimensions. They average about fifteen feet wide, with risers four and a half feet high and treads about six and a half feet deep. It is possible to ascend these stairs by means of small stone steps erected on one

THE BUILDINGS NEAR THE OUTER PRECIPICE

THE UPPER SIX STEPS OF THE GIANT STAIRWAY

end or the other of the giant step. Walls on each side, two feet wide, serve as a balustrade. A peculiarity of the construction is the locating of a huge flat stone in the centre of the riser of each step. The view to the eastward from this stairway is particularly fine. Perhaps the rising sun, chief divinity of the Incas, was worshipped here.

Beyond the stairway are terraces, alley-ways, walls, and story-and-a-half houses, filled with niches and windows. The length of the first terrace is slightly over two hundred feet and its height is twelve feet. The second terrace above it has a height of ten feet and a length of one hundred and twenty-nine feet. Above these are two long alley-ways or halls with niches in their walls and windows looking out over the terraces. These halls are five feet wide. Back of these are buildings resembling in their construction those in the lower group. They also are decorated with irregular niches and cylindrical stone projections. Under these houses, however, there ran a small passage-way or drain twelve inches wide and ten inches deep. These two houses, although roughly built, were as nearly the same size as possible. Between them ran a narrow passage-way leading to a back alley. This was curiously paved with slabs of slate half an inch thick. Back of this is another hall five and a half feet wide with windows in front and niches on the rear, or hill, side.

The gables of the upper group are steeper than those of the lower group and are in fact quite as pointed as those seen in Dutch cities. The two gable buildings of the upper group stand on the slope of the hill in such a manner that there is no gable on the side nearest the declivity. In other words, they are only half the size of the double houses below. Nearly all of these houses have two or three small, rude windows. A narrow stone stairway leads from the back alley to a terrace above. This opens out into the upper plaza on which are several buildings that overlook the western precipices. Two of the houses have no windows and one of them contains three cells. The Peruvians said they were used for the detention of prisoners. They were more likely storehouses. On the north side of the plaza is a curious little structure built with the utmost care and containing many niches and nooks. It may possibly have been for the detention of so-called "virgins of the sun" or have been the place in which criminals, destined to be thrown over the precipice, according to the laws of the Incas, awaited their doom. The plan gives a good idea of its irregular construction.

Above it the hillside rises steeply, and on the crest of the ridge runs a little conduit which we followed until it entered the impenetrable tropical jungle at the foot of a steep hill. The water in this little azequia, now dry, coming straight down the spur, was conducted over a terrace into two well-paved tanks on the north side of the plaza. Thence it ran across the plaza to a little reservoir or bath-house on the south side. This was ten feet long by five feet wide with low walls not over five feet high and had on its north side a small stone basin let down into the floor two feet by three in such a manner as to

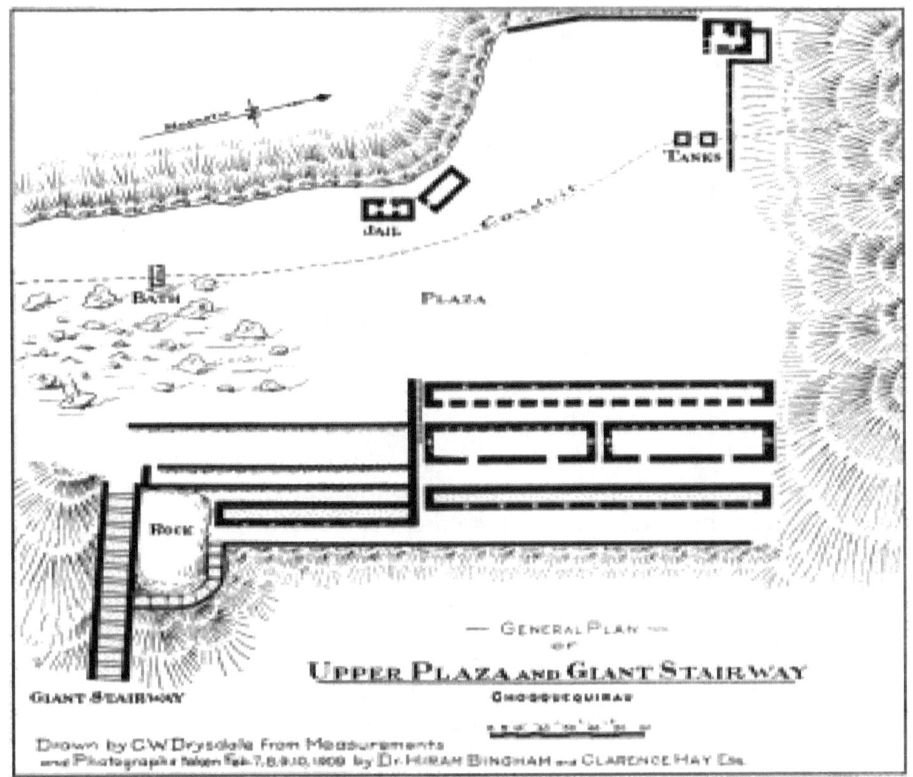

GENERAL PLAN OF UPPER PLAZA AND GIANT STAIRWAY
Choqquequirau
Drawn by C. W. Drysdale from Measurements
and Photographs taken Feb. 7, 8, 9, 10, 1909 by Dr. Hiram Bingham and Clarence Hay Esq.

UPPER PLAZA CHOQQUEQUIRAU

catch the water that flowed over the edge of the wall. A small outlet had been provided at the end of this basin so that the water could flow underneath the floor of the bathroom or tank house and then proceed on its way down the ridge to the buildings below.

As the western slope of the Choqquequirau spur is a sheer precipice, little attempt at fortification was made on that side. The eastern slope, however, is not so steep. On this side it was necessary to build enormous terraces hundreds of feet long faced with perpendicular walls twelve feet wide. Two narrow paved stairways lead from one terrace to another.

Near one of the terraces I picked up either a bola or a hammerstone nearly as large as my fist.

In the jungle immediately below the last terrace, under ledges and huge boulders, were dug little caves in which the bones of the dead were placed. I found that the bones were heaped in a little pile as though they had been cleaned before being interred. No earth had been placed on them, but on top of the little pile in one grave I found a small earthen-ware jar about one inch in diameter. It had no handles and was not closed at the top although the opening, a quarter of an inch in diameter, had been fitted with a specially well-made perforated cap. There was nothing in the jar, although it had retained its upright position during all the years of its interment. The natural entrance to the little tomb had been walled up with wedge-shaped stones from the inside in such a way as to make it extremely difficult to enter the cave from the front. I found, however, that by digging away a little on one side of the huge boulder, I could easily remove the stones which had evidently been placed there by the grave-digger after the bones had been deposited in the tomb.

The workmen had excavated under a dozen or more of the projecting ledges and in each case had found bones and occasionally shreds of pottery. In no case, however, had they found anything of value to indicate that the dead were of high degree. Probably they were common soldiers and servants. If any of the officers of the garrison or Inca nobles were ever buried in this vicinity, their tombs have not yet been discovered, or else the graves were rifled years ago. But of this there is no evidence.

All the conspicuously large rocks below the terraces have been found to cover graves. The skulls were not found alone but always near the remainder of the skeleton. The larger bones were in fairly good condition but the smallest ones had completely disintegrated. Nevertheless, ribs were frequently met with. Some of the largest bones could be crumbled with the fingers and easily broken, while others were very hard and seemed to be extremely well preserved. Some skulls likewise were decayed and could be easily crushed with the fingers while others were white and hard; all that we found were those of adults, although one or two of them seemed to be of persons not over twenty years of age. So far as has been observed, no superincumbent soil was placed on the skeleton.

1. A Hawaiian.   2-4. Skulls from Choqquequirau.   5. A Flat-head Indian.

6. Bola found at Choqquequirau. 7. Whirl-bob.

8. Jar found in a grave, Choqquequirau.

INTERIOR OF A BUILDING AT CHOQQUEQUIRAU

The Quichua Indian carriers and workmen watched our operations with interest, but they became positively frightened when we began the careful measurement and examination of the bones. They had been in doubt as to the object of our expedition up to that point, but all doubts then vanished and they decided we had come there to commune with the spirits of the departed Incas.

As a rule, the evidence of deformation of the skull was slight in a majority of the specimens examined. Nevertheless one had been much flattened behind and another extremely so in front. There was no evidence of any having been trephined or of any decorative patterns having been made on any part of either skulls or bones. Three of the skulls are now in the Peabody Museum in New Haven, with the other articles I found here.

On the steep hillside southeast of the terraces and graves, we found many less important ruins, completely covered by the forest. Were it possible to clear away all the rich tropical growth that has been allowed to accumulate for centuries, one would undoubtedly find that there is not a point which is not somehow commanded or protected by a maze of outworks. No clearing or path having been constructed in order to enable them to be seen, we could not form an adequate idea of their extent. There seemed to be, however, no limit to the ruins of the huts where lived the private soldiers and the servants of the garrison. One hall measured 75 by 25 feet while another was 30 by 10, and it is entirely possible that there are others that have not yet been located, so dense is the jungle.

On the opposite side of the valley are the ruins of Incahuasy, near Tambobamba, which have been described by M. Charles Wiener.[5] So far as I can judge from the drawings he gives of one of the "palaces," the construction is very similar to that used at Choqquequirau.

[5] Perou et Bolivie, pp. 293-5.

I believe that Incahuasy and Choqquequirau were originally frontier fortresses that defended the valley of the Apurimac, one of the natural approaches to Cuzco, from the Amazonian wilds. A glance at the map will show that Pisac and Paucartambo, northeast of Cuzco, with Ollantaytambo to the north and Choqquequirau to the west form a complete line of defence. Each is located in one of the valleys by which the unconquered Indians of the great forest could attack the sacred capital of the Incas. The Incas were never able to extend their empire far into the forests that covered the eastern slopes of the Andes or the valleys of the rivers that flow toward the Amazon. They did, however, push their empire down the valleys until they encountered the savage inhabitants of these wild forests, savage Chunchas or Antis, who with their poisoned arrows and their woodcraft were well able to protect themselves. The Incas were obliged to stop short when they reached the thick forests. The massive and complicated fortresses of Paucartambo, Pisac, and Ollantaytambo marked the extent of their sway. There were undoubtedly several less important outlying

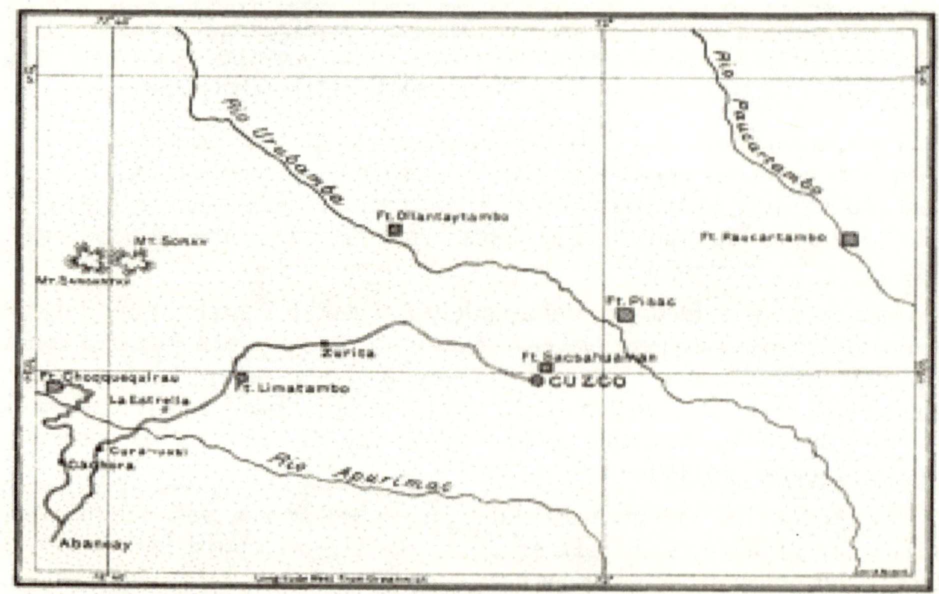

CUZCO AND NEIGHBORING FORTRESSES

fortresses lower down the rivers, situated in such a way as to be able to prevent the incursions of small parties of wild savages and give notice of any large expeditions that might attempt to march on Cuzco. They were so placed as to be practically impregnable. Choqquequirau was evidently one of these.

I fear that no amount of dynamite will ever disclose at Choqquequirau a "Cradle of Gold" or any articles of great value. It was not a temple or a treasure house, but a fortress where life was strenuous. The officers of its garrison were not likely to bring with them gold ornaments or utensils, and the poor Incas had few such baubles left at the end of their career.

Why then should it have been called the "Cradle of Gold?" One answer is that the ridge or spur on which Choqquequirau lies, when seen from a distance, looks not unlike a hammock. The setting sun often tinges it with gold and the romantic Incas might easily have named Choqquequirau from its resemblance to the only cradles with which they were familiar.

The other answer is that the name, which does not occur in any of the chronicles, so far as I have been able to discover, is a modern invention. In one of the buildings we found several slabs of slate on which visitors have been accustomed to register their names. According to these inscriptions Choqquequirau was visited in 1834 by a French explorer M. Eugène de Sartiges, and in July, 1834, by two Peruvians, José Maria de Tejada and Marcelino Leon, who may have come with de Sartiges.

Charles Wiener, in his very unreliable but highly interesting "Perou et Bolivie" (Paris, 1880), says (footnote, p. 294) that Choqquequirau has also been visited by another Frenchman, "M. Angrand whose MS. notes, with plans and drawings, were bequeathed to the Bibliothèque Nationale in Paris." I find they are merely hastily-drawn sketches. One, a route-map, is dated "30 7bre," [1847]. Angrand's name does not appear on any of the slates.

Besides de Sartiges, and the two Peruvians already mentioned, the slate records show that in 1861, on the 10th of November, José Benigno Samanez ("pro Presidente Castilla") Juan Manuel Rivas Plata, and Mariano Cisneros reached the ruins. Also that on July 4, 1885, Luis E. Almanza, J. Antonio Almanza, Emiliano Almanza, Pio Mogrovejo and a party of workmen did what they could to find the buried treasure. So much for the existing evidence of former visitors.

M. de Sartiges, writing under the nom de plume E. de Lavandais, published an account of his visit in the Revue des Deux Mondes, in June, 1850. His route, the only one possible at the time, was exceedingly circuitous. From Mollepata, a village near the sugar plantation of La Estrella, he went north across the high pass between Mts. Sargantay and Soray to the river Urubamba, to a village called Yuatquinia (Huadquiña [?]). He engaged Indians to cut a trail to Choqquequirau. After three weeks he found that the difficulties of making a trail were so great that it would take at least two months to finish the undertaking, so he and his companions made their way through the jungle and along the precipices as best they could for four days. On the fifth day they arrived at the ruins. In his projects for exploration, he had failed to take into account the fact that tropical vegetation had been at work for centuries covering up the remains of the Inca civilization, and as he was only able to stay at Choqquequirau for two or three days, he failed to see some of the most interesting ruins. The giant stairway and the buildings on the upper plaza seem to have escaped his attention entirely. He was greatly impressed with the fortifications on the south side of the lower plaza and speaks of them as though they formed a triumphal wall ("mur triomphal"). He seems to have spent most of his time hunting for treasure behind this wall. He had expected to spend eight days here, but the difficulties of reaching the place were so great and the food-supply was so limited that he had to hurry back without seeing more than the buildings of the lower plaza, the lower terraces, and a grave or two. It was his opinion that fifteen thousand people lived here once. One wonders what they lived on.

M. de Sartiges's description made us realize how much we were indebted to the labors of the treasure-seeking company for penetrating the jungle and uncovering buildings whose presence otherwise would never have been suspected.

Raimondi says that in 1862, Don Juan Gastelu, a Peruvian traveller, left Ayacucho in an effort to go up the valley of the Apurimac in a canoe, hoping in this way to reach the ancient fortress. After seven days of perilous navigation, he gave up the attempt long before reaching its vicinity.

The interesting question remains: Was this the ultimate refuge of the last Inca?

It is reasonably certain that Manco Ccapac, the last emperor, fleeing from the wrath of the conquerors, took refuge in a place called "Vilcabamba." There is a village of that name, two or three days journey over the mountains north of Choqquequirau, on the Vilcabamba River, an affluent of the Urubamba. It has never been explored so far as I know.

Peruvian writers like Paz Soldan and the great geographer, Raimondi, are positive that Manco Ccapac's "Vilcabamba" was really Choqquequirau. They base their belief on the fact that in 1566 an Augustinian Friar, Marcos Garcia, undertook to penetrate to "Vilcabamba," where poor old Manco Ccapac had found a refuge. In describing his tour, Father Calancha, the author of the "Chronica moralizada del Orden de San Augustin, Libro III, Cap. XXIV and XLII," says that Garcia founded a church in Pucyura, "two long days' journey from Vilcabamba." Raimondi calls attention to the fact that Pucyura is only two leagues from the present village of "Vilcabamba," and while he admits that it is possible that Father Calancha wrote "days' journey" instead of "leagues" by mistake, he believes that the reference is to Choqquequirau which is in fact two long days' journey from Pucyura. It is at least a very roundabout method of inference.[6]

Raimondi may be correct, but until some one shall have explored the present village of Vilcabamba and its vicinity, I am inclined to the opinion that Choqquequirau was merely a fortress.

Since writing the above I have received, through the kindness of Prof. Roland Dixon of Harvard University, a copy of a pamphlet by the distinguished Peruvian historian, Carlos A. Romero, entitled "Las Ruinas de Choqquequirau," which gives the result of his careful researches through all the works of writers who refer to Choqquequirau. It does not add to our actual knowledge of the early history of the ruins.

---

[6] Raimondi, Peru, vol. ii, p. 161.

CHAPTER XXIV
ABANCAY TO CHINCHEROS

One of the conditions on which we had based our decision to visit Choqquequirau was that the Prefect was to see to it that animals should be ready for our departure as soon as we got back, and that his officials along the road should facilitate our progress in every possible manner. To his credit be it said that he kept his promise faithfully, notwithstanding all the rules in the books to the effect that a South American rarely remembers his promise.

The next day after our return to Abancay, we spent in re-arranging our luggage and making ready for a rapid march to Ayacucho. The Prefect sent in an official request for a report on the ruins of Choqquequirau. Not being a Latin-American, I was unable to sit down and dash off a "thorough satisfactory official report" in an hour and a half and had to explain that it would take days and even weeks to draw plans from the data in our field-books and from the ten dozen negatives we had exposed.

On the following day, much refreshed in body and mind, we succeeded in getting an early start. We were accompanied out of town by a score of enthusiastic friends whose interest in our undertaking was perfectly ingenuous and of whom we had learned to be very fond. They not only decided to extend

OUR CAVALCADE ON THE BRIDGE OF PACHACHACA

the customary "mile of courtesy" to a dozen or more, but later they followed us up with congratulatory telegrams speeding us on our way.

Our cavalcade clattered gayly out of town on a fine brisk morning when for some reason or other it did not happen to be raining. A short stop at Yllanya to enable us to pay our respects to the kind Letona family, who had given us a pleasant banquet the week before, was rewarded by the young master of the house having his horse saddled at once and insisting on taking us by a short cut through his own canefields. These looked prosperous enough, but a swarm of locusts that had just made their appearance was pointed out to us, and the planter feared greatly for his crops.

At ten o'clock we reached the river Pachachaca, the first large affluent of the Apurimac. We crossed it on a stone bridge whose magnificent single arch was erected under the direction of a Jesuit architect, two hundred and fifty years ago. It is said to be one of the longest spans in the Andes. Here we stopped to have a round of drinks and to enjoy the scenery.

It was a beautiful spot: green mountains on both sides of a valley filled with waving sugar-cane through the midst of which ran a roaring, rushing torrent. A few miles farther up this valley there are a number of small Indian towns in which General Sucre had his headquarters a few weeks before the battle of Ayacucho.

An hour's brisk trot brought us to Auquibamba, a sugar mill and plantation, owned by Don Federico Martinelli who was unfortunately ill in bed and not able to see us, although his engineer and manager did the honors most hospitably. Quantities of delicious oranges were brought to appease our appetites while an elaborate lunch was being prepared for the dozen more people than had been expected.

After lunch we all mounted at once. The custom of taking a siesta does not seem to prevail at this altitude, 7000 feet. After all were on horseback, affectionate good-bys had to be said, and notwithstanding the nervousness of some of the more high-strung animals, their riders succeeded in embracing the departing guests with true Spanish fervor.

Our road from Auquibamba led through a charming country until it gradually climbed out of the valley and across a pass, at an altitude of 11,700 feet, where there was a small lake but no signs of tropical vegetation.

We saw no llamas at all. Mules, horses, and burros were the pack animals that we met carrying out kegs of aguardiente and loads of sugar and bringing in foreign merchandise. Thanks to the rainy season, the fields were covered with flowers, many varieties of which have been imported for our own gardens at home. Wonderfully large begonias, excelling in size anything I had ever seen before, lupins, cosmos, and many others added great charm to the scene and partly made up for the frightful condition of the roads.

Every one with whom we talked expressed surprise that we should attempt a journey at this season of the year when all good Peruvians stay at home. Not only are the roads positively dangerous in places, but the heavy rainfall insures a thorough daily drenching unless one is so fortunate as to be protected by a very heavy rubber poncho. As the natives depend almost entirely on woolen ponchos for protection against the rain, it may be imagined that they get well soaked after two or three hours' riding, notwithstanding the fact that the best and most expensive vicuña ponchos are beautifully and closely woven and will shed an ordinary shower.

At half past four we began the descent into the pretty cultivated valley of Huancarama. The descent was steep and the path extremely slippery, and we were paying so much attention to the manner of our going that we barely noticed the cavalcade of eight horsemen riding at full gallop up the valley. The Gobernador had been informed of our approach by the kind-hearted Prefect, and had brought with him half a dozen of his friends to do us honor. We were taken at once to his house, a small adobe hut, and treated most courteously. The priest of the village and two of the leading citizens were urged to remain and dine with us, which they readily consented to do. After dinner we were piloted through the muddy streets to the plaza where a room, evidently used for various governmental purposes, was placed at our disposal. All went well until the next morning when we were told that one of the animals which the Prefect had furnished us belonged to the Gobernador, who had lent it to the Secretary of the Department for the expedition to Choqquequirau, and he was unwilling to have it go any farther. He said that "one of his friends" had an excellent horse which he would rent us for that day. The Gobernador was firm, and as he had sent the animal to pasture, he had more than "nine points of the law" on his side. Anyhow we had no desire to impose on him, and requested him to have his "friend's horse" brought around. There seemed, however, to be some sort of an understanding between the Gobernador and his "friend," as the horse, a fairly good-looking beast, was brought out from the Gobernador's own backyard. We suspicioned that the "friend" was probably a confederate in graft, if not actually a servant. The price asked for the use of the horse for one day was five dollars. Evidently we were considered to be "easy." We appealed the matter to the soldier who had been sent as our escort, but he would only shake his head sadly and shrug his shoulders. So we told the Gobernador the price was outrageous and that rather than pay it, we would settle down in Huancarama and live at his expense. With this terrible alternative staring him in the face he sent his servant to another "friend" with orders to bring up another animal. This time the price asked was only $1, and although the soldier said that was twice as much as the regular charge, we preferred to pay it rather than be delayed any longer.

The day was very rainy. It may have been for this reason, or it may have been because he was disappointed at his unsuccessful attempt at "legitimate graft," that the Gobernador did not assemble his friends and escort us out of town. In either case we did not blame him. It was rather a relief to escape the oft-repeated expressions of sincere sorrow at departure which one can make two or three times, but which somehow lack spontaneity and sincerity when they must be repeated to a cavalcade of sixteen.

The road was no improvement on that of the day before. A long climb through the rain and sleet, a long descent through the clouds into the valley of the river Pincos, whose tantalizing roar helped us to realize what magnificent scenery we were missing; a little glimpse of green fields, a dilapidated village, an old bridge, and another long steep ascent led us finally to a bleak paramo where we were as uncomfortable as cold winds and drenching rain could make us.

Just before four o'clock we were gladdened by the sight of a good-sized town and hoped that it was Andahuaylas, our destination, but our escort said it was only San Geronimo, a suburb of Andahuaylas. We found it to be a densely populated Indian town of the usual type. Before we had much of an opportunity to take in its points of interest, however, we were surrounded by twenty horsemen, including the sub-Prefect of Andahuaylas, the secretary of the province, and their friends who had ridden to meet us. Much as we appreciated their courtesy and the liquid refreshments they brought with them, we were still more gratified by being asked to dismount and allow the soldiers to put our saddles on two fresh horses. It may have been because the rain had stopped its torrential downpour, or because our tired, jaded animals had made us lose all sense of proportion, or it may possibly have been that those two horses really were the finest animals in Peru; whatever the cause, we both of us agreed that we had never enjoyed any ride so much as that last mile to Andahuaylas, and that we had never ridden such magnificent, fiery steeds that so closely resembled the high mettled war-horse that one usually sees surmounted by General Bolivar either in bronze or in historical paintings.

The good people of Andahuaylas had heard by telegraph of the banquet which had been "tendered us" in Abancay and of the enthusiasm with which the Prefect had welcomed us back from Choqquequirau. They determined not to be outdone. If an additional reason was needed to spur them on to do their utmost, it came in the press despatches that day which stated that Chile was about to throw down the gauntlet to Peru by definitively announcing her permanent occupancy of the provinces of Tacna and Arica. To the minds of the older Peruvian generation who had felt the cruel lash of the Chilean conqueror in 1883 and had witnessed the burning of the Lima Library and the stabling of Chilean horses in Peruvian churches, there seemed little hope of a satisfactory settlement of the dispute and no desire to engage in another war. Their one idea seemed to be that the United States, with its love of fair play, would see to it that Chile did not take advantage of the weakness of Peru to rob her of her southernmost province. As we were the only Americans in sight, and as there was about us a certain reflected glamour of officialdom, we were treated as though we were diplomats, instead of being, as they knew perfectly well, merely a delegate to a Scientific Congress, and his "secretary." Anyhow, they had done their best to provide a banquet that should eclipse the glories of Abancay; the table was set for forty-five and it may safely be assumed that most of the leading citizens of Andahuaylas were present. Little American flags, made for the occasion, were crossed with Peruvian flags on the walls of the room. Portraits of President Roosevelt and President Leguia, suitably framed, decorated the wall immediately behind us. "Ice cream," made of snow brought from the Nevada of Chillihua on the backs of llamas, was on the menu. There was enough food and drink to last until 2.30 A.M. Unfortunately I had to leave early for I was simply used up with the amount of "entertainment" that I had had to undergo during the preceding week.

Our hosts came to call rather late the next morning and looked pretty mournful. It was not due entirely to the fact of the pouring rain. Nevertheless the sub-Prefect was most kind, and had us take all our meals at his house, a picturesque old compound whose large patio was surrounded by one and two-storied buildings. The roofs, with their heavy old-fashioned mission tiles, had long ago lost any straight line they ever possessed. To add to their beauty, rain and sun and mosses had given them every variety of color. In a corner of the patio, an Indian man-servant and a little girl were busy grinding meal by rocking one stone upon another in the same fashion as did the builders of Choqquequirau and with stones almost the exact counterparts of those we found there.

In the afternoon, our friends felt a little better, and the rain held up enough for us to be shown the sights of the town. A well-proportioned stone church, designed by the same architect who had built the bridge near Abancay, testified again to the excellent crafts that the Jesuits taught in this country two hundred and fifty years ago. Some of the booths on the plaza were extremely picturesque, the various colored wares offered for sale being protected from the sun by umbrella-shaped shelters rudely made from old sticks covered with faded ponchos or with the dried skins of animals, cured with the hair on.

Some one with a great fondness for Lombardy poplars had lived here years ago and the view of the town which we got from the heights across the river was most attractive. On the side of a mountain to the north were many farms. The fields of corn divided from each other by hedges gave a very pleasing background; the roaring rapids of the little river formed the foreground; while in the middle distance the red-tiled roofs, white walls, poplar trees, and fine old stone church made a charming picture.

The sub-Prefect and his secretary, who had most generously placed his own very comfortable quarters at our disposal, took great pleasure in showing us two new alamedas or avenues which had been laid out recently under his direction. It is pleasant to remember these signs of progress even though we also remember a little old street through which we had to pass after leaving the alameda. The old street, scarcely as wide as the sidewalks of the new, had no conveniences whatsoever for foot-passengers. Owing to the recent downpour, part of it had been converted into a pond, and we had an amusing and not altogether successful time getting across dry-shod.

All our friends promised to be on hand the next morning to accompany us out of town although we assured them that it was quite unnecessary. When they woke up and saw the rain coming down in sheets, they decided we were right. The sub-Prefect came through the downpour to bid us good-by, but was still suffering from dyspepsia and excused himself for not mounting his horse. By his orders, the Gobernador of the neighboring town of Talavera, through which we passed half an hour after leaving Andahuaylas, accompanied us on our way.

Talavera is noted for the manufacture of the finest grade of Vicuña ponchos.

Mr. Squier gave it a bad name and was impressed by the evil looks of its inhabitants, but we saw nothing to differentiate it from the other crowded little towns of the interior. Wherever possible, the land is occupied. There is, in fact, very little evidence that there was a much larger population in Peru before the arrival of the Spanish conquerors. Although it is true that some of the irrigating ditches have been destroyed, it does not seem likely that this region could ever have supported a much more numerous population than lives here to-day. Those writers who believe that the Peruvian Indians were reduced "from upwards of thirty millions to three millions within the space of two centuries," must have forgotten to make allowances for the fondness for exaggeration in the Spanish chronicles. The country is actually as crowded to-day as its resources will allow. In fact, most of the Indians are half starved all the time. It is difficult to believe that twice as many, to say nothing of ten times as many Indians, could find support on these bleak highlands, even when they were forced to practice an extensive cultivation of the soil by Inca laws and usages, which provided for almost every action of their lives.

Since writing the above I have been reading Prof. Bandelier's remarkable book, "The Islands of Titicaca and Koati," and am glad to notice that he says, p. 27: "The conclusion is reached that the Indian population, of that district (Chucuito) at least, has not at all diminished since the early times of Spanish colonization, but has rather increased. It shows how unjustified is the hue and cry about extermination of the natives of Peru by the Spaniards. I could easily furnish more examples of the kind from all over Peru and Bolivia."

It is pleasant to have my amateurish opinions substantiated so unexpectedly and from such a high authority.

In the valleys above Talavera there was abundant pasturage and we saw many flocks of sheep and herds of cattle. Some of the sheep had very long curly horns, reminding one of the Rocky Mountain

SOME OF THE SHEEP HAD VERY LONG CURLY HORNS

goats, while others were distinguished by having four horns instead of two. From Talavera the road turned northward and followed for some distance the valley of the Andahuaylas River, then crossed it and climbed out of the valley, passed the ruins of a tambo at a place called Monobamba, and surmounted an exceedingly bleak plateau, a veritable paramo bravo where the barometer showed an elevation of 14,500 feet. The neighboring hills, the summits of the Andes, were covered with snow. More snow began to fall before we left the paramo.

The descent to Chincheros was particularly difficult owing to the fact that a little mountain torrent, usually easy to ford, had become very much swollen. Furthermore, the mud was so deep in places that we should have found it impossible to proceed had it not been for our excellent guide, the Gobernador of Talavera, who knew how to avoid the worst places and was able to pilot us across stretches of treacherous pasture-land where the soggy soil barely sustained the weight of our animals.

It was a long forty-mile ride. The Gobernador of Chincheros, who had come out, with a dozen of his friends, to meet us two miles from his town, had been waiting in the shelter of a hut for more than an hour before we appeared. Nevertheless our tardy arrival in no wise interfered with their welcome, and the long wait had not even induced them to make any lighter the load of the Indian servant who had brought on foot a basket-load of bottled beer and coñac. We had learned by this time, from sad experience, that our stomachs, well emptied by a long day in the saddle, would rebel at being treated to fire-water even though it was "the custom of the country." Although a refusal would have been misunderstood, no objection was offered to the fact that we merely touched the fiery draft and did not drain the glass. With the kindly escort was an officer who had been sent all the way from Ayacucho bearing a letter of welcome from the Prefect of that department, with orders to attend to our comforts on the way. We felt as though we were in the hands of our friends, but at the same time we were not prepared for what was to follow.

After paddling painfully along for a mile or so through awful mud and slush, we came to a roadside inn whose proprietor had stretched a line of flags across the road and erected a primitive framework for them. As it was late in the afternoon, we did not tarry long to return his courteous greetings but trotted on down the valley. A sudden turn in the road brought us into view of a charmingly situated town. Deep green valleys, high mountains, and pleasant trees gave a fine setting to picturesque Chincheros with its little old church and its red-tiled roofed houses. We had to cross a stone bridge just before entering the town, and here we were met by an Indian bearing on a pole an enormous flag. Although it had less than twenty stars and only eight stripes, it was unmistakably intended to be "Old Glory." Welcoming us with a loud shout, the bearer turned about and marched at the head of our cavalcade. Flags fluttered from every house. The streets were thronged with people, many of whom showered us with rose-leaves! As we entered the plaza, the church bells, which had been ringing ever since we rounded the turn in the road, redoubled their noise; the shouts increased, and we were almost carried from our horses on the shoulders of the crowd. We realized perfectly the spirit with which our arrival was celebrated, and knew that it was merely an expression of cordial goodwill toward the United States, arising from a mistaken idea that we were the official personification of that great country; but it was all we could do to keep our faces straight.

After we were finally lodged in a comfortable room belonging to the little local club, we thought the crowd would disperse. Not at all. Nothing would satisfy them but that one of us should make a speech which, however feebly delivered, was received with great enthusiasm. More rose-petals were thrown, the bells were rung again, the flags waved, the people cheered, and we were made to know what it must be like to be a returning military chief and to hear the band play "Lo the Conquering Hero Comes!"

The little group of Chinchereños, whose public spirit had established the club, tendered us a banquet that evening. They had determined to outdo the celebrations which they had heard of as taking place in Abancay and Andahuaylas, but they insisted that the outside celebration was quite spontaneous, and that the Indians had taken it into their own heads to improve on that which the club had planned. After the banquet that evening, there was a display of fireworks consisting of a set piece fixed to a pole which was held by a poor Indian who did not seem to mind in the least the shower of sparks that fell on every side. To prolong his danger, the rain kept putting out the fuse so that it had to be lighted six or seven times. If he felt any pain, however, he failed to show it, and seemed only too delighted to be the centre of attraction.

The celebration had a strange witness. In the crowd that welcomed us near the bridge there was a haggard man with German features who called out in English, "Hurrah for the United States!" He soon came to call on us and told quite a tragic story.

He said his name was Emilio Smith (or Schmidt) and that his home was in Düsseldorf on the Rhine. With three companions, he had made a wager in New York that they could walk from Buenos Aires across both continents to New York City without funds and without begging. He said that the New York "Herald" and the Buenos Aires "La Prensa" had offered a prize of five thousand dollars, if they would accomplish the feat. They had had no particular difficulty in crossing Argentina, but one of them succumbed at Tupiza soon after they reached Bolivia. Nothing daunted, the other three pressed on over much the same road that we had followed from Tupiza to Potosí and thence direct to the Antofagasta railway. At each place they had secured the signature of official witnesses to the effect that they were not riding and were not begging but were conducting their overland tramp fairly. They raised money by giving lectures and

THE CLUB AT CHINCHEROS

entertainments in the towns through which they passed, and had frequent-ly been given food and lodging by kindly disposed Indians, although often they had been very rudely received. They had walked around Lake Titicaca, and had reached Cuzco, followed the old trail to Lima, walked up the coast, and penetrated the equatorial rain-belt in Ecuador before disaster overtook them. Weakened by months of exposure, they were in no condition to encounter tropical fevers, and all were soon flat on their backs. Two of them never recovered and were buried in Ecuador. Smith, now alone, cabled to the New York "Herald" for instructions, stating that he was too weak to continue the journey alone, and had no funds. The answer came back: "Return to Buenos Aires." Although he had been dismayed by the difficulties that lay ahead of him in Ecuador and Colombia, he knew enough of the road over which he had come to believe that he could safely get back to Bue-nos Aires and that then the "Herald" and the "Prensa" would probably reward him for his foolhardy excursion. Accordingly, he was retracing his steps, and had reached Chincheros that noon. He had intended to go along further in the after-noon, but hearing of the expected arrival of two Americans, and being invited to the banquet, he had stayed over.

It was a dismal story that he told, but he took great pride in it, and his eyes flashed as he recounted his exploits. The only bitter in the sweet was that he had lost his friends, and that we had not heard of him.

"What, you don't know about me? Why, I am the foot-walker. I go from Bue-nos Aires to New York. I don't get there. I go back to Buenos Aires. You haven't heard of me? You haven't heard of me, Emilio Smith, the foot-walker? That is very strange. And the Prefect of Abancay? He is a good fellow. Didn't he tell you about me? Didn't he show you my picture? My picture of me and my two friends?"

I think he felt that we really hadn't been to Abancay after all. Poor fellow, living for months on the narration of his exploits, it was a hard pill for him to swallow that the only Americans he had seen who had come over the road where he had passed several months before, had never heard any mention made of his overland journey. The reason was not far to seek. He travelled on foot. No one but an Indian travels on foot. It is perfectly inconceivable to the Spanish mind that any one should do any feat of pedestrianism unless compelled to, either by poverty or the instincts of a vagabond. Poor people and vagabonds are too common to attract much attention. We never heard of him again. He left early the next morning.

CHAPTER XXV

BOMBON TO THE BATTLEFIELD OF AYACUCHO

T HE next morning we were furnished fresh horses by our kind hosts, and accompanied by five or six of them, climbed out of the beautiful valley of Chincheros up to the heights of Bombon overlooking the river Pampas. Here in 1824, the patriot forces under General Sucre, marching along this road to Lima, encountered the Royalists under La Serna, trying to cut off their retreat. The advance guard of each army met on the 20th of November on the heights of Bombon. The Royalists were driven down into the valley and across the river Pampas.

After reaching the level of the river, our path followed the Pampas, down stream, in a northerly direction, for some distance among groves of mimosa trees and cacti. This is a famous place for mosquitoes, and there is said to be a great deal of malaria in the vicinity. The altitude is slightly over six thousand feet.

My interest in the Pampas valley was considerably increased by finding the trees and cacti covered with white land shells, some of them reminding me of those tree shells that I had gathered as a boy in the beautiful valleys of the Island of Oahu. I filled my pockets, and later spent the evening clean ing the shells, much to the amusement of my hosts. My labor was amply rewarded by finding, after reaching home, that among the shells were three new species which Dr. Dall, the Curator of the Division of Mollusks in the United States National Museum, has named and described.[7]

The bridge over the Pampas has long attracted the notice of travellers. The approach to it is at the foot of perpendicular cliffs. The surrounding scenery although not so imposing as that of the Apurimac is nevertheless magnificent. The bridge is about 150 feet long, and at the time of my visit, February, 1909, was 50 feet above the river. There are two pictures of the old bridge in Mr. Squier's book, and although wire rope has replaced the old cables that the Incas made from maguey fibre, it is still the most unwelcome feature of the road from the point of view of the mules.

One of our mules simply would not cross the bridge. No amount of pushing and pulling, beating and shouting, would make him budge an inch. Finally he was

---

[7] "On some Land Shells Collected by Dr. Hiram Bingham, in Peru"; Proceedings of the U. S. Nat. Mus., xxxviii. 177-182. The shells "comprised various species and varieties of Bulimulus and a single species of Clausilia." The latter was described by Dr. H. A. Pilsbry

blindfolded and a rope tied to each front leg. His hind legs were tied securely together, to prevent him from kicking, and by alternately pulling the ropes attached to his front feet, he was forced in a most ignominious manner to come onto the bridge and go a third of the way across. Then the ropes were loosened and the blind taken off.

THE LARGE PLAZA OF AYACUCHO

THE BRIDGE OVER THE RIVER PAMPAS

We expected to see him turn and bolt for the nearest side but he was too frightened to do anything of the sort, and became at once most docile, and finished the trip in peace.

He was not the only one who did not like the bridge. The priest of Chincheros, who had been delayed from accompanying us by the arrival of a visiting cleric that morning, overtook us here. Although a sturdy native Indian, he was rather portly and preferred not only to leave to some one else the leading across of his mule, but even to have a poor Indian bearer give him his shoulder to steady him on the swaying structure.

From the other end of the bridge we ascended the precipitous cliff by a narrow winding path and found ourselves on a lofty terrace where the enterprising Parodi Brothers have planted waving fields of sugarcane. Here we were met by the Gobernador of Tambillo and the Parodis who escorted us to their sugar factory at Pajonal, a most attractive hacienda nestled in a valley at the foot of beetling crags. Our hosts had inherited from their father an unusual stock of energy and skill. Owing to his efforts, a good irrigation ditch had been constructed that furnished the canefields with an abundant supply of water. The houses were in good repair and everything bore the marks of prosperity. It was a pleasure to see such evidence of enterprise and energy in this wild region. One brother, who ordinarily practices medicine in Lima, was here on a visit. Another brother is being educated in the States.

We left Pajonal the next morning, accompanied by the Gobernador of Tambillo, a very agreeable person of German-Peruvian descent. From Pajonal the road ascends a little valley and then climbs a mountainside to the village of Ocros, a most forlorn and wretched place, with an elevation of nearly ten thousand feet.

The adobe church, like that at Chincheros, was set back from the plaza, and had a new adobe wall around it. Earth for this seemed to have been taken right out of the plaza. No attempt had been made to fill up the huge holes that remained. The only building at Ocros that seemed to be in any kind of repair was the local telegraph office where the officer from Ayacucho who accompanied us, went to send a despatch to the Prefect.

On the way we had been struck by the extraordinary method of hanging telegraph wires that prevails in this country. The linesmen had thought nothing of planting three poles together on the top of one hill and the next three not less than a quarter of a mile away on the top of another, stretching their wire across the intervening distance in midair. This occurred not once or twice but whenever they could save poles by so doing. The strain on the wire must have been tremendous. We learned that the service was "frequently interrupted."

The road up from Ocros was the worst that we encountered anywhere. It was really the bed of a mountain stream and our animals had the greatest difficulty in picking their way among the rocks and boulders. It was hard to imagine that this was really the highway between Cuzco and Lima. The "road" grew worse and worse until it reached a bleak paramo at an elevation of thirteen thousand feet, where snow, hail, and sleet, driven in our faces by a high wind, added to our discomforts. A steep descent on the other side of the range greatly tried the patience of our animals. The ground seemed to be a hard clay that offered no support to their feet and they slid and slipped, sometimes eight or ten feet at a time, without being able to stop. Night was falling as we reached the little collection of wretched huts called Matara. No one seemed to have any desire to receive us. In fact, the Indian who had charge of the only dry hut in the place, locked the front door and disappeared into the night. Unlike vigorous Caceres, who would sooner have died than allow an inhospitable Indian to refuse admission to the foreigner in his charge, the officer from Ayacucho was a timid soul who had gone through the world bemoaning his ill fortune and doing nothing to make it better. He could think of no solution of the problem except that we make ourselves as comfortable as possible in the shelter of a kind of a porch in front of this thatched hut. So we passed an exceedingly uncomfortable night and experienced some of the hardships that the British soldiers, who aided the patriot army in that last campaign against the Spanish viceroy, must have suffered in this very locality.

The next morning our road led across half a dozen deep gulches whose streams feed the river Colpahuayo. In one of these I was so fortunate as to find in a gravel-bank at the side of the road, which had been heavily washed by recent rains, a portion of an ancient Inca stone war-club shaped like a huge doughnut.

The road continued to be extremely slippery and was not improved by the almost continuous rain. At half past two we reached Tambillo. Here we were welcomed by the pleasant wife of the Gobernador who had ridden ahead to have a good breakfast prepared while we had waited in vain on a hilltop hoping the rain would hold up sufficiently to let us photograph a magnificent panorama that included the distant city of Ayacucho and the heights of Condorkanqui and the famous battlefield.

After lunch we crossed another gulch whose treacherous sides more than once caused our mules to fall heavily. In the village of Los Neques, we were met by a very courteous emissary of the Prefect of Ayacucho who turned out to be proprietor of the hotel. He had been sent out in the rain to apologize for the fact that there was no committee to meet us and to explain that the notables had mounted and ridden out to await us until driven back by the inclemency of the weather, for all of which we were duly thankful, as it meant that we had escaped the necessity of hurting anybody's feelings by declining to drink more copitas of brandy on an empty stomach.

Here at Los Neques the Indians were getting ready to celebrate the days of Carnival which were soon to be upon us. A hundred men and women had gathered in the courtyard of an old house. In one corner a red cloth shelter had been erected

AYACUCHO

THE COURTYARD OF THE HOTEL

under which sat the old men around a table on which was scattered popcorn, roast maize, and dishes of succotash. The other men and women squatted on the ground with dishes of succotash and bowls of chicha in front of them. As long as we looked on, all was orderly and quiet except that two musicians with a violin and a primitive old harp were endeavoring to cheer them up.

Soon after dark, in a pouring rain, we passed the high walls of the Ayacucho cemetery, clattered over the cobble-stones of the narrow streets, entered the plaza, and were ushered with a flourish through a stone arch into the courtyard of the hotel. Acting on the orders of the Prefect, the proprietor had reserved for our use an enormous parlor or reception room where at least forty people could be comfortably seated, and a great bedroom of nearly the same dimensions in which were four large bedsteads. Notwithstanding the attractiveness of the hotel bedsteads, such is the perversity of human nature that I decided to use my own little "Gold Medal" folding cot that had served me faithfully for many weeks, and my own blankets which, as they were folded up every morning as soon as I arose and not unfolded until I was ready to sleep, could be relied upon to be free from fleas, etc.

The plaza of Ayacucho is surrounded on three sides with private houses that have arcades supported by stone pillars. The ground floors are taken up with shops, while over the arcades are balconies that lead to the principal rooms of the dwelling houses. Our hotel had been once occupied by one of the principal families of the town and was a good specimen of the old Spanish method of building. It had a large courtyard from which a flight of stone steps led up to the galleries, and was ornamented by potted plants and caged birds.

Hardly had we examined our rooms when we received a call from the Prefect, Don Gaspar Mauro Cacho, a tall, finely proportioned Peruvian with a remarkable sense of humor and an unfailing store of courtesy. On the following day he took upon himself to show us the sights of the town, including the fine old cathedral, the large public market, clean and well kept, the picturesque old churches, and the Prefecture, a large double quadrangle where were located the offices of the Department, the barracks of the few troops stationed here, and the rooms allotted for the use of himself and his family.

His wife and children had arrived from Lima not many months previous, and the terrors of the overland journey were vividly in their minds. His señora assured me that she had feared she would never reach Ayacucho alive, notwithstanding the fact that the government had made every possible provision for their comfort on the journey. One of the "guides" lost his way, and they were quartered at an abandoned tambo where there was nothing to eat or drink and no firewood. Having lived in Lima all their lives, they felt the discomforts keenly. It was an interesting commentary on the state of the roads that even a Prefect could not be sure that his family would travel with a moderate degree of comfort.

I had sometimes felt that the life of an official in Peru was as easy as the life of the poor Indians was hard, but I had to reverse that opinion before leaving the country. While the Prefects are appointed directly by the President and are responsible only to him, they are likely to be considered troublesome by the local magistrates who, although elected by the citizens, exercise very limited prerogatives. Were it not for the dozen or more soldiers that take their orders directly from the Prefect, he would often be in a precarious position. He must govern as well as he can, and yet if he does not make himself popular with the people of the city in which he lives, his lot is not at all an easy one. With such men as the Prefects whom we met in Arequipa, Abancay, and Ayacucho, the central government is fortunate in being able to be sure that the power which it delegates to them will be used firmly and wisely and without causing friction.

This city, one of the largest in Peru, occupies an excellent central situation and from it diverge roads in every direction. Yet so great is the difficulty of bringing foreign merchandise over these mountain roads, that we found few shops here of any importance, and almost all seemed to be owned by natives of the country. The streets were all of the same pattern, paved with rough stones, sloping, not away from the centre as with us, but towards the centre, where in the middle there is invariably a ditch, practically an open sewer. For those walking on the sidewalk, it is certainly much pleasanter to have this ditch in the middle of the street.

In anticipation of the joys of eating and drinking connected with Carnival, Indian women with huge cauldrons of chupe and immense jars of chicha were preparing to take up all-night stands, sometimes in the centre of the street or else on a busy corner where they would be sure to attract trade. The effect of the women's head-gear was most curious. It was exactly as though the lady had found her shawl a bit too warm and had taken it off, folded it into a square, and proceeded to carry it on her head for convenience. We went through one old crumbling archway, attracted by some beautiful clay jars, and found ourselves in a backyard that would have delighted a painter. Not all painters, but the kind that loves a natural combination of picturesque ruins, fine old jars tumbled about helter-skelter, dirty little Indian children in dirtier hats and ponchos, very much too big for them, a cat, and a long-legged pig who nosed about among the jars trying to see which one contained chicha fit to gratify his thirst.

From the tower of one of the oldest churches we secured a splendid view of the city and the surrounding country including nearly the entire region occupied by the forces of Sucre and La Serna in the week preceding the final battle of Ayacucho.

The old name of Ayacucho was Guamanga, which is said to have been a Spanish adaptation of the Inca Huaman-ca (Take it, Falcon), a name that was given to the district by an incident that followed a fierce battle in which a warlike tribe of this vicinity was defeated and almost annihilated by the armies

A PICTURESQUE CORNER IN AYACUCHO

CROSSING THE PONGORA RIVER ON THE SHAKY SUSPEN-SION BRIDGE

of the Inca Viracocha. It is said that when serving out rations of flesh to his troops after the battle, the Inca threw a piece to a falcon that was soaring over his head, saying "Huaman-ca." However this may be, the town of Guamanga was one of the earliest to be founded by Pizarro and was later the site of a bloody encounter between Vaca de Castro, the legitimate Viceroy, and young Almagro and his followers, who had assassinated Pizarro.

The name Ayacucho was given to the town after the famous battle of December 9, 1824, which was fought near the village of Quinua, thirteen miles north. "Ayacucho" means "corner (or heap) of dead men" and refers to the bloody character of this conflict and of those that had preceded it in the Inca Conquest and in the Spanish Conquest of Peru.

On February 21, the three days of Carnival began. Although I had often read of the impossibility of doing anything in Peru during that period of jollification, I succeeded in persuading the kind-hearted Prefect to procure us animals that we might ride to Quinua, thirteen miles away, and spend a day or so investigating the battlefield. He tried to dissuade us, but as he knew that it was for this purpose that we had come to Ayacucho, everything was soon ready. The Gobernador of Quinua had been given orders to be on hand, to act as our guide. Accompanied by him and the Secretary of the Department and a small military escort, we left the hotel and took the road to the northwest.

Our little cavalcade was strung out over a block or more by the time we reached the suburbs as the streets were narrow and not in particularly good repair. Suddenly the horses of our guides wheeled and bolted and were with difficulty kept in the road. The cause was a characteristic piece of carelessness on the part of somebody. A horse had recently died and his thrifty owner had at once skinned him to save his hide, leaving the hideous carcass in the very centre of the narrow road. It was necessary to make a considerable detour through the neighboring fields, for none of our animals would go within fifty feet of the disgusting spectacle.

For the first two leagues we followed the regular road to Lima and the north, branching off when we reached the ford over the Pongora River, then passing through several small plantations and near two vineyards, we crossed the river Yucaes on a new suspension bridge and climbed the face of a steep cliff by a zig-zag trail. We had good animals and kept them going at a comfortable trot so that we arrived at the little village of Quinua in three and a half hours after leaving Ayacucho.

The plaza of Quinua is surrounded on three sides by houses and ruins, the fourth side being taken up by the church. Like the other houses in the vicinity, these were built of stone and earth and roofed with red tiles. Many of the roofs had been allowed to fall into decay, and the house which was pointed out as the place where the truce was signed after the battle, and where the Spanish General surrendered to General Sucre, had entirely lost its covering.

A hasty lunch was prepared for us at a little mud hut called a tavern, and as soon after as possible we re-mounted and rode north for half a mile up the face of a little hill and found ourselves on the plain where was fought the last great battle of the South American Wars of Independence. A monument, apparently made of some kind of plaster, and naturally in a very bad state of repair, marked the centre of the plain. Near by was a kind of shed or shelter for the horses, and a little to the westward the walls of a memorial chapel that had not yet been completed. North of the plain the heights of Condorkanqui rise abruptly. A new road had recently been constructed over them to the warm valleys beyond, but it was still perfectly possible to see the old trail down which the Spanish troops marched in their attack on the patriots.

The altitude of the field is nearly eleven thousand feet, and romantically inclined writers have sometimes spoken of this as the "battle above the clouds." As a matter of fact, we had considerable difficulty in taking photographs owing to the low hanging clouds that continually swept down from the summits of Condor-kanqui. Fortunately it did not rain all the time.

Few battles have ever been fought on a height that offered such a magnificent view. From all parts of the battlefield, a superb panorama is spread out to the east, south, and west, embracing the entire valley of Ayacucho.

After spending the afternoon on the field, we returned to the little tavern where the evening passed very pleasantly and we were entertained by the Indian villagers who were celebrating the Carnival. They came in throngs bringing us parched corn, popcorn, and chicha, swearing eternal friendship, and expressing their appreciation that we should come such a long distance to see their famous battlefield. The village appeared to be divided into three wards, and the alcalde of each ward was anxious that we should eat and drink just as much of his offering as we had of the others.

They were easily satisfied, however, and appeared to be having a very good time. I never saw Indians enjoy themselves more. As a conclusion to the entertainment, two Indian women were instructed to sing for us. Their performance consisted in a wailing duet, beginning loud and high, ascending with a powerful crescendo to screeching falsetto notes and then gradually descending and diminishing into a wheeze like a very old parlor organ with leaky bellows.

We spent the next morning photographing different parts of the battlefield and trying to get a better idea of the reasons for Sucre's victory. I was very forcibly impressed by the skill with which he had chosen his position.

The little plain, really a plateau, is literally surrounded by ravines. It was just large enough to allow Sucre to use his seven or eight thousand men to the best advantage. An enemy attacking him must perforce come up hill on every side, even though it would seem as though the Spanish troops descending from Condorkanqui would have had some advantage. But they were under fire all the time they were descending to the plain, and just

THE BATTLEFIELD OF AYACUCHO

THE BATTLEFIELD AS IT APPEARED TO THE SPANIARDS

before they reached it, they found themselves in a little gully up the sides of which they had to scramble at a disadvantage before they could actually be on a level with the defenders. La Serna was too good a general not to have appreciated the strength of Sucre's position. In fact, as General Miller points out, the mistake of the Viceroy in attacking originated in allowing himself to be over-persuaded by the eagerness of his troops. Their patience had been exhausted by terrible marches which seemed to them to be endless. Only a few days before the battle, the tents of the Viceroy and his chief general had had lampoons pasted on them, accusing them of cowardice. It may fairly be said that he was goaded into action contrary to his own judgment.

The battle of Ayacucho, besides being the final combat, was one of the most brilliant in the history of the Wars of Independence. The troops on both sides were well-seasoned veterans. The generals in command were among the ablest that the long wars had developed. Every man fought with bravery. Although the Patriots were outnumbered, they made up for it by enthusiasm and by a knowledge that there was no opportunity for them to retreat. They were aided by the lay of the land, but the result was due to a most determined valor and a heroic daring that must always gratify lovers of Peruvian history.

We returned to the city in the middle of the afternoon in time to take a little walk in the streets and be bombarded by little Carnival balloons filled with scented water, egg-shells filled with colored powder, and the other missiles that are commonly employed to bear witness to the fact that Lent is approaching. The ladies and children, who occupied points of vantage in the second-story windows, kept up a brisk fire on everyone who ventured along the streets, and we had to do some very rapid dodging to avoid being entirely soaked and colored with all the hues of the rainbow.

In the evening, notwithstanding a terrific downpour of rain, the "society of Ayacucho," including the Archbishop, the Prefect, and fifty or sixty of their friends, "tendered us" an elaborate banquet which quite took the palm for variety of food and drink. There were no less than fourteen courses besides seven kinds of wine including champagne. The after-dinner speeches were also quite remarkable. Hitherto, the chief interest in us had been the fact that we had "visited the lost city of Choqquequirau," but here Choqquequirau meant little or nothing. The battlefield of Ayacucho meant everything, and the fact that we were delegados from a country whose aid Peru hoped to receive in case Chile became troublesome meant a great deal more. Whether it was at this banquet or at one of those that preceded it in the past three weeks, I do not remember, but the opinion was expressed more than once that, rather than have another war with Chile, they would surrender to the United States and become a protectorate. I mention this not as an indication of national sentiment, but merely to show the state of feeling that prevailed in the interior of Peru at the time, and the attitude with which they regarded the possibility of another war with Chile.

A large part of the hatred that exists between Chilean and Peruvian is due to their native ancestry. In the Chilean there is a large percentage of Araucanian blood. In the Peruvian there is as much of the blood of the Quichuas. The Araucanians are the hereditary foes of the Quichuas. For centuries there was no peace between them. The Incas pushed their army of Quichuas as far south as possible, but they never could conquer the lands where the Araucanians roved. Even the all-conquering Spanish soldiers were blocked in southern Chile. It is not necessary to repeat here the long story of the Araucanian wars and the heroic deeds of Lautaro and his kinsmen. Instead of being easily conquered by the handful of Spanish adventurers as were the Incas and Quichuas, the Araucanians kept the Spaniards at bay for centuries, and were in fact never subdued.

The Araucanians and the Quichuas had as different racial characteristics as can be imagined. Although the Araucanians did not constitute a nation in the proper sense of the word but were divided into a large number of clans, each independent and recognizing no master, they never allowed any outside people to interfere with their national life. They were intensely independent. Even the chiefs lacked authority in time of peace. There were no serfs or slaves. More important still, there were no laws; private wrongs had to be settled privately. All of these elements must be taken into considera tion when contemplating the character of the Chilean of to-day. His Spanish ancestors brooked no interference and recognized no central government, but his Araucanian forebears were still more intensely fond of individual liberty. His Spanish ancestors were brave and fearless. No better soldiers existed in Europe in the sixteenth century. The Araucanians were even more warlike, and after their first few defeats by the invaders, they successfully assumed the offensive, storming Spanish towns and carrying off cattle and horses. They organized troops of cavalry, learning to excel on an animal that their fathers had never heard of, and which the Quichuas even now rarely dare to mount. The entire Araucanian nation was less numerous than the army of Quichuas that surrounded Atahualpa when he was successfully attacked by Pizarro, yet they killed more Spanish soldiers than fell in the conquest of the entire remainder of the continent. With such an ancestry, it is not remarkable that the Chileans are notoriously the best fighters on the continent to-day. Contrast their inheritance with that of the Peruvians.

The Quichuas were and are a timid, peaceful folk lacking in dignity, defending themselves rather with cunning and falsehood than by deeds of arms. The servile sentiment is deeply rooted in the Quichua nature. He maintains a sense of loyalty for his former masters, but he has absolutely no idea of liberty or independence. The Quichuas had reached a higher state of culture than the Araucanians but their manly characteristics were far less developed. In fact, at the time of the Spanish conquest, they seem to have been already in a decadent condition. With such blood in their veins, it is not surprising that the Peruvians were easily defeated by the Chileans, their country overrun and humiliated, their valuable nitrate fields seized, and the seeds of intense national hatred planted that will take generations to eradicate.

CHAPTER XXVI
AYACUCHO TO LIMA

Every one had told us that it would be "absolutely impossible" to leave
Ayacucho until two or three days had elapsed after the end of the Carnival. Possibly because we were a trifle homesick, and possibly because we had been assured
so positively that it could not be done, we determined to try to leave Ayacucho
on the last day of the three devoted to Carnival. I must confess that it was rather
cruel, not only to the two soldiers who were ordered to accompany us, but also the
arriero who was informed that he must provide us with mules and go when we
were ready to start. The morning was spent in a great row over the mules and the
question as to how far they were to go with us, in which many tears were shed by
drunken Indian women who declared that they were sure they would never see
their husbands or animals back again. If it had not been for the Prefect's willingness to help us, we could never have persuaded any one to go, but he did his part
splendidly. We at length got off just at noon. The Prefect and his friends, to the
number of fourteen, escorted us for the first league out of the city. Then we bade
them an affectionate farewell and started off on the last stage of our journey, determined, if possible, to travel henceforth as much like private citizens as we could.
To be sure, we had our little military escort. Without them we should have found
it almost impossible to proceed at all for the next few days. Our first two leagues
were over the same road which we had used in going to Quinua, then, instead of
fording the river, we kept on its left bank until we reached a shaky suspension
bridge. Its floor was made of loose planks that were so easily misplaced by the
mules that Hay declared he had to set them all over again after I had passed in
order to avoid falling into the river.

We met on the road many Indians, celebrating Carnival, marching along gayly, beating primitive little drums and blowing on bamboo-fifes. They stopped at
almost every house they passed, shouting and hullabalooing and getting a few
drinks of chicha.

As we were crossing the rocky bed of a little stream we met an itinerant musician, a blind harpist, who was being helped across by a friend. His harp was very
curious, being a wooden box shaped like half a cone with two wooden legs tacked
into its base, and two eye-holes on the flat side which made it look very much like
some dwarfish animal. With great difficulty we tried to persuade him to set up his
harp in the dry bed of the stream and play us a tune while we took his picture.

Not having the slightest conception of what we were trying to do, the poor blind musician was rather frightened, and as he understood no Spanish whatever, we should not have succeeded had it not been for the kind offices of a pleasant-faced mestizo family party who were picnicking on the bank of the stream and who translated our poor Spanish into Quichua. In the evening we reached Huanta, an historic little town where savage Indian tribes from the Amazonian forests have frequently come into collision with armed Peruvian forces. Although we hoped to be able to slip into town unnoticed, we were met, a mile out, by the usual dozen of hospitably inclined caballeros who, with the Gobernador at their head, had been "celebrating" for the past two or three days. We were by this time so fatigued by the labors of crossing Peru in the wet season, that we found it very difficult to be as polite as we were expected to be to the reception committees that had been our lot hitherto. However, in this case, to put it bluntly, the Gobernador was very drunk, which made him only the more friendly, and he insisted that we were two "princes of America," and that his house would be everlastingly famous in history as having been the place where we stayed!

His wife and daughters behaved splendidly. They seemed to realize that we knew it was customary for all the men to get drunk at this season of the year. At the same time they did their best to make us comfortable and to see that the male members of the family did not annoy us any more than they could help.

Naturally, the "morning after" was a sad occasion, and had it not been for our excellent soldiers, who had gone to bed sober, it would have been very difficult to have persuaded our hosts to let us go. The Gobernador was extremely cross. He had

THE BRIDGE OVER THE HUARPA

forgotten all about our princely lineage, and only remembered to charge us treble for everything he could think of. Although we had gotten up at five o'clock, no Indians sober enough to act as guides could be found for several hours, and it was after ten before we finally left Huanta.

The son of the Gobernador was the only person who had energy enough, or had sufficiently recovered from the debauch of the night before, to do us the honor of escorting us out of town. This had come to be such a regular feature of our travels since leaving Cuzco that we always looked forward with curiosity to see what would happen. This young fellow was very polite and went with us as far as the entrance of the local cemetery, a bizarre white-washed adobe gate, protected from the weather by a little covering of red tiles. There must have been something prophetic about his bidding us good-by at the gates of a cemetery, for he was the last honorary escort that we had in Peru.

Our road led us through a thickly populated region. Here and there on the roadside, unfortunate individuals, both men and women, who had been too far gone to reach home the night before, were sleeping off the effects of the Carnival. Ordinarily one does not see much drunkenness in Peru, but this certainly was an exception.

Small towns and villages followed in quick succession. Then we descended into the valley of the Huarpa River and across a well-built toll-bridge. The bridge was so long and so high above the stream that my mule concluded he would stay on the east bank. He yielded to our combined efforts, but only after much beating. We now passed through a semi-arid region of cactus and mimosa trees like the basin of the Pampas River, until we began to climb an extremely steep ravine. Several times we lost our way, and in places the path had been completely washed out by the rains. The crux came at a little waterfall only five feet high. So smooth was the face of the rock over which the little stream of water trickled that our sure-footed animals found it impossible to reach the upper level until we had built a rude stone stairway which they cheerfully essayed to climb. Their energetic scrambles were finally rewarded by success. For three hours the trail wound upwards as steeply as it was possible to go, until we reached the bleak paramo near Marcas.

A magnificent panorama lay spread out before us. In the foreground were hillsides dotted with thatched huts and fields where sheep and cattle grazed; in the middle distance, deep valleys whose rivers had cut their way down into gorges out of our sight; and far beyond, a magnificent range of mountains, some capped with snow and others with clouds. It was a little after five o'clock when we entered the picturesque little village of Marcas with its two dozen huts scattered about under the lee of the rocks or clustered near the road. We recognized it as just the sort of village where we would have been refused both food and shelter had we been alone. But as we were accompanied by an energetic sergeant who did not propose to allow any poor Indians to stand in the way of our progress, a hut no dirtier or more comfortless than the rest was soon put at our disposal, and the sergeant did his best to get us all a good supper out of our own provisions.

Our baggage animals had had a frightfully hard day of it and our soldiers assured us that if we intended to catch the weekly train out of Huancayo, it would be necessary to have at least one more beast of burden, for although our luggage could be conveniently carried by two mules going at a walk, if we expected to make forty miles a day, as we hoped to do, one animal must be rested every other day. Accordingly the Indian alcalde of Marcas was instructed to get us a mule. "But there are no mules here" he replied. A horse then. "Very well, there is one old one which I will have ready for you in the morning." Soon after breakfast an old white horse appeared, accompanied by a weeping Indian woman who had no desire to take our money and who was thoroughly convinced that she would never see her horse again. It was finally agreed that the horse should go only to the next town where we could get another beast and send this one back by one of the Indian alcaldes that now accompanied us from village to village, returning as their task of acting as guides was taken up by the alcaldes of the next place.

With the aid of the fresh horse, we made good time and skirted the slopes of a high range of hills leaving the trim little town of Acobamba far off on our left. It lies in the valley of the Lircay which is quite densely populated and seemed to be very fertile. In the middle of the afternoon we reached Urumyosi where there are curious great rocks shaped like sugar loaves. They are of soft sandstone which is easily worked, and a number of caves have been made by poor people at the base of the rocks. After a long cold ride and ten hours in the saddle, we came in sight of a mud-colored town called Paucara which has long had a very evil reputation. Whether this is deserved or not we did not endeavor to discover. The sergeant persuaded the owner of a rude little hut, half a mile from the town and on the direct road, to let us spend the night there. One of our neighbors brought freshly cut barley-straw for the mules, another brought a dozen eggs, and with the aid of our own supplies and cooking utensils, we fared splendidly.

The night was excessively damp and as bitterly cold as it can be only in a genuinely tropical country when the temperature drops forty degrees after the sun goes down and an icy wind penetrates your very bones, even though you have hurriedly put on two or three sweaters and a couple of ponchos as it grew dark. There is no cold like the cold of the tropics. Furthermore the carcass of a recently killed sheep hung dripping in the hut. The floor was wet and muddy, there were no windows and only a small door. We wished we had a tent.

There being no incentive to linger at this charming country-house, our Indians were actually up and away before six o'clock. We had saved four eggs the evening before to be cooked for our breakfast, and after loading our pack animals and seeing them safely off with all our supplies, we handed our

URUMYOSI

THE HUT NEAR PAUCARA

eggs and some tea to the housewife and asked her to prepare us a frugal meal. Alas! it was quite impossible. The cooking activities of the evening before had used up every stick of firewood within a radius of a mile, and there was no way in which water could be boiled. The only provisions for our breakfast were the raw eggs. We had before us a ride of forty miles over an exceedingly rough country, part of which lay at an elevation of fourteen thousand feet above the sea, so we hastily swallowed our eggs as best as we could and started off with the prospect of twelve hours in the saddle.

At first the road wound slowly up the valley of Lircay, until finally it climbed over the edge of the hills to a great bleak plateau where hundreds of llamas were feeding. When you come to a llama range you may be fairly certain that the altitude is not far from that of the top of Pike's Peak. Add to this a blinding snowstorm that keeps you from seeing more than six feet ahead of you, a wearied mule, a very hungry rider, and the uncertainty as to whether you are on the right road or not, and you will have a picture of our predicament during part of that never-to-be-forgotten day. At length, to our great delight, the trail began slowly to descend from cheerless paramos and little mountain lakes into a great valley where, thousands of feet below, we could see huts and cultivated fields.

Skirting the hills half-way up the valley and avoiding the attractive little trails that led down to Indian villages, we kept turning more and more to the westward until we rounded a spur and came on a magnificent view of the great river Mantaro that on its way to join the Apurimac has cut a wonderfully deep cañon through this part of Peru. A tortuous descent of two thousand feet brought us to the new toll-bridge of Tablachaca and onto an excellent road. Of course, this does not mean that it could be used for wheeled vehicles, for of carts there are none in this part of the world. It simply means that a trail four or five feet wide and reasonably free from rocks and holes allowed the mules to jog along at a gait of nearly five miles an hour. So slow had been our progress over the paramo that it was considerably after dark before we reached the picturesque old stone bridge of Yscuchaca, re-crossed the Mantaro, and clattered over the cobble-tones of this well-built little town.

We had rather flattered ourselves that no one here knew we were coming and so we had avoided an official reception and all possible attacks on our digestive faculties. But we had to pay for it by finding that it took nearly two hours longer than usual before we were able to secure any accommodations whatsoever for the night. The Gobernador of Yscuchaca lived a mile or more out of town on his country estate, and learning finally that there were two "distinguished foreigners" in town, sent his head servant to welcome us, gave us the use of a room in his town house, provided our mules with pasturage, and the next morning charged us three times the regular tariff. I regret to say that we took advantage of the absence of the Gobernador to pay his major-domo what our sergeant told us was the

THE TOLL BRIDGE OF TABLACHACA

legitimate price and left him wondering why he had not been able to over-charge us as he had certain American civil engineers who had been here not long before, surveying for the extension of the central railway of Peru.

At present, that railway, begun many years ago, goes from Lima to Oroya and thence south to Huancayo which is nearly fifty miles from Yscuchaca. It is proposed now to continue it from Huancayo to Yscuchaca and thence due south to Huancavelica where there are mines of quicksilver and copper. Eventually it will form one of the links in the chain of the Pan-American Railway.

Our mules were pretty tired and so were we, but when one is on the home stretch it is easy to travel from early to late. We rose before five o'clock. Our road first crossed the Mantaro, ascended the left bank of the stream for several miles, passed several mineral springs, and then climbed out of the narrowing cañon up toward the village of Acostambo. At one place where the road had been cut through what looked like a fossil bed, I was so fortunate as to find, in situ, a fossil bivalve. Professor Charles Schuchert of Yale University has been so good as to identify it for me as allorisma subcuneata. It has been found also in Brazil. Its geological horizon, the upper carboniferous, is widely distributed in South America and is well known about Lake Titicaca. The location of this fossil here may indicate the presence in this vicinity of coal-beds. If any could be found, it would be the greatest benefit, not only to the railway that hopes some day to pass through this valley, but also to the copper-smelters in the vicinity. As a matter of fact, Peru does not need the coal for power; these great and rapidly flowing rivers like the Mantaro, the Pampas, and the Apurimac offer an abundant water-power that, transformed into electricity, would run all the railroads and factories that could possibly be crowded into Peru.

Personally, I do not believe in the construction of steam railroads in this country. The difficulties of overcoming steep grades are serious, and the cost of building is necessarily all out of proportion to the traffic that is likely to be developed. I do believe, however, that the future of Peru depends upon the development of her water-power and the building of light electric railways that would be sufficient to handle economically the product of the mines and to accommodate passengers. If the region were one where extensive crops could be cultivated and a large amount of heavy freight developed, this argument would not hold. Under the circumstances, however, I believe that it is a much safer investment for capital and a much more practical work for the government to develop electric traction.

At Acostambo, a town of perhaps two thousand inhabitants, we tried to buy something to eat for lunch, but there was nothing to be had except some dough cakes that had been "cooked" in cold ashes. After passing through two or three small villages where most of the Indians seemed to be in a state of intoxication, we crossed the Cordillera Marcavalle and found ourselves on the well-travelled road to Pampas. Before us, spread out in a magnificent panorama, the fertile, densely populated valley of Jauja. Watered by the Upper Mantaro River and its affluents, there are over fifty villages, towns, and cities, clustered together in this rich plain. Immediately ahead lay four towns almost exactly in a straight line and less than ten miles apart: Pucará, where we stopped long enough to buy some parched corn and freshly roasted pork for supper, Sapallauga, Punta, and Huancayo. Instead of the desolate region in which we had passed most of yesterday, we were now in one of the most thickly populated parts of Peru, and felt as though we were back again in civilization. This sensation was increased when we began to clatter down the long street of Huancayo. It seemed like an age before we finally reached the business centre of the city at 9 P.M. and surrendered ourselves into the hands of a courteous Austrian hotel proprietor.

We had spent nearly fourteen hours in the saddle. This was quite forgotten when we learned to our delight that there was to be a train for Oroya the next day, for the first time in two weeks.

We had heard that the train from Huancayo left usually on Sundays, so we had promised our soldiers a sovereign apiece if they would see to it that we reached Huancayo by Saturday night. As they had to accompany the slow-moving pack animals, they did not arrive themselves until the next morning, somewhat in fear lest they had lost their promised reward. When they were assured, however, that we had caught our train, and when they had received their gold and what was left of our kitchen utensils and supplies, their delight knew no bounds, and they were constrained to embrace us in truly oriental fashion.

Sunday morning is a great event in Huancayo. Before sunrise, thousands of Indians come in from the surrounding towns and villages for the weekly Fair. Two large plazas are crowded with vendors of every conceivable kind of merchandise: oxen and mules raised nearby, toys "made in Germany," pottery and ponchos made in Huancayo, and beer made in Milwaukee. Overflowing from the crowded plazas the Fair extends for nearly a mile through the main street of the city. The picturesque Indians in their brilliantly colored ponchos, thronging the streets and alternately buying and selling their wares, offer a field for diversion that no one should miss who reaches Lima.

Like the Mexican Indians, so vividly depicted by Mr. Kirkham in his artistic "Mexican Trails," there are many among the throng who will "sell a hen, later to bargain for a sombrero, presently to go upon their knees within the church yonder, candle in hand; lastly to lie by the roadside, overfull of pulque and oblivious of this world, or the next."

The type is the same whether it be seen on a Sunday in the Andes of Mexico, Peru, or Colombia. Only here it is chicha that is the favorite beverage instead of pulque.

The long expected train was due to arrive at noon and "to leave soon afterwards." The platform and the newly constructed booths near the little corrugated-iron station were crowded for hours by

SUNDAY MORNING IN HUANCAYO

intending passengers and friends of expected arrivals. But it was late in the afternoon, almost dark in fact, before the belated little train pulled into the station and the runners from the three Huancayo hotels had the satisfaction of greeting their "friends." We were informed that the train would not leave before six o'clock the next morning so we tried to possess ourselves in patience at our comfortable little hotel.

We were on hand, bright and early, just in time to see the train pull out of the station. Happily it was only a false alarm, and the train soon backed down to the platform again and waited for three quarters of an hour for intending passengers to arrive. At length the conductor decided he could wait no longer, and at 6:40 we pulled out, just before the sub-Prefect and his friends arrived on the scene. A young politician on the train, who thought that the sub-Prefect wanted to go to Lima, pulled violently at the bell-rope. The engineer, accustomed to that form of stopping the train, had detached the ropes from the locomotive so that all that the friends of the sub-Prefect were able to do was to pull several yards of it into the rear coach. Rather characteristically, the only four people who were on hand at six o'clock ready for the train to start on time, were all Americans. The two besides ourselves were artisans from the great copper mines of Cerro de Pasco who were enjoying a week's vacation.

At Jauja there is a spur track which runs from the main line a mile or more back to the historic old city, celebrated in the annals of the Spanish Conquest and the Wars of Independence. The good people of Jauja, not yet accustomed to the necessary rules of a railroad train service, flocked on board the train to say "good-by" to their departing friends and chat as long as possible. Taking no heed of the screams of the engine and the cries of the conductor, more than twenty ladies, who had no intention of leaving town, were still on board when the train pulled out of the station. The conductor took them a mile and a half down the track to the main line; then, fearing that the mere fact that they would have to walk home would not sufficiently impress them, he made each one pay for riding! Twenty more sheepish-looking individuals than the garrulous ladies, whom the conductor lined up in the field a short distance from the tracks and charged for their short ride, would be hard to find.

At eleven o'clock we came to a wash-out and had to cross the Oroya River on planks hastily thrown over the unfinished new railroad bridge. A train was waiting for us on the other side, and with very little delay, all the passengers and luggage were safely carried across and we reached Oroya before four o'clock that evening.

Although there are rich mines in the vicinity and it is the terminus of the new line, built by American capital, to the great Cerro de Pasco smelters, Oroya is chiefly famous as the terminus of "the highest railroad in the world," and we looked forward with interest to our journey on the morrow.

The magnificent great viaduct which has frequently been pictured as formerly one of the highest railroad bridges in existence, had come to grief only a short time before, in a rather tragic manner. A car, loaded with bridge-construction material and occupied by several American engineers, was standing on the bridge to which repairs were being made. A run-away engine came flying down the grade, struck the car, jumped into the air, crashed back on the frail viaduct, which gave way and allowed a tangled mass of men and metal to fall into the cañon two hundred and twenty feet below.

This accident necessitated many delays, as all the passengers and freight had to be transferred by mules or on foot down into the cañon and up the other side to the train for Lima.

The ride from Oroya to Lima has been so frequently described by many travellers and the excitement of coasting down from the summit tunnel where the altitude is 15,666 feet to the Lima station, which is only a little above sea level, is so well known, that I will not attempt to give my own impressions here. Suffice it to say that the excitement was increased if anything by the fact that besides the bridge accident another had occurred only a few days previously in which a locomotive had left the tracks and rolled down an embankment.

Owing to these accidents our train was provided with a very old engine whose boilers were so leaky that we had a hard time climbing up from Oroya to the divide. Several times we stopped; once for three quarters of an hour to allow enough steam to accumulate to pull us around a curve. We did not object, however, for the scenery was wonderful. The great craggy cliffs, their slopes covered with snow and ice, made us realize that this was really the roof tree of the continent. Just before entering the summit tunnel, the train stopped again, and we had a chance to enjoy a magnificent panorama of snow-capped mountains.

A hand-car with two workmen was sent down the road just ahead of our train so as to give us some sense of assurance. It is well known that most people coming up this road from Lima suffer greatly from soroche before they reach the summit. On our way down, however, most of the passengers were so well accustomed to high elevations that not more than three or four, and they Peruvian ladies from Jauja and Oroya, seemed to be affected. So far as I could judge, their trouble was due more to car-sickness and the lack of ventilation than to the elevation.

We reached Lima about half past eight on the evening of March 2d. Who can describe the comfort and luxury of those first few hours in the excellent Hotel Maury?

My first duty the next day was to call on President Leguia, report on what I had seen at Choqquequirau and tell him how very hospitably we had been received in the interior towns and cities. After talking with him for a few moments, we were no longer at a loss to understand why the Prefects and sub-Prefects of Peru had been so courteous to us, for their chief is himself the soul of courtesy. Well-travelled, well-educated, speaking English fluently, a trained business man, not in the slightest degree the type of South American President with which novel-readers and playgoers are familiar, he impressed us as a man who would do his best to advance the welfare of Peru without caring in the least how his own affairs might prosper in the meantime.

The door-keeper was a fine, tall, gray-haired soldier who had the manners of a general, was rather suspicious of us at first, but returned almost immediately after taking in our cards and, with a magnificent bow and a courtly gesture, ushered us at once into the inner reception room, greatly to the disgust of several pompous, perspiring politicians who had been warming their heels in the gilded salon for some time before we arrived. We did not stay long, and on our way out were again given a demonstration of interest by the courteous old brigadier. To our sorrow we read a few months afterward that in the unsuccessful revolution already referred to in the chapter on Arequipa, which began by seizing the presidential offices and in securing the President himself and his Minister of Foreign Affairs, the revolutionists had ruthlessly killed the old door-keeper.

Like every visitor to Lima, we too went into the cathedral to see the mummified remains of Francisco Pizarro, the Conqueror of Peru, and then we took a little victoria, drawn by a pair of speedy little trotters, and explored the parks and boulevards. We saw the monuments and the new public buildings, called on the American Minister, whom we found to be a charming southern gentleman, exceedingly well suited to his diplomatic profession; admired the many substantial foreign banks and business houses, and regretted that so much of the flavor of the old colonial Lima had been lost in the Chilean war and in the recent era of business prosperity. With electric lights and electric cars and abundant foreign capital, it is not easy to preserve those picturesque features which are so charming in the interior cities.

At last my journey overland from Buenos Aires had been completed. I cannot claim to know it as well or as intimately as the poor "foot-walker" who, if he has been successful, must by this time have reached Buenos Aires and walked on foot twice over this long dreary road. Nevertheless, I can appreciate keenly some of the difficulties of travel in Spanish-America during the colonial period when Lima was the gay capital and Buenos Aires was merely a frontier post. It is small wonder that there was little sympathy between Lima and Buenos Aires in those days.

Like my journey across Venezuela and Colombia, this taught me to feel anew the stupendous difficulties that lie in the way of advancing South American civilization. It made me admire tremendously the courage and determination of those heroes of the Wars of Independence who marched up and down this road for fourteen years until they had driven from it the last vestige of a foreign army.

CHAPTER XXVII
CERTAIN SOUTH AMERICAN TRAITS

As one travels through the various South American republics, becomes acquainted with their political and social conditions, reads their literature, and talks with other American travellers, there are a number of adverse criticisms that frequently arise. I shall attempt here to enumerate some of them, to account for a few, and to compare others with criticisms that were made of the people of the United States, half a century ago, by a distinguished English visitor.

Although it is true that the historical and geographical background of the South Americans is radically different from ours, it is also true that they have many social and superficial characteristics very like those which European travellers found in the United States fifty years ago. The period of time is not accidental. The South American Republics secured their independence nearly fifty years later than we did. Moreover, they have been hampered in their advancement by natural difficulties and racial antipathies much more than we have. Although the conditions of life in the United States, as depicted by foreign critics seventy-five years after the battle of Yorktown, were decidedly worse than the conditions of life in South America seventy-five years after the battle of Ayacucho, the resemblances between the faults that were found with us fifty years ago and those that are noticeable among the South Americans of to-day, are too striking to be merely coincidences. It is surely not for us to say that there is anything inherently wrong with our Southern neighbors if their shortcomings are such as we ourselves had not long ago, and possibly have to-day.

The first criticism that one hears, and the first one is likely to make after getting beyond the pale of official good breeding in South America, is that the manners of the ordinary South American are very bad. Lest the traveller be inclined to take such a state of affairs too seriously, let him read what Dickens wrote about us and our ways in 1855. It was a faithful picture of a certain phase of American life. It should be confessed that it paints a condition of affairs worse than anything I have seen in South America.

Travellers who are prone to find fault with the service at South American hotels and restaurants will enjoy Dickens' description of the dining-room of a New York boarding-house. "In the further region of this banqueting-hall was a stove, garnished on either side with a great brass spittoon.... Before it, swinging himself in a rocking-chair, lounged a large gentleman with his hat on, who amused himself by spitting alternately into the spittoon on the right hand of the stove, and the spittoon on the left, and then working his way back again in the same order. A negro lad in a soiled white jacket was busily engaged in placing on the table two long rows of knives and forks, relieved at intervals by jugs of water; and as he travelled down one side of this festive board, he straightened with his dirty hands, the dirtier cloth, which was all askew, and had not been removed since breakfast."

It is indeed hard for us to overlook the table manners of the average South American. But how many years is it since North Americans were all reading and conning "Don't! A Guide to Good Manners"? It is less than a quarter of a century since our self-conscious use of the fork on all possible (and impossible) viands showed that we felt the need of improvement.

To one inclined to criticise the speed with which a company of South Americans will dispose of their food, let me recommend Dickens' American boarding-house table where a "very few words were spoken; and everybody seemed to eat his utmost in self-defence, as if a famine were expected to set in before breakfast-time to-morrow morning, and it had become high time to assert the first law of nature. The oysters, stewed and pickled, leaped from their capacious reservoirs, and slid by scores into the mouths of the assembly. The sharpest pickles vanished; whole cucumbers at once, like sugar-plums; and no man winked his eye. Great heaps of indigestible matter melted away as ice before the sun. It was a solemn and awful thing to see. Dyspeptic individuals bolted their food in wedges; feeding, not themselves, but broods of nightmares, who were continually standing at livery within them. Spare men, with lank and rigid cheeks, came out unsatisfied from the destruction of heavy dishes, and glared with watchful eyes upon the pastry."

The conversation of a group of young South Americans is not such as appeals to our taste. There is usually too much running criticism on the personal qualities and attractions of their women acquaintances. To them it seems doubtless most gallant. At all events, it is not sordid, as was that conversation which Dickens describes as "summed up in one word—dollars."

When Dickens visited America, he remarked the frequency of the expression "Yes, sir" and made a great deal of fun of us for our use of it. Singularly enough, the Spanish "Yes sir"—si señor—is so extremely common throughout South America as to attract one's attention continually.

Another thing that Dickens noticed was our tendency to postpone and put off from day to day things that did not have to be done. Yet there is no more common criticism of Spanish-Americans than that known as the "Mañana" habit. You will hear almost any one who pretends to know anything at all about Spanish-America say that the great difficulty is the ease with which the Spanish-American says "Mañana." Personally, I do not agree with this criticism for I have heard the expression very seldom in South America. It is true that it is hard to get things done as quickly as one would wish, but I believe that the criticism has been much overworked. Undoubtedly Dickens was honest in re porting that the habit of postponing one's work was characteristic of the middle west as he saw it, but it would be greatly resented to-day and would not be true.

In many South American cities one is annoyed by the continual handshaking. No matter how many times a day you meet a man, he expects you solemnly to shake hands with him just as did those western Americans who annoyed "Martin Chuzzlewit."

So also with "spitting." I have been repeatedly annoyed, not only in the provinces, but also in the very highest circles of the most advanced Republics, by the carelessness of South Americans in this particular, even at dinner parties. But how many years is it since "The Last American" was prophetically depicted by J. A. Mitchell as sitting amid the ruins of the national Capitol with his feet on the marble rail, spitting tobacco juice? One can hardly ride in our street cars to-day without being reminded that only recently have the majority of Americans put the ban on spitting. The fact that there are already printed notices in some of the principal South American cathedrals begging people, in the name of the local "Anti-Tuberculosis Association," not to spit on the floor, shows that this unpleasant habit will undoubtedly be eradicated in considerably less than fifty years after we have ceased to offend.

We also dislike intensely the South American habit of staring at strangers and of making audible comments on ladies who happen to be passing. Unfortunately, this is a Latin habit which will be hard to change. The South American has a racial right to look at such customs differently. But if some of his personal habits are unpleasant, and even disgusting from our point of view, there is no question that we irritate him just as much as he does us. Our curt forms of address; our impatient disregard of the amenities of social intercourse; our unwillingness to pass the time of day at considerable length and inquire, each time we see a friend, after his health and that of his family; our habit of elevating our feet and often sitting in a slouchy attitude when conversing with strangers, are to him extremely distasteful and annoying. Our unwillingness to take the trouble to speak his language grammatically, and our general point of view in regard to the "innate superiority" of our race, our language, and our manufactures, are all evidences, to his mind, of our barbarity. We care far too little for appearances. This seems to him boorish. We criticise him because he does not bathe as frequently as we do. He criticises us because we do not show him proper respect by removing our hats when we meet him on the street.

Furthermore, he regards us as lacking in business integrity. We are too shrewd. Our standard of honor seems low to him. In fact, a practical obstacle with which one accustomed to American business methods has to contend in South America, is the extreme difficulty of securing accurate information as to a man's credit. Inquiries into the financial standing of an individual, which are regarded as a matter of course with us, are resented by the sensi tive Latin temperament as a personal reflection on his honesty. It seems to be true that the South American regards the payment of his debts as a matter more closely touching his honor than we do. He is accustomed to receiving long credits; he always really intends to pay sometime, and he generally manages to raise installments without much difficulty. Yet when pressed hard in the courts, he is likely to turn and resent as an intentional insult the judgment which has been secured against him. I have known personally of a case where a debtor informed his creditor that it would be necessary for him to come well armed if he accompanied the sheriff in an effort to satisfy the judgment of the court, for the first man, and as many more as possible, that crossed the door of his shop on such an errand would be shot. This we criticise as defiance of the law. To the South American, the law has committed an unpardonable fault in venturing to convict him of neglecting his honorable debts.

It is unfortunate that the South Americans themselves are generally quite unaware of their failings—a species of blindness that has frequently been laid at our own doors. It is due to a similar cause.

South American writers who have travelled abroad and seen enough to enable them to point out the defects of their countrymen rarely venture to do so. The South American loves praise but cannot endure criticism. It makes him fairly froth at the mouth, as it did the Americans in the days of Charles Dickens' first visit. So the pleasant-faced gentleman from Massachusetts, Mr. Bevan, told young Martin Chuzzlewit. "If you have any knowledge of our literature, and can give me the name of any man, American born and bred, who has anatomized our follies as a people, and not as this or that party; and has escaped the foulest and most brutal slander, the most inveterate hatred and intolerant pursuit, it will be a strange name in my ears, believe me. In some cases, I could name to you, where a native writer has ventured on the most harmless and good-humoured illustrations of our vices or defects, it has been found necessary to announce, that in a second edition the passage has been expunged, or altered, or explained away, or patched into praise."

There is a story in Santiago de Chile of a young American scholar who spent some time there studying localisms. When he returned to New York he ventured to publish honest but rather severe criticisms of society, as he saw it, in that most aristocratic of South American republics. As a result, the university from which he came received a bad name in Chile and his visit is held in such unpleasant memory that his welcome, were he to return there, would be far from friendly. This seems narrow-minded and perverse but is exactly the way we felt not long ago towards foreigners who spent a few months in the States and wrote, for the benefit of the European public, sincere but caustic criticisms. American sensitiveness became a byword in Europe. Possibly it is growing less with us. However that may be, South American sensitiveness is no keener to-day than ours was fifty years since.

I am willing to admit that it ill becomes an American to offer serious adverse criticisms of the people of any country. Our own defects have been so repeatedly pointed out by foreigners, many of them with distressing unanimity, that we cannot afford to set ourselves up as judges of what South Americans should or should not do. It is true that the South Americans have certain graces of manner which we lack. They are more formal in their social intercourse, and use more of the oil of polite speech in the mechanism of their daily life than we do.

Climatic conditions and difficulties of rapid transportation have had much to do with the backwardness of the South American republics. With the progress of science, the great increase in transportation facilities and the war that is being successfully waged against tropical diseases, a change is coming about which we must be ready to meet.

It is particularly important that we should realize that the political conditions of the larger republics are very much more stable than our newspaper and novel-reading public are aware of. Lynchings are unheard of. Serious riots, such as some of our largest American cities have seen within the past generation, are no more common with them than with us. It is true that the Latin temperament finds it much more difficult to bow to the majesty of the law and to yield gracefully to governmental decrees than the more phlegmatic Teuton or Anglo-Saxon. But the revolutions and riots that Paris has witnessed during the past century have not kept us from a serious effort to increase our business with France. The occasional political riot that takes place, of no more significance than the riots caused by strikers with which we are all too familiar at home, is no reason why we should be afraid to endeavor to capture the South American market.

There is not the slightest question that there is a great opportunity awaiting the American manufacturer and exporter when he is willing to grasp it with intelligent persistence and determination. South America is ready to take American goods in very large quantities as soon as we are ready to take time to give attention to her needs. As Mr. Lincoln Hutchinson aptly says: "There is no quick and easy remedy; money must be spent, thoroughly equipped export managers must be employed, export houses specializing on South American trade must be established, efficient travellers must be sent out, technical experts employed, agencies established, credits be given, minutiæ of orders attended to, and, above all, trade connections adhered to in spite of allurements of the home market, if we would succeed in the face of our competitors. Half-way measures can accomplish but little, and that only temporary."

Germany teaches her young business men Spanish or Portuguese and sends them out to learn conditions in the field. American Universities long ago learned the advantage of adopting Germany's thorough-going methods of scientific research. American business men have hitherto failed to realize the importance of adopting Germany's thorough-going methods of developing foreign commerce. It is high time that they took a leaf out of the experience of the "unpractical" universities.

Finally, a word of caution to those in search of information regarding the history, politics, or geography of South America. The most unfortunate result of the seven centuries during which Arab, Moorish, or Mohammedan rule dominated a part or the whole of the Spanish peninsula, is the truly Oriental attitude which the Spanish and the Spanish-American maintains towards reliable information, or what we call "facts."

The student of the East realizes that Orientals, including Turks and Celestials, have no sense of the importance of agreeing with fact. They have furthermore a great abhorrence of a vacuum. If they do not know the reply to a question they answer at random, preferring anything to the admission of ignorance. If they do know, and have no interest in substituting something else for what they know, they give the facts. When they have no facts they give something else. They not only deceive the questioner, they actually deceive themselves.

The same thing is true to a certain degree in South Americans. Sometimes I have thought they were actually too polite to say "I don't know."

In South America as in the East it is of primitive importance to reach the men who know and to pay no attention to any one else. No one really knows, who is not actually on the spot in contact with the facts. The prudent observer must avoid all evidence that is not first hand and derived from a trustworthy source.

I do not bring this as a charge against the South Americans. I state it as a condition which I have found to be nearly universally true. So far as the South Americans are concerned, it is an inherited trait and one which they are endeavoring to overcome. They are not to be blamed for having it, any more than we are to be blamed for having inherited traits from our Anglo-Saxon ancestors which are unpleasant to our Latin neighbors and for which they have to make allowance in dealing with us.

In offering these adverse criticisms of the South American as he appears to me to-day, I must beg not to be misunderstood. There are naturally many exceptions to the rule. I know personally many individuals that do not have any of the characteristics here attributed to South Americans in general. I have in mind one South American, a resident of a much despised republic, whose ancestors fought in one of the great battles of the Wars of Independence, who has as much push and energy as a veritable New York captain of industry. He has promoted a number of successful industrial enterprises. He keeps up with the times; he meddles not in politics; he enjoys such sports as hunting with hounds and riding across country. The difference between him and the New Yorker is that he speaks three or four languages where the New Yorker only speaks one and he has sense enough to take many holidays in the year where the New Yorker takes but few. I know another, a distinguished young lawyer who gives dinner parties where the food is as good, the manners as refined, the conversation as brilliant, and the intel lectual enjoyment as keen as any given anywhere. He, too, speaks four languages fluently and could put to shame the average New York lawyer of his own age in the variety of topics upon which he is able to converse, not only at his ease but brilliantly and with flashes of keen wit. I know another, a distinguished historian, who has been described by a well-known American librarian, himself a member of half a dozen learned societies, as the "most scholarly and most productive" bibliographer in either North or South America. But these are exceptions to the general rule.

When we look at South Americans at close range we may dislike some of their manners and customs, but not any more so than European critics disliked ours half a century ago. And not any more so, be it remembered, than the South American dislikes ours at the present day.

In this chapter and, in fact, throughout the book, I must confess to having spoken more frankly and critically than will please some of my kind friends in South America. Although they placed me under many obligations by their generous hospitality, I feel that it is better for all concerned that the truth should be told, even when it is unpleasant. We cannot have confidence unless we have facts. I cannot pretend to have succeeded in always finding the facts, but it has not been for lack of endeavor. I have had no interest in concealing anything favorable or unfavorable which I thought would make the picture clearer or more distinct. Were we not already deluged with so much official propaganda, it would have been my privilege to tell more of the wonderful natural resources which all the South American republics possess. But just because it has not been the business of "boosters" or promoters to advertise difficulties or obstacles to progress, it becomes the more necessary for the unprejudiced traveller to lay more stress on the existing human handicaps, than on the wonderful natural resources. It is an unpleasant task, but I believe it is worth doing. I have no patience with those writers who paint everything in glowing colors and leave others to discover the truth at their own expense. Nor have I any sympathy with those who distort or emphasize disagreeable truths for the sake of creating a sensation. I will, however, plead guilty to being a prejudiced observer in so far as I am an ardent advocate of closer and more intelligent relations between the United States and the South American republics, and a firm believer in the truth that international friendships, in order to be lasting, must be built on an honest understanding of prevailing conditions and racial tendencies.

INDEX

A

J

K

L

Z

Lector House believes that a society develops through a two-fold approach of continuous learning and adaptation, which is derived from the study of classic literary works spread across the historic timeline of literature records. Therefore, we aim at reviving, repairing and redeveloping all those inaccessible or damaged but historically as well as culturally important literature across subjects so that the future generations may have an opportunity to study and learn from past works to embark upon a journey of creating a better future.

This book is a result of an effort made by Lector House towards making a contribution to the preservation and repair of original ancient works which might hold historical significance to the approach of continuous learning across subjects.

HAPPY READING & LEARNING!

LECTOR HOUSE LLP
E-MAIL: lectorpublishing@gmail.com

www.ingramcontent.com/pod-product-compliance
Lightning Source LLC
Chambersburg PA
CBHW031449160726
47994CB00005B/1952